Overcoming the Odds

Overcoming the Odds

*Raising Academically Successful
African American Young Women*

FREEMAN A. HRABOWSKI, III
KENNETH I. MATON
MONICA L. GREENE
and GEOFFREY L. GREIF

2002

OXFORD
UNIVERSITY PRESS

Oxford   New York

Athens   Auckland   Bangkok   Bogotá   Buenos Aires   Cape Town   Chennai
Dar es Salaam   Delhi   Florence   Hong Kong   Istanbul   Karachi   Kolkata
Kuala Lumpur   Madrid   Melbourne   Mexico City   Mumbai
Nairobi   Paris   São Paulo   Shanghai   Singapore   Taipei   Tokyo   Toronto   Warsaw

and associated companies in
Berlin   Ibadan

Library of Congress Cataloging-in-Publication Data
Overcoming the odds: raising academically successful African American young women/
Freeman A. Hrabowski III . . .[et al.].
p. cm.
Includes bibliographical references and index.
ISBN-13: 978-0-19-512642-6

1. African American women—Education. 2. Education—Parent participation—United States.
3. African American women—Family relationships. 4. Academic achievement—United States.
I. Hrabowski, Freeman A.

LC2731.O94 2001
649'.15796'073—dc21
2001032152

Book design by Adam B. Bohannon

Printed in the United States of America
on acid-free paper

CONTENTS

This book represents the second part of a study that began in 1995 as the result of the success of the Meyerhoff Scholars Program at the University of Maryland, Baltimore County (UMBC). This exciting program, created in 1988, was designed to increase the numbers of minorities, especially African Americans, who become research scientists and engineers. As a result of the program's success, the university has received numerous inquiries from school systems and parents about the backgrounds of these extraordinary students. In fact, over the past ten years, increasing numbers of parents of young children and adolescents have asked the program's staff for advice on how to improve their children's academic performance, in general, and in math and science, in particular. The recurring question was, "How did the Meyerhoff Scholars become such high-achieving, committed students in science and engineering?" Clearly, the best people to answer this question were the students themselves and their parents.

In 1989, the first year of the Meyerhoff Program, only African American young men were selected to participate, reflecting the particular interest expressed by Robert and Jane Meyerhoff, the program's cofounders and most substantial private donors. Their interest focused on the plight of young Black men in American society. Beginning with the second year of the program, young African American women started participating. (While the program continues to be approximately 65 percent African American, 35 percent of the students are from other ethnic and racial backgrounds, reflecting additional selection criteria that focus on talented students in the sciences who have an interest in working with minorities underrepresented in these fields.)

Each year, between 40 and 60 Meyerhoff freshmen are competitively selected from across the country from over 1400 nominations and applications. Preference is given to students with strong grades and SAT scores, who have taken advanced placement math and science courses, have research experience, and have strong references from science and math instructors. Other criteria include a commitment to remain in the sciences and a desire to participate in community service. Admitted students benefit from various kinds of support, ranging from scholarships and academic and personal advising to intensive mentoring by faculty and professional scientists and opportunities for substantive research.

In our first book about the Meyerhoff students, *Beating the Odds: Raising Academically Successful African American Males*,[1] we chose to write about young Black men because of the major challenges this group faces in our society (e.g., in many states, there are more young African American men in prison than in college) and because they tend to be on the lower rungs of the K-12 academic ladder nationally. Since the publication of *Beating the Odds*, we have had the opportunity to discuss the book's findings throughout the United States with numerous state and local school boards, professional associations, and a variety of other educational and community groups. The book has received overwhelmingly positive responses not only from policymakers and teachers but also, not unexpectedly, from parents of both minority and other children. Most important, people have found the book responsive to their search for answers to questions about academic achievement, especially concerning young Black men. At the same time, we have received numerous questions about our research and plans for a second book focusing on African American girls and young women, recognizing that there are both similarities and differences among the circumstances of young Black men and women, and that the nation faces significant challenges regarding the academic performance of African American girls and the status of African American women in particular, and of American girls and young women in general.

Overcoming the Odds is especially timely from the standpoints of (1) current research on girls and young women in America, (2) the nation's continuing struggle with achieving diversity in higher education (e.g., race-sensitive admissions policies) and in the work force, and (3) the nation's commitment to eliminating the gap in health status between minorities and other groups of Americans and the related shortage of minority biomedical scientists and health professionals. The book complements important perspectives of recent scholars, including those associated with the American Psychological Association's 1999 Task Force on Adolescent Girls,[2] who focus on a strengths-based model in examining how girls are raised by their parents. Regarding minority achievement in higher education—our primary focus—it is especially important to identify and replicate those parenting and educational practices and strategies that have been most effective in producing success. In this area, former university presidents Derek Bok and William Bowen, in their book *The Shape of the River*,[3] provide a wealth of information on the successful performance of African American undergraduate students, both in a sample of selective universities across America and in their subsequent careers. In addition, they highlight the value of a diverse student body in preparing students to live and work with people from other races. Finally, *Overcoming the Odds* also suggests how we can produce more minority scientists, which is one of the major challenges experts contend we must address in order to focus more effectively on the biomedical problems of minorities in America.

From their first day in the program, the female Meyerhoff students appeared far more assertive and comfortable with their academic success in science than their male counterparts (though significantly fewer demonstrated interest in engineering or computer science). As we interacted with these "daughters" and their families, we began thinking about the roles that the students' parents played in instilling such confidence and the sense of security they exhibited. In fact, over the past ten years, we have been astonished by the impressive abilities of these students to lead balanced lives. Over this period, we have surveyed hundreds of young women in the program through personal interviews and questionnaires. The results of these efforts helped to inform the process for developing interview and survey questions for our research in this book. Furthermore, our analysis of the data collected over the years through both the surveys and our personal experiences with Meyerhoff students and their families have helped us to understand more fully the information we obtained in the current study. On the one hand, the young women have focused heavily on their laboratory research and course obligations, also serving as role models and tutors to countless girls and boys in the state of Maryland and beyond; on the other hand, they have successfully grappled with all of the pressures, issues, and questions associated with moving into womanhood—from developing self-esteem to making choices related to their futures as professionals, wives, mothers, and daughters.

Because of its focus on young women, this book presented some very different challenges from those we faced in writing the book about young men. We found through our interviews with the young women, as has generally been the case in the program, that they were more forthcoming than their male counterparts in responding in an in-depth manner to questions regarding their sources of motivation, their backgrounds, and even their feelings about being high academic achievers. As a result, we had to cull from literally thousands of pages of interviews those comments and insights that would best reflect the thinking of the variety of young women and families we studied. Our intent was to provide as much information as possible about the success of these young women, including the problems and obstacles they faced at different stages in their lives and the strategies they used to overcome them.

We spent considerable time thinking about the best way to give readers a sense of the differences and similarities among families, parenting strategies, and the perspectives of the students and parents we studied, because they come from a wide range of educational, socioeconomic, and family backgrounds. In addition to focusing on the more traditional two-parent, middle-class homes where at least one parent attended college, we worked to ensure that we had substantial representation of single-parent families or families where neither parent attended college.

Regardless of the educational backgrounds of these parents, we found in our research (for both books) that many of the parents became discouraged from time to time when their children did not meet their expectations or think and act as the parents wished. Despite the parents' efforts to instill certain values in their daughters, it was very clear that some of the daughters in our study had different opinions and approached problems differently from their parents—simply because they were growing up at a different time and facing different kinds of challenges. From what we observed, it is not surprising that the parents of many young girls are searching for answers to questions not simply about how to help their daughters with their academic work, but also about how to support them emotionally as they grow and develop into womanhood. African American families, in particular, will find that the book provides superb examples of successful practices and insightful comments from the young women, their parents, and others who played a significant role in the young women's lives.

The book also offers many inspiring stories about the unusual strength and determination of these young women to overcome the odds—in some cases even after they have come to college. One young woman, for example, was diagnosed with non-Hodgkin's lymphoma during her sophomore year and did her homework from her hospital bed and faxed it back to her professors. She depended on friends and classmates to take notes for her but was determined that her disease would not deter her from her goal of earning a degree in chemical engineering. "I told myself I didn't have time to be sick," she said. She endured three surgeries, weeks of chemotherapy, and the loss of her hair but remained in school and even enrolled in a summer session. Her grades remained high, and she managed even to continue her research internship at the National Institutes of Health, scheduling her medical appointments around her work. Today, her sights are set on earning an M.D./Ph.D. in biomedical engineering.

In another case, two Meyerhoff women—sisters four years apart—were inspired in different ways by their mother's uncommon academic perseverance. The mother, newly married and pregnant in 1973, had left Drexel University with a year of study to go. More than twenty-five years later, in spring 1999, and nearly 46 years old, she earned a degree from Wellesley College, completing a program for women of nontraditional ages. Inspired by their mother's persistence, both daughters—one majoring in math, the other in biochemistry and molecular biology—graduated a few days later in spring 1999, each having taken a different path. The younger daughter consistently carried heavy course loads in order to graduate early, while the older daughter, like her mother, had left school early but decided to return and earn her degree. Adding to the mother's pride and excitement about the sisters' simultaneous graduations was the element of total surprise—she knew nothing about her older daughter's return to school and graduation. The daughter simply said, "Mom knew firsthand what it meant to leave school, but her one lesson to me was to do what makes me happy. She always said, 'Never stop dreaming.'"

We are hopeful that *Overcoming the Odds* can serve as a valuable source of information about what parents, schools, and even universities can do to produce African American female scientists and engineers. We hope also that the book will add substantially to the growing body of research and dialogue on critical issues involving education and diversity in America—issues certain to have a profound influence on the nation's future.

ACKNOWLEDGMENTS

This book is the result of the collaboration of four authors, including a university president, a professor of psychology, a faculty research associate in psychology, and a professor of social work. All four have focused considerable attention on issues related to minorities in American society. One of the four authors is the father of daughters (two are fathers of sons), two are African American, and one is a woman.

Freeman A. Hrabowski

Since the first group of young women entered the Meyerhoff Program in 1990, I have often thought of and referred to these students as "my daughters." For the past ten years, they have taught me a great deal about inner strength, persistence, and the importance of believing in oneself. I have been very impressed by the parents of these young women, who have devoted their lives to teaching their daughters how to succeed in a society that does not necessarily expect them to succeed and achieve at high levels. As I listened to parents and educators around the country responding to our first book on young Black men, it became increasingly clear that people were anxiously waiting to learn about the rearing of successful young African American girls and about their families. I want to thank the young women and their families for allowing us to study their lives and their family relationships over an extended period of time.

It has been a gratifying experience to collaborate with my coauthors as we have talked and worked together on this project over the past three years. I especially want to thank Mr. and Mrs. Robert Meyerhoff, who have been far more than benefactors of the Meyerhoff Program. They have been an inspiration to my colleagues, students, and me as they have given generously of themselves through their encouragement, their interest in the issues, and their enthusiasm about the students' success. It is hard to describe the special effect of their personal attention to the Meyerhoff Scholars. Suffice it to say that they have been instrumental in helping us to show these young people how special they are.

I also am grateful to the staff of the Meyerhoff Program, all of whom work very hard to ensure the success of these students. Special commendations go to Earnestine Baker, director of the program, and LaMont Toliver, associate director, who have been invaluable in the interviewing and general research for this book. They and the other Meyerhoff staff members are the professionals who work most closely with, and inspire, these young women on a day-to-day basis. I also want to thank Doug Pear, my associate, for his special commitment to the Meyerhoff Program, especially involving his invaluable editorial comments on drafts of this book. Doug was particularly invaluable in helping us to express ourselves clearly and precisely, understanding the wide-ranging backgrounds and perspectives of potential readers. Also, I am grateful to Linda Gorham, a doctoral student in psychology at my university, who provided both invaluable assistance with the literature search and insightful perspectives gained from having reared an African American girl who is now a successful professional. My colleagues among the faculty, not only in science and engineering but across disciplines, and staff in general at UMBC, have contributed substantially to the Meyerhoff Program and can rightfully take ownership of its successes and the national visibility it has received. My coauthors and I also are grateful to President's Office staff, including Karen Wensch for her general support and encouragement, Kathleen Raab for providing outstanding technical support on numerous drafts, and Susan Bosley for her assistance in transcribing many pages of interview data. I will always be grateful to my wife, Jackie, for continuing to believe in me, and to my son, Eric, through whose eyes I have come to see and understand so much more about young people.

Finally, we dedicate this book to all of the young women in the Meyerhoff Program and their families, and to families like them throughout the nation who are striving every day to support their daughters.

Kenneth I. Maton

It has been a special privilege to read the interview transcripts which formed the basis of the current book. The young women and their parents are impressive in so many ways—their strength of character, resilience, integrity, and persistence have been a source of great delight, hope, and inspiration to me. And, as I noted in the preface to our first book, *Beating the Odds*, I see a lot of myself in the Meyerhoff students—especially their educational focus growing up. Although my ethnic heritage, as a Jewish white male, is quite different in many ways from theirs, I feel a kinship concerning a shared personal and family focus on the importance of education, and the overarching reality that education's benefits can never be taken away, no matter how hostile the environment. I am grateful for the willingness of the daughters and parents to contribute to this endeavor, and hope the book begins to capture and communicate the importance and specialness of what their lives and dreams—to date—have accomplished.

An important source of inspiration for this work has been my family. My two sons, Nathan and Tyler, provide opportunities every day to apply the helpful parenting practices and approaches delineated in this book. My wife, Mary Kay, is a true friend, and has unfailingly provided the extra support and space needed when chapter deadlines loomed near, and time was precious. My sister, Nori, and my parents, Edith and Oscar Lang, and Norman Maton, are my "Meyerhoff" Family—growing up, and to this day, I could not have had more support and love than they provided.

A large and diverse team of colleagues and students has contributed importantly to the development of all aspects of the current book. We fully appreciate the commitment, enthusiasm, and insights provided by Hibist Astatke, Anne Brodsky, Linda Gorham, Troy Green, Colleen Loomis, Susan Lorentz, Dewi Smith, Wendy Stevenson, and Elise Vestal.

Monica L. Greene
When I was a graduate student, I spent several years assisting in all aspects of research involving the Meyerhoff Program. Through my interactions with such an impressive group of students, I learned of their successes, their challenges, and the multiple resources on which they relied for support. As I fervently completed my doctoral dissertation on the race-related experiences of the Meyerhoff students, I believed it was the end of a very meaningful experience. Thus, less than two years later, when my colleagues invited me to contribute to this exciting project, I was not only surprised but was also quite honored and intrigued. For me, this book represented an exciting opportunity to integrate two subject areas with which I could readily identify, the Meyerhoff Program and the developmental process of successful Black women. I am grateful to my coauthors for a truly enjoyable collaborative process.

I thank the Meyerhoff Program staff for their continuous assistance and support, and especially Earnestine Baker, director, and LaMont Toliver, associate director, for their critical and generous contributions to this endeavor. I am especially grateful to graduate student Elise Vestal for her invaluable assistance at all levels of this process. I express my deep appreciation to Anne Brodsky, Colleen Loomis, Hibist Astatke, Dewi Smith, Wendy Stevenson, Susan Lorentz, and Juanita Tennyson for their valuable insights and contributions as members of the research and coding teams. My thanks go to Linda Gorham and Christina Wilmer for their assistance in the coordination of research literature. I also acknowledge Tracey Drummond, Mary Johnston, Sylvia Mallonee, Terri Harold, Alice Graham, and Heather Dimmig for their critical help in transcribing thousands of pages of interview data.

Finally, I give thanks to my supportive network of family and close friends. Special thanks go to my husband, André Smalls, for his abiding love, support, and faith in my abilities. I am thankful to my parents, Marion and David E. Greene, Jr., and my brother, David K. Greene, for instilling in me the importance of faith, education, and family, and for raising me to become a successful African American woman.

Geoffrey L. Greif

My first exposure to the Meyerhoff Program came in 1995, when work began on *Beating the Odds*. Over the years, I have come to appreciate, through my eyes as a researcher, social worker, and parent, how remarkable the Meyerhoff students are. They are remarkable not only for their academic achievements but also for what many of them have overcome in order to reach their potential. They have not done it alone by any measure. Parents, other family members, teachers, mentors, religious leaders, and peers have all played a part. As I reflect on my parenting of two daughters who are about the same ages as the young women who are the focus of this book, I wonder what kind of a father I have been. On the basis of their skin color, many more doors are immediately open to my daughters. But I wonder if I have given them a sufficient sense of community and heritage. I learned from the parents in this book how they encouraged their children and wonder if I have encouraged mine while also supporting them unconditionally. And I wonder if, as a father, I have taught them enough about the world.

I realize that somewhere along the line, most parents wonder about these things no matter how accomplished, loving, and lovable their children are. Parenting is an imperfect endeavor—there are no perfect children just as there are no perfect parents. Readers of this book should not feel distressed if their families have not always taken the steps that these families have taken. No single family in this book has followed the steps that are described cumulatively by all the families. Parenting is a dynamic process that calls for different responses throughout life. What is appropriate at one point is rarely appropriate at another. It is the wanting to be a good parent that is key. I thank the Meyerhoff families and my daughters for helping me to learn this important lesson.

Overcoming the Odds

CHAPTER ONE

Successful African American
Young Women and Their Families

"Your uncle's hooked on crack" says my mother as we park in front of his
house. As I walk towards my house, I look to my right and see a couple of drug
addicts sitting on what used to be my aunt's favorite couch and enjoying the
comforts of her once humble abode. On the steps, there sits a high-school
dropout, no older than the age of 17, counting the money he earned from sell-
ing drugs. At the corner, the mother of a local drug kingpin took on his
responsibility after he was killed in cold blood....

My parents always stressed the importance of a good education and taught
me to strive to be the best.... I have witnessed the effects of alcohol and drugs
firsthand, and it has taught me that drugs are not the way to deal with life's
bleak realities. I use society as my motivation to excel in all that I do because
as a teenage Black female I am not expected to do well. There is a sense of sat-
isfaction in knowing I achieved more than was expected, but more impor-
tant, I achieved more than I expected. My hard work paid off....

MEYERHOFF SCHOLAR

When we read or hear about young African American women in our society, we usually find that the emphasis is on problems—from welfare and teenage pregnancy to violence and drugs. Rarely do the media focus on the success of young Black girls in school or of African American women in professional careers. For example, despite the fact that the nation's teenage pregnancy rates have steadily declined since 1991,[1] and that the majority of the nation's pregnant teenagers are not Black,[2] it is common nevertheless for the American public immediately to associate the expression, "babies having babies," with young Black girls. This association is largely created and reinforced by images presented in the media of young African American women in trouble, either as unwed mothers or, in more recent years, as gang members.

Less well known are the significant accomplishments and value of African

American women and the enormous role they can, and do, play in our nation. Consider the prose of Nobel Prize-winning writer Toni Morrison, and the courageous voice of one of America's most eloquent child-advocates, Marian Wright Edelman. African American women are achieving at the highest of professional levels, from college presidencies to cabinet posts. Consider, for example, the appointments of Dr. Shirley Jackson, a physicist and the first African American female to earn a Ph.D. in any field at the Massachusetts Institute of Technology, as president of Rensselaer Polytechnic Institute, one of America's major technological universities, or of Dr. Condoleezza Rice as the President's National Security Advisor.

Notwithstanding these positive accomplishments, most Americans—Black and White—still know very little about these high achievers. Increasingly, entertainers—both women and men—send mixed signals to young Black girls about who they should aspire to become as they move toward womanhood. Often, these images, which tend to be unflattering and even at times degrading, focus on a culture that is excessively influenced by glamour, sex, and violence. In *Reviving Ophelia*, Mary Pipher discusses the powerful influence of the media in shaping girls' definitions of themselves through teen magazines, advertisements, music, television, and movies.[3] Indeed, walking through a high school and looking at the clothes and listening to the conversations of young adolescent African American girls, one cannot help but notice the enormous influence of the media and entertainers.

One career aspiration mentioned frequently by African American girls from various geographic settings is to become a cosmetologist, or beautician, because they have seen many examples. Other young women, like their male counterparts, dream of becoming young professional basketball players, and as the role of African American women in professional sports grows, we can expect increasing numbers of girls to aspire to that profession, notwithstanding the lack of realism associated with this choice. In contrast, one study, focusing on the lives of rural and urban African American girls,[4] found that the girls raised in rural areas most frequently cited teacher, nurse, doctor, and lawyer as their career aspirations. For urban Black girls, career aspirations most often included such professions as doctor, day-care worker, teacher, lawyer, model, and astronaut. Given the significant impact of television on children, it is unfortunate that only a handful of shows provide constructive examples of African American women in the professions, and even those shows superficially reflect what the professions actually involve. Whether on television or elsewhere, rarely does the public hear about the success of African American women in their careers or about the efforts of millions of African American families who are working hard to raise their daughters to excel—families that are doing all they can to give these girls all possible opportunities and to protect them from the dangers of growing up in our society today.

Significance and Purpose of the Book

In her essay, "When Girls Talk: What It Reveals About Them and Us,"[5] Joan Jacobs Brumberg discusses a series of books that focus on the voices of girls and young women, including some based on social science research and others on actual biographical statements. According to Brumberg, "By listening to their voices, we should be able to learn a great deal about the ways in which the girls' developmental processes are shaped by social life and cultural values in different class strata and ethnic communities." We have captured the voices of many of the young Meyerhoff women, and in reporting what we have learned, we hope to contribute to the existing body of literature.

Moreover, according to the American Psychological Association's recent Presidential Task Force on Adolescent Girls, most of the literature on this group focuses on the problems and stresses in their lives. The Task Force suggests that much more attention should be given to the success of adolescent girls in handling the stress and challenges they face.[6] Moreover, the Task Force asserts that, "An adolescent's ethnicity has intense influence on her development, as it affects her sense of belonging in a world that often determines inclusion and exclusion on the basis of skin color. . . . [I]t is important to assess the interplay of what occurs within families and what occurs in the political, economic, social, and racial climates in which young girls are challenged. Perhaps the most resilient factor common to all ethnic minority groups is identification with family and community."[7] By focusing on the young girls' strengths and resiliency and on child-rearing strategies and practices that actually work, we can help parents, schools, and girls themselves during these critically important developmental years.

Overcoming the Odds strives to answer the question about African American girls and young women on the minds of countless parents, educators, and policy-makers: What does it take for these children to succeed academically? Far too often, we hear from both young African American women and men that it is not "cool" to be smart and that many African American children who work hard to achieve academically are either isolated or ridiculed by their peers.[8] In fact, for young African Americans, the influence of peers—in this case, the lack of peer support for academic achievement—is so strong that even when they are positively influenced by strong parenting, their academic performance still suffers.[9]

Our book asks in-depth questions of both the academically successful young women in our sample and their parents regarding what has made the difference in their lives. It looks carefully at effective approaches taken by both the students and their parents. We focused on the families of young African American university women majoring in science or engineering and participating in the Meyerhoff Scholars Program for talented students in these fields at the University of Maryland, Baltimore County. Our efforts proved to be exciting given that few Americans in the general public have the opportunity to observe closely successful young African American women and their families—people who strive every day to overcome what appear sometimes to be insurmountable odds, ranging from peer pressure focused on sex, drugs, and violence to messages that permeate society and discourage high achievement, particularly among minorities and women.

Two recent books which provide refreshing perspectives on growing up as a young African American woman during the last quarter of the twentieth century are J. Okwu's *As I Am: Young African American Women in a Critical Age* and Rebecca Carroll's *Sugar in the Raw: Voices of Young Black Girls in America*. Consider, for example, the voice of a young 14-year-old girl who spoke about why Black girls do not lose their self-esteem:

> I never have the luxury of knowing what it's like to not be branded in society. I read somewhere once that young White girls lose their self-esteem around this age and that Black girls don't, which is kind of weird, since Black girls have so much more to deal with. Maybe it's because we have so much to deal with that we don't want to risk giving up our self-esteem because then we'd really be in trouble. We'd still have all the issues we have to negotiate with no self-esteem. Sounds grim. I'm not saying that I've got this huge amount of self-esteem; I'm saying that what amount I do have is mine.[10]

What makes the young women we studied so special is that they are excelling academically and planning to pursue professional and graduate degrees in science and engineering. *Overcoming the Odds* reports the findings of our research and offers concrete strategies on how to increase the numbers of young Black girls who succeed in these areas, thus enhancing a significant and precious national resource.

Why is it important to look at this group? First, it is imperative for the nation to know the reality about the achievement level of young Black women in American society today. It is encouraging that substantially more young Black girls over the past twenty-five years have been succeeding in school and going on to college and beyond. Approximately 74 percent of African American women, 18 to 21 years old, had graduated from high school as of 1997, compared with only 65 percent in 1975. By comparison, for the same age cohort, 63 percent of Black males and 82 percent of White females had graduated from high school as of 1997, compared with 55 percent of Black males and 81 percent of White females as of 1975.

Regarding SAT performance, more African American students are taking the SAT than ever before (approximately 115,000 in 1998 compared with almost 98,000 in 1988).[11] However, the 1999 mean combined math and verbal score for this group was only 856 compared with 1055 for Whites.[12] Moreover, only 4 percent of African Americans who took the exam earned combined scores of 1200 or higher, compared with almost one quarter of White students. African American women in 1999 had a mean combined score of 850, compared with combined scores of 866 among Black male high school students and 1036 among White female students.

Regarding college-attendance rates, despite the low average test scores, the number of African American women attending college has grown substantially the past twenty-five years. While approximately 26 percent of Black women, 18 to 21, who had graduated from high school as of 1975 were enrolled in college that year, 38 percent of those who had graduated as of 1997 were attending college that year. The 38 percent figure among African American women in 1997 compares with 28 percent and 49 percent of Black men and White women, respectively.[13]

Data regarding the college-level progress of African Americans, especially young Black women, also are encouraging on the whole.[14] Blacks account for approximately 11 percent of the total college enrollment, and they earn roughly 8 percent of all bachelor's degrees, slightly under 4 percent of all doctoral degrees, and 6.5 percent of first-professional degrees. African American women earned almost two thirds of all bachelor's degrees awarded to Blacks in 1997, including nearly half of the degrees awarded to

African Americans in computer science and 30 percent of the degrees in engineering. In contrast, among Whites, women earned only 23 percent of the bachelor's degrees in computer science and 15 percent of the degrees in engineering. It is not surprising that the proportion of these degrees going to African American women compared with African American men would be higher than their White counterparts, primarily because African American men experience substantially more academic problems than their White counterparts.

Data from the most recent National Science Foundation report (2000)[15] show that once in college, African Americans accounted for 7 percent of all science-and-engineering bachelor's degrees in 1996. At the doctoral level, only 3.0 percent of all science and engineering degrees were earned by African Americans in 1997 (607 of 20,233). Black women accounted for 1.6 percent (280) of all science and engineering doctorates, compared with 29.6 percent earned by White women (5,180). Among African Americans who earned science and engineering Ph.D.s in 1997, women accounted for 46.0 percent, and men accounted for 54.0 percent (328). Data on preparation of medical doctors[16] show that 7.1 percent of all medical degrees awarded in 1996-97 were earned by African Americans (1,107 of 15,571). Of these, African American women received 4.4 percent (684) compared with 27.6 percent earned by White women (4,292). Among African American medical-degree recipients, women earned 61.8 percent, and men 38.2 percent (423).

A second compelling reason for studying high-achieving young Black women in science and engineering is to understand the special support often required for success in these fields. In our recent study focusing on Black students—both those in the Meyerhoff Program and those with comparable backgrounds who attended other institutions without the level of support provided by the Meyerhoff Program—we found that nearly 90 percent of the Meyerhoff students graduated in science while fewer than 50 percent of the comparison group had done so.[17]

Third, it is important that we learn more about those students who are succeeding at the highest levels in order to identify best practices and to encourage families, schools, and communities—working independently and together—to focus on these best practices. By focusing on high-achieving young African American women, we can pinpoint strategies and perspectives—even habits and behaviors—that can be useful to educators, parents, and policy-makers in combating the problem of low academic achievement among Black children.

In this connection, it is significant that we often assume that high-achieving students do not need much attention or support and that they will succeed on their own. Given this assumption, it is understandable that most of the attention and resources placed on minority education go to remediate the skills of students at the lower end of the academic achievement spectrum (who, all too often, also are at the lower end of the socioeconomic spectrum). Miller, in his book on minority educational advancement, points out that, "as a nation, Americans must be concerned with improving the educational prospects not only of those living in poverty and those whose parents have little education but also of those who are middle-class minority students,"[18] since many of these students are also not succeeding academically.

This important theme is echoed by the College Board in its 1999 study, *Reaching the Top: A Report of the National Task Force on Minority High Achievement*,[19] which finds that although top students typically come from educationally and economically advantaged families, this is not the case for minority students. Minority students from middle-income families are not achieving at the same levels as their White and Asian American counterparts. In other words, the achievement problem exists at all socioeconomic levels within minority groups.[20] Some attribute this low performance, and the resulting achievement gap, to problems of values held by African Americans,[21] though clearly there are many other factors that need to be considered. What is especially significant, as the report points out, is that,

> Until many more underrepresented minority students from disadvantaged, middle class, and upper-middle class circumstances are very successful educationally, it will be virtually impossible to integrate our society's institutions completely, especially at leadership levels. Without such progress, the United States also will continue to be unable to draw on the full range of talents in our population during an era when the value of an educated citizenry has never been greater.[22]

Moreover, few predominantly White universities have examined the question of why so few underrepresented minority students are among their top graduates each year, or what it takes to increase the number of African American and other underrepresented minorities among the high achievers. In response to this lack of attention, the College Board study calls upon both the higher education community and our elementary and secondary schools to make high academic achievement a top priority for minority students.

Finally, *Overcoming the Odds* is meaningful because many of the lessons we learned through our research are relevant to any family, school, or university interested in improving the academic performance of young African American students. When talking about success and high achievement, we must keep in mind that the definitions depend on the context. The young women in the Meyerhoff Program were in the top 10 percent of their high school graduating classes, earned combined SAT scores of 1200 or higher, and have maintained higher than a B average in university-level science and engineering courses. Obviously, when talking about success in general terms, we want to increase the number of students who do well and go on to college to major in the programs of their choice. This book focuses specifically on the pipeline of young women who are future scientists and engineers.

Importance of the Family

One of the primary assumptions of this book is that the family is crucial to the academic success of children. As was true in our first book about young Black men, *Beating the Odds,*[23] the most important and most frequently mentioned source of strength for the young Black women we studied has been the students' mothers. The following quote, from one of the students, reflects the important contributions of mothers to the academic success of their daughters (in this case, in terms of selecting an area of study).

> *I guess my mom has always encouraged me. I wouldn't say she forced me, but she has always strongly influenced me to be in the sciences. Ever since I was little, she would tell me, "You're going to be a scientist. What kind of scientist do you want to be?" So it really just got ingrained in my head.*

Several researchers who describe the important role mothers play in raising their daughters have found that there is strong communication between the mothers and daughters and that these mothers raise their daughters to be economically independent, strong, self-confident, and capable of handling family responsibilities.[24] This socialization of African American girls tends to place less emphasis on cultivating stereotypical qualities of femininity (e.g., limiting displays of assertiveness) and more emphasis on encouraging a combination of self-sufficiency and the traditional roles of nurturing and child care. These mothers often encourage the girls to stand up for themselves as a means of survival.[25] In fact, one study found that as these girls get older, they often tend to continue talking openly to their mothers and perceive their mothers as talking openly with them and telling them about their lives.[26] Another study, by Signithia Fordham, found that parents of high-achieving African American girls tend to limit their daughters' friendships and encourage their involvement in religion, while parents of underachieving girls tend to allow, even encourage, many friends and dates and are generally indifferent about religion.[27] Fordham also found that families of high-achieving girls tend to prepare their daughters in such a way that while the girls are aware of the larger society's perception of them, they are able to deemphasize the possible limitations that might be imposed on them and to focus more heavily on developing strong academic skills.[28]

Regarding the families of the Meyerhoff students we studied, it is significant that in those families where there were two parents living in the home, often both parents played important roles in helping their child develop self-esteem and in setting expectations as well as limits. Throughout the interviews, we found numerous examples of fathers and mothers who were actively involved in their daughter's education; in fact, many of the daughters speak about the important roles both of their parents played in their success.

In our study, we found it important to examine a variety of issues related to preparing African American girls to be successful, including health (physical and mental), education, and socioeconomic status.

Physical and Mental Health

While it is not surprising that some young African American girls experience a variety of health-related problems, it may be somewhat surprising that this group actually fares better in certain areas than other groups of girls. Research indicates, for example, that Black girls have higher self-esteem, healthier body image, and greater social assertiveness than their White counterparts,[29] and they express fewer concerns related to image and appearance (e.g., weight, style, clothing) than do White or Asian American girls.[30] In fact, one study found that 40 percent of Black girls considered themselves attractive or very attractive in contrast to only about 9 percent of

White girls.[31] Nevertheless, the fact remains that 60 percent of the Black girls did not consider themselves attractive or lacked self-esteem. In addition, the vast majority of eating disorders (90 percent) are found among White rather than Black girls and young women.[32]

Also, the overall rates of drug use for Black schoolgirls are actually lower than those of their White counterparts, and Black schoolgirls who are involved in extracurricular activities are less likely to use alcohol and marijuana than White girls similarly involved.[33] As might be expected, both Black and White female adolescents who illicitly abuse drugs are more likely than nonusers to avoid going to class, break school rules, be suspended, have problems at home (particularly with mothers), and have a greater number of sexual partners.[34] Other studies have also found that fewer Black teenage girls smoke than their counterparts of other races,[35] and Black girls are less likely than White or Hispanic girls to contemplate suicide, although the percentage remains high (22 percent).[36]

Self-esteem, as noted, is an important issue among young girls, and it is pivotal for high-achieving African American girls. Although girls generally enter puberty feeling self-confident, they become less so during adolescence, and they tend to have fewer positive feelings about themselves than do boys during this period. In contrast with other girls, however, African American high-school girls report higher feelings of self-worth.[37] In particular, girls who identify strongly with their ethnicity tend to have higher self-esteem than those who do not. However, African American girls classified as gifted, in contrast to African American girls generally, sometimes have more difficulty than their White counterparts developing social and racial identity because they have a variety of demands placed upon them.[38] Besides often having to handle conflicting cultures between home and school, they frequently feel isolated in gifted classes where they see few others like themselves.[39]

Regarding sexual behavior, a significant number of American girls report having sexual intercourse between the ages of 15 and 19. In fact, about half of both Hispanic and non-Hispanic White girls and two thirds of Black girls report engaging in intercourse between 15 and 19; and, even before 15, we find that about 25 percent of White and Hispanic girls and 39 percent of Black girls report having sex.[40] As might be expected, girls who have earlier sexual intercourse are more at risk of unplanned pregnancies and sexual victimization. Clearly, the most talked about challenge facing these young women is teen pregnancy, which has numerous negative factors associated with it, for example, poor academic performance, substance abuse, disciplinary problems in school, absenteeism, and poor communication between children and parents.[41] Teen pregnancy also contributes heavily to school drop-out rates, though African American girls appear to be slightly less affected in this regard than other girls. Thus, while well over half (62 percent) of young women giving birth during high school drop out, the figure is slightly lower among African American girls (54 percent).[42] It is especially noteworthy that the largest decline in teen birth rate since 1991 has been among Black teens.

One of the more recent and most troubling issues facing young women today is violence. Although girls generally are still far less likely than boys to be arrested—nationally, they accounted for approximately one quarter of all youthful arrests in the mid-1990s—they appear to be involved in substantially more violent crimes than they were a decade ago. In fact, during this period, arrests of girls were up 64 percent for murder, 114 percent for robbery, and 137 percent for aggravated assault.[43] Factors related to this increased violence include girls' physical and sexual victimization, negative attitudes about school, lack of academic success, and a perceived lack of opportunities.[44] In a study of delinquent African American youth, girls involved in delinquency and violence were more likely to talk about dissatisfaction with their school experience than were their male counterparts, who more readily cited poor family relationships.[45] In another study of young Black and Latino women incarcerated for serious offenses, most of the women discussed feeling alienated from their families and peers and tended to suffer from low self-esteem.[46] The increasing involvement of girls in gangs is seen by many of these girls as a solution to a limited occupational future, feeling subordinate or isolated in the home, having sole responsibility for children, and the threat of victimization from crime.[47]

Education
A National Perspective

This book examines the families and lives of high-achieving young Black women who have overcome the odds of being placed in low-level classes, of underachieving in school, of becoming too popular and "cool," of dropping out of school, and of becoming pregnant. This group is particularly special not only because its members have avoided these pitfalls but also because they are among a much too small group of African American high achievers in math and science who intend to become scientists, engineers, and physicians.

On a national scale, we find that African American girls represent approximately 8.4 percent of all children attending public elementary and secondary schools. While they also account for 10.4 percent of the children suspended from school and 13.2 percent of those placed in classes for the mentally retarded, they represent only 4.1 percent of students placed in gifted-and-talented classes and only 4.6 percent and 5.0 percent of students taking Advanced Placement (AP) math and science courses, respectively. [48] In contrast, White girls represent 30 percent of the nation's children enrolled in public elementary and secondary schools, yet constitute only 13.2 percent of those suspended and 22.8 percent of those placed in classes for the mentally retarded and make up almost 40 percent of students enrolled in gifted-and-talented classes and 35 percent or more of students in AP math and science courses.[49] Finally, as might be expected, Black girls fare slightly better than their Black male counterparts, who represent 8.6 percent of the nation's public elementary and secondary school enrollments, yet 21.7 percent of those suspended, 20.0 percent of those in classes for mentally retarded, 3.2 percent of gifted and talented enrollments, and 3.6 percent and 3.5 percent, respectively, of those in AP classes in math and science.[50]

Despite the bleakness of some of these statistics, it is encouraging that high school drop-out rates among African American girls and boys have declined substantially over the past thirty years—by 40 percent.[51] Further, Black girls have significantly lower drop-out rates and higher college-enrollment rates than Black boys.[52] While 86 percent of Black high school seniors who are eligible completed high school in 1996, compared with 93 percent of White students and 61 percent of Hispanic students,[53] this statistic for African American students is somewhat misleading because a very high percentage of students drop out between the ninth and eleventh grades. In Baltimore, Maryland, for example, only 40 percent of the Black ninth graders graduate four years later, compared with almost 62 percent statewide in Maryland's school systems. Further, as might be expected, Black girls drop out less frequently than Black boys, though once Black girls leave, they are much less likely than their Black male counterparts to return and earn a high school equivalency diploma. Of the African American women who drop out of high school, 92 percent cite being held back in school as the reason for leaving school,[54] and almost half (47 percent) live in poverty.[55] Moreover, young women who drop out are more likely to become pregnant than those who stay in school.[56]

Importance of School Environment and Expectations

We find also that school environment is a significant factor influencing the academic performance of girls, and of Black girls in particular. The attitudes and expectations that teachers, administrators, and school staff convey through their words, actions, and body language have a strong influence on the behavior and achievement of students. In their study of expectations and change in high school, Weinstein and colleagues make this point eloquently:

> One important factor that places certain groups of children at risk is the operation of differential and very low academic expectations for what they can accomplish. Minorities and children from lower socio-economic classes are largely over-represented as the target of low expectations. The dynamics of teacher expectations and how they can become self-fulfilling prophecies have been well illustrated within classrooms (toward individual children and between reading groups) and between classrooms (in the tracking system of high schools). Studies of effective schools have also pointed to the expectations of principals and teachers as powerful influences on student performance.[57]

Differential treatment of girls and boys in general also is an important and very real aspect of school environment. One study[58] found that generally teachers tend to allow boys to talk and interrupt more than girls, that teachers are more likely to punish girls for academic mistakes and boys for being disruptive, and that they tend to comment to girls on their appearance and to boys on their performance. The study also observed that teachers tend to give boys more specific feedback while spending less time on suggestions to girls. Further, according to an American Association of University Women study,[59] boys receive more attention than girls primarily because boys demand more attention, at times even by shouting out answers to questions. Boys also receive more specific comments regarding instruction and their conduct.

In general, gifted girls are not encouraged as often as boys to pursue careers in science and engineering.[60] According to Callahan and Reis,[61] they also tend to drop out of gifted programs after ninth grade. These girls frequently cite peer pressure as a reason for not continuing, and many report under-using their skills to avoid competition, which they think might threaten their relationships. It is not surprising, then, that teachers sometimes learn that gifted girls purposely conceal their abilities. One study has found that over half of academically gifted African American girls are teased by other Black students, and about a third are accused of "acting White."[62] Also, teachers of these girls sometimes expect them to be leaders among the African American students, which may at times be an unrealistic expectation.

Black girls also have less interaction with their teachers than their White counterparts, although Black girls try to initiate more interaction with teachers than either their White counterparts or their male peers. When teachers do not respond favorably to the young Black girl, she reacts by "often becoming the class enforcer or go-between for other students."[63] Overall, African American students receive more reinforcement for their social behavior while their White counterparts receive more reinforcement for their academic achievements.[64]

Despite the large numbers of African American female students who may not be doing well, it is important to focus on students who, like the female Meyerhoff Scholars, represent success stories. In this way, we gain a better understanding of what can be done to increase the numbers who succeed. It is encouraging, for instance, that those African American women who are classified as gifted in mathematics tend to expect positive results as a consequence of being successful in this area, even more so than their male counterparts. They do not view math as a male-dominated subject; they do not have a fear of success in math; and they view their intellectual capacity positively.[65]

The need to examine why women in the Meyerhoff Scholars Program have been successful becomes even more compelling when we consider the recent findings of the American Association for the Advancement of Science (AAAS) regarding minorities in science. In its 1998 report, *Losing Ground*, AAAS asserts,

> While increased enrollment of underrepresented minority American students in graduate education in science and engineering was expected, in light of increased baccalaureate degrees awarded to Black

and Hispanic Americans over the previous years, declining enrollments were seen, especially for African Americans.... [A] precipitous one-year drop of over 20% was seen in the data collected for all S&E fields and a 19.3% drop in the NSCSME&E [natural sciences, computer sciences, mathematics, and engineering] first-year graduate enrollments of African Americans between 1996 and 1997. The overall decline observed in first-year S&E and NSCSM&E graduate enrollment did not approach the magnitude of the decline for African American students.[66]

These data are cause for national concern when we consider the 27 percent increase in the number of science-based jobs since 1996, the 36 percent increase in the number of jobs requiring a significant background in math, and the 26 percent decline in the pool of science and engineering bachelor's degrees awarded in the late 1990s.[67]

Socioeconomic Status and Issues

We know that there is a strong correlation between the socioeconomic performance of parents and the level of academic resources available to their children and the children's academic performance: typically, the higher the parents' socioeconomic status (SES), the higher the children's grades and SAT performance. Conversely, poverty's impact on academic achievement is often devastating. It is not surprising, therefore, that among low SES Black boys and girls, 34 percent and 29 percent, respectively, were held back at least one grade.[68] Nor is it surprising, as Phillips points out,[69] that almost all American students in the highest income quartile (95 percent) complete high school compared with only 65 percent of those in the lowest quartile.

Financial status also is an important determinant of college enrollment and college students' persistence and academic achievement. Slightly more than half (53 percent) of all African American college students in 1995 came from families whose total household income was below $30,000, whereas only 19 percent of White college students were from families with similar household incomes. Even more telling, 34 percent of African American college students in 1995 were from families with household incomes less than $20,000, compared with only 8 percent of their White counterparts. Also, families with household incomes above $50,000 accounted for 21 percent of Black college students and 52 percent of the White students.[70] Even when students from low-income families do begin college, they often drop out because of financial problems. In fact, it has been estimated that a student from the highest income group is nearly twenty times as likely to complete four years of college by the age of 24 than is an unmarried student, 18 to years old, who is from the lowest income quartile.[71]

Regarding the challenges girls face, it is important to consider the fact that girls from poor families, unlike their male counterparts, often are expected to care for siblings or ill or elderly family members, and that these responsibilities sometimes interfere with the girls' ability to study or attend school regularly. Moreover, the economic factor is especially critical for minority families (Black and Latino in particular) because over one quarter of these groups (26 percent) fall below the poverty line in comparison to fewer than 10 percent of White families.

Regarding the economic status of African American women generally, what we observe in recent years is encouraging in some respects and discouraging in others. Latest U.S. Department of Labor data[72] show that in 1996, there were approximately 7,900,000 Black women, 16 years of age and older, in the labor force (a 60.4 percent participation rate). It is encouraging that during the preceding decade, many more Black women entered higher paying, career-oriented managerial and professional occupations. In fact, between 1986 and 1996, this number increased nearly 80 percent—from approximately 900,000 to 1,600,000—and constituted 20 percent of all African American women in the work force. Despite this progress, nearly 60 percent of Black women, 25 years old and above, have never attended college, and only 15 percent are college graduates. Moreover, the median family income ($25,970) for Black families is only 61 percent of what White families earn, and the ten leading occupations for Black women, in rank order, are as follows: (1) nursing aides, orderlies, and attendants, (2) cashiers, (3) secretaries, (4) personal service occupations, (5) retail sales workers, (6) janitors and cleaners, (7) cooks, (8) maids, (9) registered nurses, and (10) elementary school teachers and social workers. It is especially noteworthy that by the mid-1990s, nearly half of African American families in the United States were headed by women, and almost half of these households were living in poverty. In fact, African American women are nearly three times as likely to live in poverty and twice as likely to be unemployed as their White counterparts.

Social Science Issues

In contrast to some of the negative images of young African American women in the media, a number of researchers point to the strengths of Black families in their examination of the role of these families and how they prepare their children for success. Billingsley[73] asserts that the strengths of these families are much more influential than their weaknesses, and the strengths will help these families to thrive in many cases. What he found among strong African American families is certainly consistent with what we see in the families with daughters enrolled in the Meyerhoff Scholars Program—a deep commitment to education, a supportive environment in the home, strong spiritual beliefs, and a focus on self-help. We found both two- and one-parent families with wide-ranging educational backgrounds raising high-achieving young African American women.

One of the questions researchers frequently ask about raising girls, in general, focuses on differential treatment of boys and girls by parents. Phillips observes that during childhood, parents' interaction with boys tends to encourage independence and self-confidence, while interaction with girls fosters dependence by restricting exploration, prematurely intervening in problem-solving tasks, and providing toys that emphasize beauty and nurturing rather than skill-mastery and action.[74] Lips notes, for example, that "boy" toys tend to be oriented toward competition and aggressiveness, while toys for girls are more closely linked to nurturing and creativity.[75]

Among African Americans, however, it is significant that girls are reared to be much more independent and resourceful than boys.[76] In this regard, they often are encouraged to be strong, self-sufficient, willing to stand up for themselves, and to fight back if necessary. At the same time, they are taught to be nurturing and to be capable of taking care of children. Also, their mothers often work to prepare them to handle the realities of discrimination and to be prepared to fend for themselves economically. Phillips finds that African American girls are socialized toward independence, strength, and resourcefulness,[77] while Reid notes that African American college women expect to combine marriage, child-rearing, and a career and are much less likely to express ambivalence about their role than are their White counterparts. In fact, the mother's role in the Black community typically combines toughness and assertiveness with tenderness and nurturance.[78] Black fathers, although reporting a preference for male children, tend to be more involved with their daughters, according to Reid. In general, unlike their

White counterparts, Black families that are strongly oriented toward authoritarian parenting styles produce independent and assertive children, both boys and girls.[79] And regarding academic performance, Lips notes that African American parents' expectations about mathematics have been found to be less gender-stereotypical than is the case in White families.[80] Lips's finding is especially significant because the expectations of Black parents about their daughters' achievements in math were found to be significant predictors of the daughters' academic self-image.[81]

Notwithstanding these influences, which for the most part appear to have a positive influence on academic performance, Reid[82] notes that racial stereotyping of African American female characters in children's books often casts them in negative roles, such as domestic servants. Not surprisingly, even Black female characters appearing in comedy programs on television tend to be portrayed as lacking in academic ability and as dominating the home. These images certainly can have an adverse impact on the aspirations of young Black girls.

Methodology and Observations

This study is based on interviews and questionnaires completed by young African American women who are students in, or graduates of, the Meyerhoff Scholars Program, their parents, and some of the other adults who influenced the young women's lives, including teachers, principals, guidance counselors, church members, and others active in the community.[83] We both personally interviewed and surveyed by questionnaire 66 young women and 73 parents (46 mothers and 27 fathers). An additional 34 students only completed the survey questionnaire. Interviews with students were primarily conducted one-on-one. They completed questionnaires prior to starting the Meyerhoff Program and again during the year they were interviewed.

We also invited mothers and fathers of the students to participate in group interviews, with the groups ranging in size from two to six people. The interviews were conducted between fall 1998 and fall 1999 by staff members in the Meyerhoff Program, one of the coauthors, and an African American graduate student. We separated mothers and fathers during our interviews because previous experience with the program showed that when mothers and fathers met together, most of the fathers were much less active in the discussions than the mothers. We also wanted to look carefully at the role of gender by focusing on the relationships between fathers and daughters and between mothers and daughters from the perspectives of the different groups interviewed. In some cases, individual interviews were conducted by telephone with parents who could not attend the session, but in three quarters of the cases, we conducted interviews in person. The parents also completed a questionnaire focusing on their parenting practices.

Of the 46 mothers and 27 fathers who participated in these interviews, 18 of the mothers and two of the fathers raised their daughters alone for at least a substantial portion of the daughters' upbringing. Among the fathers, 21 lived with their daughters and their daughters' biological mothers throughout the children's upbringing (i.e., through high-school graduation). We oversampled for single mothers because that group is disproportionately represented among parents raising African American children today. (In fact, only one in three African American children lives with both parents.)[84] In six cases, the parents we interviewed were either stepparents or did not have primary custody. In addition, slightly over 60 percent of the parents in our sample had a college education.

One limitation of the group interviewed is that we spoke only with those parents who agreed to be interviewed. Of the 129 parents contacted—all parents of daughters either enrolled in or graduates of the Meyerhoff Program at the time of our study—57 percent (73) participated. Those who declined our invitation to be interviewed may have had other demands on their time or may have been uncomfortable with speaking in a group context.

In addition to talking with parents, we also interviewed 66 daughters from a variety of family, educational, economic, and geographic backgrounds. Approximately half of the young women have spent some of their childhood with a single parent (the mother in 80 percent of the cases). A quarter of the daughters had at least one stepparent.

We decided to edit interview comments when necessary for easy readability, although we were very careful not to change the substance of comments. We also concealed the identities of families and individuals involved. In addition to the information gathered through interviews and questionnaires, we had already collected information on these students as a regular part of the Meyerhoff Program's research agenda.

In some cases, the home environment for the families in our study changed over the years—from two parents to single parents or to grandparents or stepparents living in the home and being engaged in childrearing—a situation frequently found among African American families today. Most of the parents we studied were raised in the southern and mid-Atlantic regions of the country. Though many of the daughters were born and educated in this country (primarily in Maryland), 13 of the 66 (approximately 20 percent) had parents who were born in other countries, primarily the Caribbean and African countries. Nearly 90 percent (59 of 66) of the young women described themselves as African American (four described themselves as Caribbean, and three saw themselves as Black-and-White or other). The sample was primarily drawn from Maryland, a diverse state with social problems and programs that in many ways make it an excellent setting for studying the issues addressed in this book.

Most people have heard the stereotype that African Americans "raise" their daughters but "love" their sons. Rarely, though, do we have opportunities to hear parents talking about how they raised their daughters. It is very clear from our interviews that African American mothers and fathers exhibit a variety of parenting styles in working with their children, and these styles are heavily dependent on the parents' backgrounds and circumstances as well as the schools their children attend and the neighborhoods in which they and their children live.

While we rarely hear the voices of mothers talking about their daughters, we hear even less about the role of fathers in raising young African American women. Our questions to mothers and fathers focused on (1) the approaches their own parents took in raising them, (2) what they learned from those approaches which, in turn, they used in raising their own daughters, (3) the role of education in their family of origin, (4) what they did to help their daughters achieve academic success, (5) how they raised their daughters as African Americans, and (6) their approaches to disciplining and communicating with their daughters. In general, the interviews with parents focused on the extent of their involvement in their children's lives and schooling.

The questions to daughters focused on their relationships both with their parents and with their peers and others in school and in the community. Key issues included (1) important topics discussed between the daughters and their parents, (2) who had the most significant influence on their academic success, (3) what their parents did specifically to encourage them academically, (4) the types of discipline used, (5) how the students see their academic achievement and their ability in math and science, and (6) the approach that their parents used in helping them understand what it means to be an African American.

From listening to the voices of the parents and their daughters, we have been able to develop a clear picture of their successes, the challenges they face, and, most important, why they are so determined to overcome the odds against succeeding. We examine some of the obstacles that these young women face—from others' low expectations of them to issues related to sexual behavior and pregnancy. Most important, we analyze those factors that explain the success of these young women, ranging from parents' attention to their daughters' intellectual development in elementary-school years and the parents' assuming a strong advocacy role to an emphasis on education in the home, strong emotional support from family and others, and the role of religion and spirituality in the students' lives.

We look at the parents' perception of their relationships with their daughters' schools, and we see a pattern of interaction that was at times assertive and forceful, particularly when teachers misunderstood their daughters or expected too little of them, or when their daughters seemed to be victimized by discrimination. We focus attention on the relationship of these students to their peers, both in school years and in college, to determine the influence of peers on academic achievement. We also pay special attention to the frequency and context in which these girls were accused of "acting White" or of being nerds and, more important, how these young women countered these pressures. We look, too, at the role played by others in the community, including that of extended family and the church. One study, for example, found that church activities such as choirs, youth groups, and missionary teams are influential in the development of social skills among rural African American girls[85] and, in contrast, that urban Black girls lack the types of out-of-school experiences, such as church involvement, that help to develop interaction skills.[86]

Some of our observations are similar to those we made in our first book on raising young African American males. The group-interview sessions lasted longer than expected—between two and four hours each—because parents became so involved. Most important, parents spent a substantial amount of the time learning about and understanding their children's strengths and weaknesses and focusing on a variety of approaches in order to give appropriate support. As might be expected, these parents often based much of their parenting styles and child-rearing practices on those used by their own parents. In most cases, there was considerable consistency. In a few cases, though, parents purposely emphasized approaches different from what their parents had used. We also learned that parents found different practices and strategies to be effective at different stages of their daughters' upbringing. Parents also wanted to hear how others had addressed a variety of problems over the years. Parents generally agreed that an approach that proved effective with one child may not be so with the next child. They also agreed that effective parenting involved modifying approaches in order to reflect the changing needs of daughters at different times and under different circumstances.

Overall, during the course of our study, we observed six key strategies, or aspects, of parenting: (1) showing love by being involved in the daughters' education, giving encouragement and support, and cultivating a belief in self, (2) creating an environment that includes clear limits on behavior and discipline when appropriate, (3) consistently setting high expectations for success, academic and otherwise, (4) engaging in open and strong communication with the daughters, (5) emphasizing positive identification as both a woman and an African American, and (6) using available community resources.

The Outline of This Book

This chapter provides the context for the book by giving an overview of the challenges facing African American girls and women as well as information about their success, with a special emphasis on their educational experiences.

The next two chapters explore the voices of the mothers and fathers of the academically successful women in this study. What is very clear is that these parents have consistently given a great deal of thought to what it means to raise daughters. Chapter 2 gives the mothers' perspective on parenting practices and strategies that were most effective in supporting their daughters. Similarly, Chapter 3 looks at father-daughter relationships, which are even more rarely examined. In both chapters, the results of the group interviews give us the parents' perspectives on the six critical parenting components that we identify as central to effective parenting. In both chapters, we learn about these parents' views about their own childhood experiences, and we look at the impact of these experiences on their approaches to parenting.

Chapter 4 provides an opportunity for readers to hear the actual voices of young, successful African American women coming from different household backgrounds: one-parent, non-college-educated; one-parent, college-educated; two-parent, non-college-educated; and two-parent, college-educated. We hear the young women from these different groups talking about those factors that have contributed most heavily to their academic success—from the role of parents and effective parenting strategies to the importance of reading and of home and academic environments.

Chapter 5 looks specifically at the science-and-math-related experiences of these young women in their homes, schools, and universities. The key question addressed is how these young women were able to do so well in math-and-science areas traditionally dominated by males, and how parents, teachers, and others contributed. We learn that in some cases, the girls performed at high levels continually, while others experienced periods when they got into difficulty—both academic and disciplinary—and did not do well. The chapter also looks at the impact of a special academic program for talented minority students in science and engineering at the University of Maryland, Baltimore County. What is very clear is that in spite of their success in high school, a number of these women experienced periods of doubt and academic difficulty, which the program fortunately helped to counter.

Chapter 6 looks at challenges these young women have faced, focusing most closely on social, cultural, and emotional issues with which they have had to grapple, both inside and outside the academic setting, as they moved from girlhood to womanhood. Most important, this chapter explores the strategies and problem-solving techniques used by these young women to handle a variety of difficult situations.

In the final chapter, we return to the key findings of the study and make specific recommendations to parents, schools, policy-makers, and communities. Our suggestions are the result of interviews and group discussions with scores of students, their parents, and families who have been associated with the Meyerhoff Scholars Program since 1989. We also had the benefit of discussions with people from community-based organizations who were identified by the students as having played a key role in their academic success.

While families in this study are not fully representative of the general African American population, we believe that many of the suggestions in this book can be helpful to parents in general. Regardless of educational or economic backgrounds, the families we studied have overcome unusual circumstances. Consider, for example, the young woman whose quote begins this chapter. She knows that many have not expected her to do well, and yet she hears her mother's voice of encouragement. She sees alcoholics and crack addicts in her neighborhood, and people her age who have dropped out of school and earn money by selling drugs. Yet, through it all, she is determined to excel in school and become a scientist. Our hope is that her voice, and those of the other young women and parents in this book, will help families, schools, and communities as they work to ensure that African American girls and young women overcome the odds.

Mothers of Academically Successful Daughters
The Mothers' Voices

I think my daughter was born with a certain proclivity towards academics.
She was a very bright child who walked early, talked early, and was highly
active. She picked up things quickly and had a very good memory. . . . One of
the things Black kids have to learn that they have to be told early is that they
cannot take anything for granted. They are always going to have to work
twice as hard as the White kid and never assume that the White kid is
smarter because that is not always the case.

MOTHER OF MEYERHOFF STUDENT

If you have a bright White female, you think doctor, lawyer, whatever. . . . .
When you have a bright Black female, what is thought of her? Maybe she'll
make it, maybe she won't. A few will make it far, but what about all the
others?

MOTHER OF MEYERHOFF STUDENT

For many of the mothers we interviewed for this book, it does not matter how talented their daughters are academically, because they believe their daughters' success will never be certain. The mother whose quote begins this chapter describes a daughter who could read at three years of age, loved educational television, and attended college-based science camps during her summers in high school. Yet, at various points during her daughter's education, the mother had to advocate on her behalf, seeking the kind of education she deserved. The second mother quoted shares the first mother's concerns about the obstacles that lie ahead for her daughter, despite her talents. These mothers are representative, we believe, of what many African American mothers, regardless of education or marital status, struggle with in helping their children to achieve. These mothers have to be constantly vigilant, making sure that their daughters receive what they deserve. They also are constantly concerned that someone or something will impede their daughters' progress because of race or gender. In spite of these obstacles, these mothers work to empower their daughters to succeed against the odds.

In this chapter, we look at the stories the mothers tell us about their daughters' upbringing. It is their voices we hear. We wanted to learn from the "experts" how their daughters came to achieve at such high levels, when so many Black youth do not. We look at the issues of race and gender, and how in both school and the broader society the two are interconnected. We first ask the mothers about their own upbringing. We then focus on how they raised their children. We inquire specifically about how much they helped with homework and how they disciplined their daughters. We delve into their status as African Americans, asking, for example, what they have taught their daughters about growing up Black and female. We also ask if they think their daughters will encounter racism and if they think it will be difficult to find a husband in the future (should they want to marry).

We often find patterns of child-rearing that have been handed down by families from generation to generation, that are being repeated with success with the Meyerhoff students. Many mothers were the products of work and education-oriented kin. Occasionally, though, we hear from mothers who have taught themselves how to raise academically successful daughters. These are mothers who did not come from families with a strong emphasis on education. The message we take from this latter group of mothers is that a parent can help her child succeed even if her own upbringing was educationally impoverished.

By asking about the generation that raised them, we begin to see how a family tapestry has been woven. We use the term tapestry as a way of illustrating the intriguing complexity that emerges in families. The tapestry is the family picture that emerges over generations where each generation contributes something unique. Each tapestry is different and multifaceted, yet some commonalities exist, as these mothers' stories will show. From the mothers' predecessors, to the mothers, and then to the daughters, we gain at least a three-generation perspective that is rich in industry, survival skills, and accomplishments, all the while fending off external and internal challenges.

Many of the mothers we interviewed have college degrees or are married to men who do. But a significant minority are not college-educated or married, and their daughters are the first of their generation to attend a four-year college. We do not describe a monolithic approach to parenting. Black families are as diverse as families from any other race.[1] Some mothers describe growing up and then raising their daughters in middle- and upper-middle-class situations, while other mothers have reared their children in more impoverished situations. What we see is a diversity of approaches to child-rearing, stemming from a diversity of experiences represented in the mothers' backgrounds.

The mothers' views of race and their views of growing up Black and female are shaped by their families as well as by their more recent experiences. Regardless of the path the mothers have taken, they, like generations before them, have played a significant role in the family and in the achievements of their daughters. We see resilience in the mothers' own behavior and, as is shown in chapters below when we hear the daughters' voices, the younger generation has had it easier in many ways than their mothers. In the midst of threats to affirmative action and questions about the future of civil rights, the mothers have kept their focus on rearing their daughters while being mindful of an ever-changing social environment. The social environment is changing in some ways for the better, in the opportunities that become available to African American women. And it is changing in some ways for the worse, with the terrible increase in crime, drug abuse, and single parenting that has marked much of these daughters' early years.

African American Mothers' Journeys

The African American mother is often seen as the bulwark of the community. Since the end of slavery, when women outnumbered men (a legacy that remains today[2]), she has fulfilled many key roles. She is a worker, a professional, a caretaker, a provider, an educator, and supporter of the men and women of her generation, the generation that precedes her, and the generations that follow. Since her early years in the Americas, she has never neglected her family. Family in the African American community has come to mean extended kinship that goes beyond the nuclear family, according to Beverly Greene. It includes blood and nonblood relations. The historian Lerone Bennett writes that once slavery ended, ". . . almost all Black women abandoned the fields and served notice that they would hereafter devote themselves to their homes and children."[3] To understand the African American mothers whom we interviewed, we need to examine the challenges that Black women and Black mothers have faced historically and continue to face as they raise their daughters. These are issues of both race and gender. Their stories are intertwined with those of Black men, as well as with White men and women.

The end of slavery did not signal immediate social changes. The strong aftereffects of slavery continued for generations and hindered opportunities in higher education and employment. Opportunities for women, and particularly women of color, were few. According to Bennett, in 1865, when educating Blacks was still largely illegal, one in twenty Blacks was literate. Thirty-five years later, at the beginning of the twentieth century, 60 percent could read and write, a significant gain given the rural and agrarian nature of life at that time. Also, at the turn of the century, 90 percent of the Black population still lived in the South, which lagged substantially behind the North in industrialization. A Black professional class, though, was developing, largely in education and the ministry, two professions that were open to Blacks. The number of physicians and dentists by comparison was quite small.

The growth of the professions does not tell the whole story. African American women lagged behind African American men professionally. The first Black man graduated from a dental school in 1867, twenty years ahead of the first Black woman. The first Black man received his medical degree in 1822, more than forty years before the first Black woman. As noted below, many of the young women we studied in this book are aspiring doctors, scientists, and engineers. Their professional role models are historically few. Other lucrative professions were also dominated by men. In 1910, there were 777 Black lawyers in the United States, two of whom were female.[4] The few women who did succeed professionally often paid a high personal cost. Stress and severe headaches were not uncommon for the early Black female pioneers, particularly those in the White colleges, such as Oberlin.[5] To understand the African American women in the Meyerhoff Program, we need to appreciate the extraordinary efforts of their predecessors who overcame racism, classism, and sexism—efforts which have helped pave the way for Black women who are succeeding today. In fact, there are more Black women in medicine and law today than ever before, and, in many institutions, their numbers exceed those of Black men. Despite these enormous strides, their numbers are still disproportionately small when compared with White women.

Work has always been available to African American women, though not in the most respected professions. Because of racism and sexism, the lowest-paying jobs in society have been what is left for African American women. They could find work when Black men, who were often the target of a more virulent form of racism, could not. The historian Gerda Lerner believes that Black women are trained early on with the notion that they must work to support themselves and their families.

The mothers we interviewed have supported their daughters, pushed them to succeed, and have set high expectations for them, in part because high levels of achievement are more possible than ever before. As we learn below, each generation sets higher expectations than the preceding one. Many of these mothers were themselves expected to attend college even though their mothers and fathers did not. These mothers expect their daughters to go to graduate school. Even with these expectations, some mothers raised their daughters to be cautious about the future and to be ready for racism wherever it may appear.

Lerner underscores this point and introduces the issue of sexism when she writes, "Black women have always been more conscious of and more handicapped by race oppression than by sex oppression. They have been subject to all the restrictions against Blacks and to those against women."[6] At the same time, Lerner believes that Black women have prepared their daughters for such a life: "[Black women's] intimate contact with White people has made them interpreters and intermediaries of the White culture in the Black home. At the same time, they have struggled in partnership with their men to keep the Black family together and to allow the black community to survive. This dual and conflicting role has imposed great tensions on Black women and has given them unusual strength."[7] Lerner believes that mothers have trained their children to feign acceptance of discriminatory patterns on the one hand while instilling in those children racial pride and a desire for equality on the other.

Do mothers who are highly successful in their professions also face the same conflicts as those who have worked in less skilled jobs? Whether as a mother or grandmother, and whether highly successful or typical in their accomplishments, mothers give family the highest priority. In her study of forty-five highly successful African American women, ranging from congresswomen to doctors and artists, Patricia Reid-Merritt found that all the mothers described motherhood as their most significant role. These mothers view their parenting as being a part of a heritage and serving to link their children to their past, present, and future. Focusing on them is integral to maintaining an emphasis that respects the great strides women have made. This is the tapestry of experiences that these mothers weave when raising their children. Not only are they aware of the past, they are concerned about the future. The highly successful women who Reid-Merritt interviewed willingly put their own status and power aside to focus on their children. They did so, though, by sacrificing some of their success.

Before we hear how the mothers in this book raised their daughters, we need to reiterate that motherhood and work and the definitions of success in both are forever changing. Patricia Hill Collins writes, "The institution of Black motherhood consists of a series of constantly renegotiated relationships that African Americans experience with one another, with Black children, with the larger African American community, and with self. . . . [J]ust as Black women's work and family experiences varied during the transition from slavery to the post–World War II political economy, how women define, value, and shape Black motherhood as an institution shows comparable diversity."[8]

The Status of African American Women

It is important to consider the economic and social status of African American women and mothers. While U.S. women earn approximately one quarter less than men with comparable education, regardless of the level of education (no high school diploma, high school diploma, or college degree), the gap is smaller between African American women and men. In 1999, Black women's median income was $14,771 versus $20,579 for black men (72 percent of the Black males' income).[9] Black women are slightly more apt to be employed than Black men and are more apt to be in managerial and professional jobs (the highest category of employment), according to census data.[10] They are, though, less apt to hold this highest category of employment than are White women. Thus, as many experts on the Black family suggest, Black women are better off than White women when their status is compared with men of the same race. Black women are more apt than men to rise professionally (though without the pay). Some believe this is the vestige of generations-old beliefs in society about the danger of Black men.[11]

Poverty and single parenthood are often interconnected for African American women. Black women who head their households are more apt to be living in poverty than Whites or Hispanics who are the heads of their households.[12] Single-parent families dominate in the Black community—53 percent of all Black families with children under 18 are headed by a single mother, as compared with 17 percent of White women and 25 percent of

Hispanic women.[13] These facts are not lost on the mothers we interviewed. They are at the foundation of many of the concerns the mothers express when they worry about their daughters' employment, marriageability, and future responsibilities.

The Interviews with Mothers

The forty-six mothers we interviewed were, on average, 49 years old at the time of the interviews and were more highly educated than the typical African American woman. Almost two thirds had a college degree. Of those with a college education, almost two thirds had attended at least some graduate school at the time of the interviews. Slightly over one third did not graduate from college, and half of those had no schooling past high school. While the overall level of education is high (only 29 percent of all women under 30 have at least a college degree),[14] it should be noted that many of these mothers did not achieve their advanced education until their own daughters were in high school or college. In some cases, mother and daughter were pursuing higher education at the same time. One quarter of the mothers were working in such jobs as secretary, salesperson, skilled worker, and unskilled worker, while another quarter were working at the highest level of professional jobs.

There were usually between two and three children living in the home with one mother raising as many as eight children. Daughters outnumbered sons in the homes by a margin of almost three to one. For most of their daughters' upbringing, almost three quarters of the mothers interviewed were married; slightly more than one quarter were either separated, divorced, never married, or widowed. Overall, this is a population of mothers who are more highly educated and more apt to be married than the typical Black mother. This would usually place a mother and her child at a great advantage. Financial resources and the presence of a father in the home would provide greater stability and support to a daughter as she grew up and, we believe, would make academic success a greater likelihood. We believe, though, that it is possible for Black young women to be highly successful without many of the resources that the mothers we interviewed had. We also need to note that the mothers we interviewed for this chapter are not representative of mothers of the full set of daughters who are interviewed in later chapters. The current group of mothers, both more highly educated and more likely to be married, responded to our requests to be interviewed at a higher rate than the single, less educated mothers. (As can be seen in chapters below, slightly more than half of the daughters we interviewed spent some of their childhood in a single-parent family.) Despite the resources that a father in the home and education may provide, the road may still have been rough for many of these families.

In listening to these mothers' (and fathers') stories, we heard about six components of successful parenting that are similar to those we learned about from the parents we interviewed for our previous book, *Beating the Odds*. These successful parenting practices reflect the following: (1) *child-focused love*—the sense that these mothers geared much of their lives around the children (as the mothers in Reid-Merritt's research did); (2) *strong limit-setting and discipline*—the mothers were very strict in terms of the limits they placed on their children, especially in relation to social life; (3) *continually high expectations*—with the emphasis on the daughters achieving their fullest potential, they were constantly told to strive and not to be satisfied with low grades for their school work; (4) *open, consistent, and strong communication*—mothers talked to their children about a number of academic and developmental issues and tried to establish a parenting relationship in which their children felt comfortable bringing issues to them; (5) *racial and gender-identity focus*—mothers not only worked hard to define racial issues productively for their daughters, but they also talked to their daughters about their roles as women carrying on a heritage; and (6) *community resources*—the mothers sought out support systems outside the family, most notably the church environment and extracurricular activities (dance, sports, academically oriented summer camps) with which their daughters could become involved, and which provided important avenues for spiritual and intellectual growth as well as physical development.

These six components of parenting are approaches that the mothers brought to their parenting experiences. They represent methods of child-rearing and ways that parenting behaviors can be conceptualized. As the mothers' experiences are articulated, we hear these components in action.

The Mothers' Own Childhood: Messages About Education

In what kinds of homes were these mothers raised? Was education important? Did these mothers receive different messages growing up because they were female, in comparison with their brothers in the home? In the lengthy interviews we conducted, we received a number of answers. We look at the generations that raised the mothers to learn about the intergenerational transmission of values and parenting practices.

Almost two thirds of the mothers said that education was emphasized in their households when they were growing up. Their parents (or the relatives and adults who raised them) either told the mothers directly that they needed an education in order to get ahead or imparted to them the assumption they would need to earn a college degree. For the other one third, the message was either that education was not particularly emphasized or that survival, which meant putting food on the table, was the most important concern. A few examples from both of these groups of mothers follow.

From a college-educated mother who was raised in a home where there was an educational focus, we hear, "*My parents believed that education was a necessity. I grew up in the South. At that time it was very difficult for Blacks to make it. We were told if you want to get a good job, you've got to get a college degree. I was one of five children and it was just assumed you were going to graduate from high school and go to college. They believed very strongly in that and sacrificed for us. That made me think if they could do this for me, I could do it for my children.*"

A second mother, also from the South and not college-educated, told us that her parents were not educated. Her mother did not finish high school, and her father finished only the third grade. What she remembers most about them is how they worked together as a team to raise her and her siblings. Even without an education of their own, they emphasized the importance of getting an education. The message she heard most clearly from them was, "*'You can be whatever you want to be, but you have to work for it.' They told me that they did not get an education, but I was going to need it.*"

A third mother, who is raising her daughter alone and attended college, received a more mixed message about education, one related to being female. While she reported that both her parents thought that education was very important, her father held a traditional view about her career path.

"*I mentioned at one point that I was thinking about becoming a veterinarian, and he surprised me by saying he was not going to pay for me to go all the way through medical school, and then I would just get married and not use it. I got the feeling that it was okay to go into certain profes-*

sions, like teaching, but that you had to know what you were going to do with it when you finished."

Not every mother received such a strong message about the importance of education. It depended greatly on the family's history of education and economic circumstances. A mother with no college education told us, *"When I grew up, going beyond high school was not talked about and college was not encouraged. I was the youngest of eight, and we were expected to go out and get a job after high school, or do the family thing if that's what we wanted. Because I went to college after I had worked for a while, I encouraged my daughter to go to college while she still had the chance, as it was hard for me going back. I stopped and found it harder to go back again because I got complacent with my job."*

One mother, from a family of five girls, said that although education was not emphasized, a sense of being able to achieve was.

"I was raised on a farm, and we were taught by our father we could do anything on that farm. We were segregated in an all-Black school, and we had to put out more of an effort. The teachers cared a great deal. But there was no emphasis on education. My parents had fifth- and sixth-grade educations, and education was not stressed for them, so they did not emphasize anything other than finishing high school. I feel very blessed that my life has turned around and that I was able to move away from that environment, and see the opportunities available for my daughters. We all went on to college. I'm thankful to my parents that they instilled in us that we could do anything. My dad said, 'Remember on your way up the ladder, if you don't do things correctly, you'll meet those same people on your way down the ladder.'" (This mother did eventually complete college.)

For an example related to a family that focused on survival, we heard from this mother, the youngest of six. She illustrates how putting food on the table was the key. *"My father was a sharecropper, so it was survival for us. He had a little farm and worked the fields for someone else. So, for me, I was just encouraged to finish high school with no mention of education after that."*

Naturally, there was also great variation in achievement within families (as we see again in the daughters' chapters, where their success is contrasted in some cases with that of their less high-achieving siblings.) The variation the mothers described was between same-sex siblings and between daughters and sons. In a few families, mothers told us that boys were expected to achieve while girls were expected to marry.

One mother spoke of the differences both between same-sex siblings and between genders. She is a twin and views herself as the less academically strong of the two. *"My sister loved going to school while school didn't matter to me. She got a Master's in mathematics and one in computer science. So, she got all the education for both of us. My parents didn't push the girls in our family."* This mother, though, was in the minority. To our surprise, most mothers said that when they were growing up, there were not great differences between the expectations placed on them and on their brothers.

Messages About Getting Ahead in Society

We asked the mothers what their families taught them regarding the need to get ahead, and whether there were any particular strategies they learned that they conveyed to their academically successful daughters. We wondered what types of barriers they may have been warned about because they were African American. Although the wording of the messages varied, the mothers' parents raised them believing that they could compete with Whites, but that they had to do so with caution, that competition might exact a price.

The mother we quoted earlier, the youngest of eight, talks about being in school when integration arrived. She then describes how her family tapestry is woven, how the past influences the present.

"My school started out being segregated. But in my last two years of high school, they became fully integrated. I came through the '60s and '70s when segregation was a hot topic. My parents' role was one of providing caution, because they were from the 'old old-school,' while I consider myself from the 'old school.' They would encourage you, but at the same time, there was hesitance. They would tell me, 'Don't rock the boat unless you have a life jacket. And a life jacket can be hard to obtain.' In other words, they encouraged me cautiously. I came up in the marching era of civil rights, with the sit-ins. They were afraid of bodily harm because we were literally threatened.

"I have shared these stories with my daughters in the hopes that they will understand where we come from, and that as an African American people there is still definitely a struggle ahead of us. The struggle may be even greater today because the awareness of racism is not as high as when I came along because we were right in the middle of integration. There are still many things that we must overcome, and you still have to be better than other races to succeed."

The wisdom passed on in other families was similar. The mother who was the daughter of the sharecropper and the youngest of six told us, *"The message I received from my parents about being an African American is that you can succeed, but there are limitations with being Black and with being a female African American on top of that. But they instilled in me to always strive to do my best."*

A third mother, who was quoted previously and whose parents had little education, said, *"When I reflect back on my family history, slavery, and Black women, I think that they were strong during that time, and our race is here today because of the Black women. We kept our race going. I encourage them to know that they came from good roots. There are obstacles that are going to come because racism still exists, but my children have to stand firm and know what they want and keep pushing towards that goal."*

The mother who was discouraged by her father from being a veterinarian contrasted her mother's and father's styles for us. Being raised by both, her job was to parse out the differences in the messages and figure out for herself what they meant.

"My mother was a little conservative. She tried to encourage me to try new things but not to make a lot of waves or conflict. My father thought we should make things work regardless—knowing that race was always a barrier. He was always doing whatever he could as a newspaper reporter to push the envelope. . . . I got the message that it was difficult being Black, it was dangerous, but you still do what you can."

This same mother tried to simplify for her daughter the series of complex messages she received.

"I probably sent all those messages but basically tried just to instill the pride in being a Black woman. She was in situations where there may

not have been many Black children so I was constantly trying to balance giving her, through dance or Girl Scouts, the experience of being with other Black children her age. I probably did emphasize that there are barriers out there, and this is the way of the world, but I didn't want to stop her. I wanted to make her aware of that and try to figure out how to move around it. I think maybe the hardest part, when I look on my mother's persona, is sometimes you have to use a little sugar, you have to look at what you want to achieve, and sometimes getting aggressive doesn't always work. And sometimes you have to figure out when to slide by someone who you know is a bigot and that part was hard for her."

A few mothers told us that being an African American was not emphasized to a great extent in their homes when they were young, and those mothers do not bring that message to their daughters today. When asked about racial identity, one mother told us, *"I can't recall my parents making that distinction, even though we were raised in southern Virginia. They never talked about color, and I guess I never talked about it in that way with my daughter. I tried to encourage her to succeed as a person. So, if you succeed as a person, regardless of what color you are, you'll be okay."*

Another mother answered that she was given a clear message about how to succeed. Like others, she was told that if a ten were needed, she would have to get a fifteen. She also got some very pragmatic advice.

"You should present yourself in the way that the status quo will accept you. It may be nice to go to the roots of Blackness, but it's not really Black power—it's green power. And one of the strongest things that they impressed on me is that you need to get in the mainstream, where the decision-making process is being made, so that you can bring about change. And you can do that if you are able to speak the language and sit at the main table where the players are."

It is important to note that not all of the mothers we interviewed were born in the United States or were raised by their parents. One sixth of the daughters we interviewed in Chapters 4, 5, and 6 had at least one African or Caribbean parent. One mother was raised by her relatives in the West Indies after her parents died when she was young. Education was not important to her uncle, so it was not emphasized with her.

"The reason education was not important is that my uncle and aunt could not read. I was not given the privilege of going to school. I hold that against them, and I was damaged because of that. Education is very important to me. When I came to the United States, I could not obtain a proper job because I did not have the education. I had to take a job as a domestic and at fast-food places.

"Based on my experiences, what I told my children was that it doesn't matter who you are or what color you are, you can achieve your goals. I always encourage them to draw a picture in their mind of who they want to be and what they can be and remember that picture and go after that goal. They may fall but they should always go back to that dream."[15]

Mothers whose parents were separated also learned different strategies about getting ahead from each of their parents. One mother lived in two different homes in starkly different neighborhoods during her early years and saw class differences as well as philosophical differences between the two living arrangements.

"I lived with my father in the middle class until I was fifteen. My grandmother helped raise me. My father did not instill in me education or succeeding as a Black person—he just told me what to avoid and to be careful in trusting any White man. Later, I went to live with my mother and learned how to survive, how to eat. Living with her taught me that I needed an education and needed to graduate. I learned about being a Black person living with my mother because of where we lived. Cops beat me up just because I was Black. What I learned from this I taught my daughter. Nobody taught me how to be a Black female. They just taught me what I couldn't do, and I had to teach myself what I could do."

The stories we heard from the mothers about their own upbringing reflect a great diversity of experiences. Both parents were not always in the home, and education was not always emphasized. In some families, women were discouraged from pursuing education while their brothers were pushed. A large number of mothers came from Southern and rural environments where "survival" was the goal. Many of the mothers, both those who were encouraged to get an education and those who were not, used their experiences as a springboard to set high-achievement standards for their daughters. Thus, mothers work to motivate their children not simply because of the educational role models their families presented to them. In some cases, their lack of a role model or the lack of an emphasis on education is their stimulus. Also, mothers acknowledge the historical thread being woven from previous generations of Black women into this youngest generation. A sense of responsibility to the race and to their gender is being conveyed. The metaphor of the tapestry is apt. Each generation builds on the previous one, has a responsibility to that generation, and weaves a "story" for the generation that follows.

Educational Attainment

"My daughter is very successful because she has set a lot of goals for herself. Ever since she was a little girl, she has set those goals."

"I believe my daughter has been successful because from early on it has been a family affair. We tried to instill in her the importance of education and being responsible."

One of the most interesting questions to consider in examining the academic success of these young women is the extent to which their natural gifts (nature) or the environment of family, community, and school (nurture) have provided the foundation. While it is impossible to single out a specific reason for a complex series of events leading to anyone's success, we did ask the mothers questions about their daughters' success and sought to learn the genesis of their success. We also sought to learn what barriers, if any, confronted them along the way. In so doing, we realize that the answers the mothers provide are dynamic. What they believe about their families and their daughters' paths to success may change over time. They may gain new perspectives on their own, or they may speak with their daughters who may cite the significance of certain events or people the mothers did not recall. We also realize that reasons for success are often linked to one other. By that, we mean that a child who is born "talented" is more likely to have academic experiences that build on each other and elicit positive learning-related responses from a parent or teacher than is a child who shows little interest or talent. At the same time, a parent who is highly invested in a child's learning will expose that child to more opportunities for growth that may, in turn, elicit positive responses about learning from the child. In this way, we see that reasons for success can be linked.

It is important to mention here that there are various theories about the reasons for children's success in school. Some theorists turn to the interactions between the parent and child that occur over the child's years at home. They assert that the parent who creates a developmentally appropriate and conducive environment over the child's first eighteen years of life will maximize the chances for success. Some theorists zero in on the first three years of life as the critical time for developmentally rich interactions to occur. If those interactions do not occur, the child will suffer in the years to follow, they believe. Others turn to the school, and place responsibility on the shoulders of the professional educators. Still others focus on the role that socioeconomic status plays in the lives of children in poor families who fare worse than those who are raised in families with wealth.[16]

We believe that a partnership between the home and school throughout a child's educational career will maximize the chances for success. We hope our findings from the interviews with parents, their daughters, some of their mentors, and teachers will encourage the building of such coalitions.

As part of our inquiry, we asked the mothers why they thought their daughters had done so well academically when so many African-American youth do not succeed. With few exceptions, the mothers gave one of two responses. Approximately half told us, like the mother whose quote begins this section of the chapter, that their daughters were highly self-motivated. This was described in several ways. Sometimes we learned that the daughters had always been interested in learning and had always liked school. Other times, the term "self-motivation" was used. We also heard that the daughters were interested in a particular profession, such as medicine or science. Finding their way into these careers was seen as a continuation of something they had always wanted. To some extent, the mothers who gave these responses were telling us that there was something wonderful that emerged in their daughters. They tended not to take a great deal of credit for their daughters' success. A few mothers said that their daughters were "naturally" bright and focused on the nature of the children. We acknowledge that modesty may have prevailed in some cases—some mothers may be reluctant to take credit for specific education-related approaches they followed with their children.

The other half of the mothers gave an answer that places the emphasis on nurturing. They said, like the other mother quoted at the beginning of this section, that the family was at the root of the daughters' success. These mothers credit family involvement, working together, and modeling the importance of education and accomplishments. To them, setting high expectations was critical. (This is one of the six parenting components to which we referred earlier.) Several mothers also credited the role of a strong belief in God and commitment to the church.

One mother stated, *"I feel she succeeded so well because we have been there behind her, never letting up, telling her what she can do and how important education is."* She even suggested an intergenerational connection by adding, *"I guess reflecting back on how our parents made education the most important thing in the world, and it has just filtered down, as we felt the same way. So we just constantly pushed her."* Here the mother is invoking the family environment in its broadest sense by saying that the success is linked not only to the current family but to the past emphases in the family.

Another mother gave a slightly different twist in her response. *"I believe she accomplished her goal because she was told as a child that whatever she wants to achieve she'll have to work very hard for. I let my children know that to achieve, you have to work."* Here the emphasis is not on family support, per se, but on educating the children about the necessity of hard work. The implication from this mother is that her daughter would have to achieve on her own to some extent. In fact, later in the interview with this mother, she recounted how she could not help her daughter in high school with her homework, because it was beyond her knowledge of the topic. Despite this, she was always a presence in her daughter's life.

As the mothers expanded on some of their answers about their daughters' successes, they frequently explained that they *"were always there as mom,"* *"always encouraged her,"* and *"made sure that learning was fun."* (This is reflective of the parenting component of child-focused love—the daughters' success was a central goal for the mothers.) They skillfully monitored homework by usually taking one of two approaches, particularly when the children were young. Some mothers (often in conjunction with the fathers) set up a schedule for their children where they were expected to do homework when they got home from school and before they went out to play. This made school work a priority. The second approach (sometimes tied to the first) was to read over the homework and sometimes to ask to have it redone if it was done sloppily or contained mistakes. As cited already, if the daughter's academic abilities outpaced the abilities of the mother or father, which they often did in the latter high-school years, this approach became less useful as an aid in completing the work. It also was less necessary, though, in high school. Many of the daughters' strong work habits and ethics were formed by the time the daughters entered high school. Struggles that mothers told us about that revolved around schoolwork and work habits usually occurred in elementary or middle school.

In fact, it is in high school that many of the daughters either excelled or received recognition for their excellence. Gifted-and-talented programs, advanced placement courses, and special, academically accelerated summer programs were typical activities for many in lower grades, but some of the daughters did not hit their stride until high school. Others had long shown a proclivity for math and science and had been excited by these fields from the first time they had exposure. Often, in fact, it was a math or science teacher who was inspirational and took a special interest in them.

The teacher would recognize and support the girls' talents or push them to new levels of achievement. The recognition made the young students feel appreciated and understood for what they had to offer. One mother recalled, when asked how teachers had encouraged her daughter, *"My daughter became part of the gifted-and-talented program because her teachers had noticed her interest in sciences. She enrolled in the elementary school program and followed it through high school. All her teachers have shown an interest in her. I remember a couple suggesting courses she might benefit from in high school or a class outside of school or a book."*

Other Information on Education

In addition to the interviews, we also gathered information about the specific role the mothers played in their daughters' academic achievements by asking the mothers to complete a questionnaire with more than fifty items focused on their parenting role.[17] The mothers' answers reflect a picture of involvement in school studies that is highest in elementary school and diminishes over the course of middle and high school. In elementary school, 91 percent of the mothers monitored the amount of time their daughters spent studying. In middle school, the number dropped slightly, to 82 percent, and by high school it had fallen to 59 percent. Monitoring the time the daughters spent playing video games and watching television also dropped as the daughters moved from elementary school, where 83 percent of the mothers monitored, to high school, where 56 percent monitored. Although the amount of time spent with friends was also watched more closely when daughters were younger, 72 percent of the mothers reported still keeping an eye on this area in high school. This appears to be an age-appropriate reduction in the mothers' involvement. As children age, they should be left to manage their homework and free time increasingly on their own.

An additional way we gained a sense of the mothers' involvement was to ask them to compare themselves with other parents in their neighborhoods. Almost two thirds agreed that they were more vigilant in monitoring homework than other parents. A slightly higher number also thought they were generally stricter than other parents in their neighborhood. While mothers lessened their watchfulness and involvement as their daughters progressed through elementary to secondary school, their "work" was clearly not finished. Almost every mother (97 percent) reported knowing how her daughter was doing academically in high school, and slightly more than three quarters also reported usually attending high-school programs designed for parents. Substantial numbers (89 percent) also attended athletic events and other activities in which their daughters participated.

In fact, extracurricular activities were mentioned by most mothers as being a substantial part of their daughters' lives. Ninety-five percent said they encouraged their daughters' involvement in these activities. The number and range of activities were extensive, including church-related events, dancing, music, sports, museums, and special classes. Mothers used these activities as a balance for the academic side of their daughters and hoped that such involvement would make their children well rounded. As one mother put it, *"I won't say her extra-curricular activities encouraged her academically, but they probably gave academics a different twist. She was involved in church, in dancing, and in Girl Scouts. With all that she was involved in academically in school, I thought she needed these as a release to help her when she got back to the books so she wasn't so stressed."*

High academic achievement, however, did not mean that some typical teenage behaviors that have bothered parents for generations were not present. For example, over 40 percent of the mothers were concerned that their daughters were spending too much time on the telephone during their high-school years.

Developing an Interest in Math and Science

As mentioned in the first chapter, women do not typically go into science and engineering as professions, and young girls are not typically expected to pursue math and science in school. Yet many of these Meyerhoff Scholars showed an early talent in these areas. In most cases, this came as a surprise to the mothers. Although a few daughters were specifically exposed by their parents or relatives to math and science (and it is believed their interest arose from that), much more typical is the mother who told us that this talent came naturally. For example, we heard, *"She was always good in math!"* and *"She just loved science. I don't know where she got it, but we strongly encouraged it."* Scientists, nurses, doctors, and mathematicians were in the families or extended families in about one quarter of these situations. In these cases, we heard that the daughter developed an interest that was fostered by relatives. Of course, it is difficult to know whether the interest initially developed because of the environment or was simply reinforced by the familial environment, which returns us to the question of whether such talent appears as the result of nature or nurture.

Most families, though, did not have scientists in the home, and, very soon into the daughters' high-school experience, the parents were trying to keep up academically with their daughters. One mother used an interesting strategy enabling her to stay involved with her daughter's learning.

"She had to teach me math sometimes. If I couldn't help her, I'd ask her to teach me. Math always came easy to her, and it's not my or my husband's forte." Regardless of how the interest in math and science developed, no mother seemed to discourage it as a pursuit for a woman. One mother, though, did have a grand plan to make sure that her daughter would never veer away from following a nontraditional field for women. She told us, *"I tried as hard as I could to guard against this 'girls aren't good at math.' I told her when she was younger that there was a secret. And that was that girls were always smarter."*

Some daughters discovered science on their own, some were heavily influenced by family, and a few had teachers who encouraged it. A few mothers mentioned the importance of the Meyerhoff Program in sustaining the interest.

Specific Ways Mothers Helped Their Daughters

Mothers helped their daughters along the path to success in many specific ways. These approaches were revealed throughout the interviews (and are also mentioned by the daughters in Chapters 4, 5, and 6). Like nuggets of gold, these twenty-one suggestions can be mined by all parents for their own children's success. Some were mentioned by a number of mothers, others by only one or two.

1. **Doing things with their daughters.** Mothers often mentioned spending time going places, taking trips, talking, and going for walks with their daughters, emphasizing the educational nature of such outings. Walks, for example, would be at nature reserves, while trips might involve exploring a historic area.
2. **Restricting or monitoring television-watching.** Mothers viewed the television as a distraction from school work, reading, and other activities.
3. **Going on specific outings.** Mothers cited science museums, parks, zoos, libraries, and dinner theaters as good destinations.
4. **Becoming involved in the life of the school.** Serving on the PTA, accompanying daughters on class trips, or visiting the classroom were viewed as fundamental to daughters' success.
5. **Encouraging and advocating for participation in gifted-and-talented programs.** Parents often had to advocate on behalf of their daughters in order to become involved in these programs.
6. **Reading at home.** Some mothers constantly read to their daughters; a few even read to them in utero. Books were carefully selected so that they would have a positive influence on the daughters.
7. **Teaching at an early age.** Mothers took every opportunity to turn experiences into learning activities. Whether talking about the stars during an evening stroll, reading words on signs, or examining plants, mothers constantly interpreted things to their daughters. When the mothers could not answer questions, they sought out the answers from reference books or the Internet.
8. **Watching educational TV shows.** *Sesame Street* was popular with a few mothers.
9. **Restricting video games.** This type of activity was forbidden in many homes because it was viewed as a mindless activity.

10. **Encouraging extracurricular participation.** As mentioned earlier, these activities played an extremely important part in the non-academic side of the daughters' lives and were viewed as enhancing the academic side.

11. **Maintaining a strict schedule in relation to homework.** Also mentioned earlier, mothers often insisted on a schedule of homework before play.

12. **Checking homework.** It was typical for mothers to ask to see their daughters' homework when the daughters were in elementary school.

13. **Providing a variety of intellectually stimulating in-home activities.** Mothers described having a range of toys, books, and games around the house to stimulate their daughters in different ways.

14. **Advocating within the school.** A number of mothers described situations where their daughters were placed in classes that were lower in level than appropriate given the daughters' knowledge. Mothers (as well as fathers) often insisted on a higher placement.

15. **Encouraging the best work.** Mothers, in checking over the homework or in setting standards, frequently set high standards.

16. **Involving the daughter in church.** A number of mothers cited church activities as an important source of support for their daughters.

17. **Giving unconditional support.** Although high standards were set, the refrain from the mothers was that it was important to "be there" for their children to be supportive.

18. **Moving to a new neighborhood where schools were better.** A handful of mothers reported relocating to another county or school district in order to enroll their daughters in a better educational system.

19. **Reinforcing family values.** Mothers conveyed the message to their daughters that the family was at the core of their upbringing and would always play an important role in their lives, and that family life was highly valued. Though, in a strict sense, this is not an educational strategy, it has implications for educational achievement.

20. **Seeking help when needed.** Mothers encouraged the use of tutors or other people in and outside of the family who might be knowledgeable about the subject matter their daughters were studying.

21. **Encouraging questions.** In all activities, the mothers urged their children to question both what was going on and why it was going on. Intellectual inquiry was highly valued.

It is important to reemphasize one point, in particular—*advocacy*. Many mothers gave examples of their daughters being placed in lower-level classes. Mothers believed teachers did not expect their daughters to do well and placed them in these classes. Over one third reported that their child was misplaced at least one time, and over 40 percent said they had to advocate for their child with a teacher or school administrator. One specific example came from this mother.

"I was insistent that they place her where she was supposed to be placed in classes or I would go to the school board. When she went to high school, she came home the first day and told me they had put her in a lower math class, and she was always in the highest. I went and talked to the principal, and he told me it was because enrollment was low that teachers were being shifted around. I told him that was his problem and he had to deal with it. He said he couldn't move her, and I said he would move her and that I wouldn't leave until it happened. He said he would talk to her teachers, and he got back to me and said they could shift her classes and get her in. He warned me that if she did not get good grades he was going to move her. And I told him to let me worry about that— it was my problem. I told her that if she came home with a C, I was going to wring her neck. Every year it was something. They were always trying to move the kids into lower classes."

For these reasons, vigilance was always needed. But such wariness can take a toll. It places a strain on the parent who has put herself on the line for her child in a way that many parents often do not have to. Rather than trying to partner with the school to educate, a wary alliance is built. This, in turn, can strain the relationship between mother and daughter. While the daughter of the mother in our example achieved, other mothers may not always be as successful either in advocating or in having their children earn good grades under pressure.

Extrafamilial Support
and Handling Developmental and Social Issues

In the African American community, the giving and receiving of support or some type of assistance is a key facet of the culture. Survival has meant the community or neighborhood having to pull together, often under the umbrella of a religious institution. The saying, "it takes a village to raise a child," is a metaphor for everyone connected to a child helping that child succeed. In some communities, the young women we studied were treasures cherished and supported. According to their mothers, they were helped along the way by many different people. It is not unusual, of course, for a parent of a highly successful child, when asked about those who helped, to name a number of specific people or institutions. These mothers were no exception. It is noteworthy who they named and what some of the comments were about the support their daughters received.

"Family," in its broadest sense, was mentioned most often as the primary source of support. Specifically, the mothers mentioned their husbands, parents, cousins, and siblings as contributing to their daughters' achievements. Sometimes, it was not a particular person but rather the entire family that was credited with being central to the daughters' academic accomplishments. The concept of the "village" was invoked in describing how a particular daughter was raised by everybody and how she was, to some extent, the responsibility of everybody.

One mother said, *"My family always encouraged her. When we'd go home to North Carolina and we'd have family times, we'd all get together and they were always interested in what she was doing. My brother took her to his lab and encouraged her to be a doctor. The whole family encouraged her."*

The church and spirituality were also cited. While a few mothers cited prayer and God as being helpful, the church community as a whole and either a church leader or a church member were most typically named (the parenting component of drawing on community support). Some churches praised a daughter's accomplishments from the pulpit. Others followed her progress over the years as one academic success was followed by another. A few church communities had members who helped the daughters with studying and homework. Mothers highly valued this spirit of cooperation and caring in a faith-based arena.

We heard, for example, *"We were very active in our church. I think in our community we believe in the 'village' concept. The church members were devastated when my husband and I split up, and everyone was trying to help out. The elder sisters in the church became mini-mothers to my daughters. So we were there on Sundays, and they were taken care of."*

Another mother focused more on the academic support.

"Everybody in the church pushed my girls. The members stood behind them. When the girls were in high school, the church encouraged them.

We had teachers and preachers, my old teachers from high school who were in the church. They were always asking me, 'Where are the girls and how are they doing?'"

After family and church, school teachers were mentioned most frequently as the primary positive support. Usually a high-school or middle-school math or science teacher was cited. In one situation, an elementary teacher and middle-school teacher were mentioned.

"These were two major forces outside of the family. One was a fourth-grade teacher who called my daughter one day and told her about the Maryland Gifted-and-Talented Summer Program. She encouraged her to apply because she worked so hard in the Aquatic Biology Program. The other person was a science teacher in the eighth grade. She left her research job to teach, mainly to encourage females to go into sciences."

Teachers were sometimes the only support. One mother told us that because she did not have a large family and moved a great deal, the teachers' role in encouraging her daughter became even more central than usual. The teachers were one of only a few stabilizing influences. Others cited the teachers for the opportunities they provided in their labs, referrals they made to special programs, and advocacy for their daughters to enroll in advanced classes. One mother gave the credit to the school counselor and principal, noting that her daughter's *"counselors and principals always made her aware of the programs, and every year there was a different principal at the school—one told her about the Gifted Program. The principal went with her to one of the luncheons for the program. Her counselors, the principals, and the teachers saw the gift in her."*

This is not to say that teachers and the school environment were uniformly supportive. As mentioned earlier, over 40 percent had to fight for their daughters because they thought the daughters had been placed inappropriately in lower-level classes. Clearly though, many teachers provided support that was seen as absolutely essential to the success of the daughters.

Finally, friends and neighbors were also mentioned occasionally (as was the staff at the Meyerhoff Program) as providing support. It should be emphasized that support often was provided by more than a single source. For example, one mother told us, *"My family was very proud of her, and I have friends in education who were really proud of her accomplishments. And neighbors would always say they wished their kids were like [my daughter] who was a role model for them."* As in keeping with "the village," many people were involved.

Developmental and Social Issues

Most teenagers, male and female, experience personal and social struggles. Resolving these struggles is part of growing up and sets the stage for young adulthood. We wondered specifically what issues these young African American women encountered. To learn the answers, we made the following statement to the mothers: "Girls face many developmental challenges while growing up, perhaps especially in the teen years. What types of challenges or difficult experiences, if any, did your daughter face, and how did you help her deal with them?" Two thirds of the mothers responded that significant issues arose for their daughters, ranging from issues involving physical appearance and treatment based on race to family disruption and family dysfunction.

In a few cases, mothers described daughters who had played the role of the perfect daughter for years and then, in high school, rebelled by acting out. One mother gave us a harrowing description about what can happen.

"That's a real touchy subject. Both my daughters had been A students, perfect, respectful young women. They would say 'yes ma'am, no ma'am.' They knew their place as a child versus adult. But when the oldest hit senior year, everything that she could have done from age five to 17 happened. I was shocked. I'm sure it had a lot to do with her father not being in our lives anymore, and I was working crazy hours. She started hooking school and missed so much that she didn't graduate. It wasn't that she couldn't do the work. She didn't want to do the work. She started hanging out with people I could not understand why she'd be attracted to. I recognized that I was not in her life 24/7 anymore, nor her in mine. The street has a lot of influence when you get a certain age and she was hanging around people who were a really bad influence. She got caught in the peer pressure between what they wanted and what her mother wanted. I was constantly going to school and talking to the guidance counselors. They knew she was brilliant, but there was something lacking in her life and in her home life.

"She did not get into trouble with the law but she got into trouble. She ultimately ran away and nobody knew where she was. There was this older person who was 29 who was controlling her life, and I could not do anything about it. I tried the police and learned what my options were. I felt lost a lot of times. Ultimately, and I believe this through prayer and through the efforts of people at church and my family, we stayed with her . . . we never left her. She graduated with honors and made it into the Meyerhoff Program. The day that happened, I thought I was going to die. I just couldn't believe it. It was like a godsend. She got focused and pulled up her grades and applied. It was like a miracle. But I never left her, and it was the relentless support of the family that worked. She was going to be a statistic on the street, and I told myself that I did not work this hard to lose my child. I came face to face to battle those people in the street who had a hold on her, and I was scared. At one point, I literally had a baseball bat and I was willing to murder. But it was to protect my child."

While this mother's experiences were extreme compared with those of other mothers whose daughters we interviewed, they illustrate the fear that many mothers believed they would face if their daughters took a misstep. For some, there was a sense that their daughters were not that far away from getting into serious trouble, that the benefits of their accomplishments were tenuous. Similar concerns about dating and levels of independence were mentioned by a number of mothers. Many mothers forbade dating until late in high school. They believed that boy-girl socializing would only get in the way of the more important goals of education and staying focused on work.

As one mother put it, *"The most difficult moment was when she was not allowed to date. I was the worst mom. Everybody else can do these things except her. So we had problems. Junior high school was tough. I encouraged her to talk to me and told her we may not like each other right now but we'll get past it. She would remind me that she had never been thirteen before and I would say I had never been a mom before. There was a two-year span of her thinking that she was missing out on everything. I needed to know whose house she was going to and who the parents were. I thought we should meet and greet her friends. Even when she started to date, I did not believe in pick up and go. If he doesn't come to the door, I don't know him so you can't go. We got through it and she came out a really good person."*

Another mother, who was born in the Caribbean, echoed some of these sentiments. *"There were times that I, as a mom, always said no to her. Not only her but the rest of my kids because there are certain principles that I do not agree with in the United States such as teenage girls going out with boys, especially if I did not know him."*

Some dating situations, though stressful at the beginning, had happy endings. This mother weathered a storm that is a concern in many communities—older men dating teenagers.

"When she was sixteen she became interested in a young man who was older than she by four years. That was a difficult period because we didn't want her focus to be broken, and she was determined to keep the relationship. It was a period when she was trying to find out who she was. She did continue to see him and we talked to him and let him know what we expected from her and what her potential and future were. He did respect that and today he's her husband."

Even if dating was allowed, in some communities a lack of eligible young men was an issue. One mother reported that there were only a few Black boys and girls in her daughter's high school and that the Black boys dated the white girls. This left the Black girls with no social life. As was mentioned at the beginning of the chapter, the availability of Black men has been an issue historically.

Not only was dating often restricted for these daughters, prohibitions were also placed on freedom and independence in general. At least some of the prohibition was driven by the cultural context. It was necessary in the eyes of at least one mother to be wary because of her race and competition from others.

"A lot of her friends had more freedom than she did. I always felt that being a young Black girl, that she could not afford to be as free as some other kids. A lot of her friends came from money. Their parents gave them more than I could afford and they had a lot more freedom. I thought a lot of her friends were envious because she was smarter and that they were trying to get her into trouble. And I thought the first time they got her into trouble they are going to laugh at her and say she thought she was so smart and call her a 'Miss Goody Two Shoes.'"

In sum, dating was not handled uniformly by the mothers. Some reported their daughters were not allowed to date at all. A few mothers who were raised in Latin America or the Caribbean gave this answer and cited cultural reasons for this prohibition. Another group of mothers said their daughters could go out only on group dates until they were in the later years of high school. One or two mothers said dating was not an issue either because their daughters were too involved in school work or sports or were not asked to go out. The final group of mothers allowed their children to date but insisted on meeting the date first and in making sure the dating experience was structured.

Teens not only struggle with their parents about developmental issues, they also struggle inwardly. Some of the young women had significant problems that were related to their physical appearance. These concerns are not unique to this group of young women but are pervasive in adolescence. One mother said her daughter coped by "hiding." The mother not only drew on her own experiences as a woman to guide her daughter but also relied on another woman for help.

"When my daughter started to develop as a pre-adolescent I noticed that she would wear big baggy tops all the time to try and cover up. We had several discussions about how she felt about her body and the fact that boys were noticing. I think it improved when she realized she wasn't the only one to have gone through this—that I had experienced the same thing and that she had nothing to be ashamed of, that it was all natural and normal. I mentioned it to her female pediatrician and they talked about it, too."

Having a period of low self-esteem and being concerned about physical beauty is also something mothers are in a unique position to discuss (as compared with the fathers interviewed in Chapter 3 who assume a more protective role.) One example is the mother who related, *"At some point in middle school, she felt she was this ugly duckling and seemed to have little confidence in herself. I was surprised when I found out because I had no idea. So I talked to her and built up her confidence. It took probably two years to get her back on track and really believe in herself."*

Weight was given as a concern, too, as we heard from this mother.

"When she went into high school, she had a weight problem. I never pressured her about it because I was afraid she would get an eating disorder. It was a fine line. She wore pants all the time, but then when she went to

the store she wouldn't fit in the junior department anymore and that was a problem.

"One day she was watching TV and she said she wanted to get some diet pills. I told her we were going to the doctor instead. The doctor told her she had not gone through puberty yet, and it would be okay but that she should cut out sweets. So she cut out sweets and began feeling better about herself."

Another mother reported a more significant weight problem.

"My daughter was obese and obesity is hereditary in our family. She still is obese. She had to face not being asked on dates, and lost some friends in high school because of it. She did find one male friend who seemed to be attracted to her personality and the fact that she was smart. He stuck with her and that basically got her through high school. They are still friends now." This mother helped her daughter by encouraging her to go with the people that accepted her and ignore those who did not.

We also learned about daughters who, because they were sometimes one of only a handful of African American girls in a gifted-and-talented program, would be harassed by other African Americans. One mother whose daughter was in this situation told us, *"It was a challenge being a minority and the only one in her classes. In elementary school the other African-American kids would get jealous of her and would pick on her. We had to work out this situation with her which was probably the most challenging because she initially responded by getting sick and not wanting to go to school. We worked with the counselor and the teacher. My daughter didn't want us to get involved because she thought it would make it worse, but she was being bullied and I thought it couldn't get any worse. Once she stood up to them, it was over."*

Occasionally problems that developed for the daughters were beyond the capacities of the family and school personnel. Outside professional help was then sought. One mother recounted taking her daughter for therapy when her daughter's best friend told the mother how depressed her daughter was. When a second daughter became depressed, the whole family went for family therapy.

Finally, mothers talked to us about family crises that affected their daughters: the breakup of the family, divorce, and substance abuse. These issues are, unfortunately, all too common today. Even with the talents of these daughters, they posed serious threats to their daughters being able to maneuver successfully through adolescence.

In relation to family breakup, one mother recounted, *"The separation of her father and me was difficult. Kids don't like to be different and she saw herself then as different. Most of her friends and family were growing up with two parents. As she grew older she appreciated my efforts and was able to cope with the fact that she was raised by me. Last week I was touched when I overheard one of her friends saying that I was so strict. My daughter said I had to be strict because I was both the mother and the father."*

Alcoholism was present in a handful of families and proved to be quite difficult to confront. One mother noted, *"The biggest problem for her as a teenager was her father who was an alcoholic. She wasn't able to handle that so I tried to keep them apart. When he was drinking, he wasn't abusive, he just liked to drink, especially on weekends. Sometimes he would come when the kids would have friends in the house and embarrass them. She couldn't understand why he would drink, and wanted him to go someplace else. We finally separated and that affected her, and now she doesn't like to see anyone drink and won't touch it. He eventually died from drinking."*

Raising a Daughter to Deal with Sex and Drugs

The challenges that exist for teenagers, including African American teens, are well documented in the literature, in the media, and in the minds of parents and teachers throughout the United States. Unwed teen pregnancy, substance abuse, violence, and crime are prevalent in cities and on the rise in suburban areas and rural areas. At the least, sexual activities and drugs distract and, at the most, consume the lives of many youth. These temptations and dangers exist for this population.

We wanted to know how these parents handled these issues with their daughters. There was great variety in the responses which reflect differing parenting philosophies and different personal experiences of the mothers (and fathers) in the home.

Sometimes issues around sex and dating (discussed earlier) were talked about together. One mother specifically tied the two together.

"We talked about all these things in the family over the years. Dating was not acceptable until they got to the point where they knew what they were

doing, which was not until they were sixteen or seventeen. Premarital sex never became an issue because you couldn't do it if you were home with your parents."

But more open and frank discussions about sex also occurred. Most of the mothers interviewed reported talking to their daughters about sexual activity and using educational materials as necessary. When we talked about sex with the mothers, two common themes were noted. First, the mother-daughter relationship was seen as the building block to communication. Mothers held the expectation that they would learn from their daughters about social pressures being placed on them to have sex and also about any sexual experiences their daughters were having (if they were having them). Trust was seen as the key issue, with many mothers reporting that they and their daughters could discuss everything.

Second, almost every mother discussed concerns about pregnancy. Many referred to the high rate of pregnancy in the Black community and worried that their daughter would become another statistic. One mother told her daughter she was *"one in a million"* and that *"sharing her body was a special invitation that she could only give for the first time once."* Some told of high-achieving friends of their daughters who became pregnant and whose success was derailed. Mothers encouraged their daughters to stay focused and kept watch over them vigilantly.

A few mothers reported taking what they described as a "realistic" approach to dating. These mothers assumed that premarital sex was going to happen and helped with obtaining birth control. One mother reported, *"I was always very vocal and very informative to my daughters when they were coming of age. When they were eight and nine we went to the library and talked about reproduction and sexuality. I was as graphic as I felt necessary at this time and age. Each year, I would become a little more specific. They've always felt comfortable coming to me to talk about anything. When my youngest had her first sexual encounter, I was upset, but life is life. I remember when I was a teenager, so I wasn't going to pass judgment. But she knew I wanted her to wait and that I was adamant about not having unprotected sex. I'm not always ready for everything they want to tell me, but that's the environment that I brought them up in. So, sex is okay and we've talked about many female issues."*

This same mother, in talking about her daughter's socializing, revealed the deep conflict it touched off in her relations with her husband. Clearly, parents do not always agree about what should occur on a date or whom their daughter should be dating.

"Dating was an issue for her father, who did not want her bringing home any White boys. He had a dislike for interracial couples that I didn't know about. We came into serious opposition because I believe if they treat you like a lady and are nice to you, then the color of the skin is not important. He has dark skin and I am light, so it became an issue between us as I was trying to get him to understand that I have White people in my family."

A number of mothers emphasized consequences with their daughters—that if they played with fire they were going to get burned. They encouraged their daughters to resist being pressured and taught them that they had a choice with their actions.

While issues about sex education seemed to be handled through communication and a strong mother-daughter relationship, issues about drugs were handled through education and strict prohibition. Dating will be allowed at some point, even if it is not until college, so relationships can be seen on a continuum. Drug use, on the other hand, is illegal and is more easily forbidden. A great deal of literature on drugs is available and was shared with the daughters. Interestingly, this literature is often based in science and had a particular appeal to this group of young women. While a few mothers admitted they were not convinced that their daughters had not tried drugs, generally this did not pose as large a problem as did issues around sex.

Personal appeals were also used in relation to drugs. One mother told us, *"With drugs I just told her basically what our life was like because my husband and I used to be on drugs. He especially had a $100-a-day habit. How the Lord delivered us from that I don't know. And she knew about my mother being an alcoholic. I didn't hide anything from her. She knew that was not the type of life to get into, and she didn't hang around people like that. We moved out of the apartment complexes into the suburbs, so that helped."*

Special Challenges Raising an African American Daughter

One premise of this book is that female African Americans face unique challenges in society as women and as people of color. We wondered to what extent these families, with their high-achieving daughters, would be buffered from these challenges, if at all. Growing up female in America exposes a young woman to social pressures related to appearance and dating. Growing up also includes balancing family and community loyalties with academic and work pursuits. The mothers were asked what they saw as the special challenges raising a Black daughter.

On one end of the spectrum were mothers who felt there were no particular challenges and who had not specifically raised their daughters with an awareness of race and gender. On the other end were those who were keenly intent on teaching their daughters about the dangers of the world and warned against a young Black woman ever relaxing her guard or taking anything for granted.

A number of mothers spoke specifically about a common concern of many Black parents, one we identified in *Beating the Odds*—namely, that Blacks have to work harder than Whites and be better at what they do in order to get ahead. The mothers and daughters in our study had this feeling, especially in largely white academic settings. As one mother told us, *"Sometimes she would go places and there would be just a few African American people there, and we would talk about that and how you always have to work hard to excel and that people aren't going to give you a fair chance. You have to be twice as good or you always have to be your best. Don't ever think when you are in a majority environment that you have to be second to anyone. You can set goals on being whatever it is that you want to be within that context. Don't let people hold you back."*

This mother is also citing another point that mothers made to us. They encourage their daughters to believe they can achieve as much as anyone and not to listen to racial stereotyping that Blacks are not as competent.

Other struggles were also mentioned. A few mothers whose daughters went to predominantly White schools told us that their daughters had a hard time fitting in if they were one of only a handful of Black students in the class. Their social lives were greatly restricted because their Black friends saw them as trying to act White. Other parents told their daughters to make sure they socialized with the "right crowd," a reference to avoiding African Americans who were more interested in socializing than schoolwork. One mother said her hardest challenge was teaching her daughter to be tactful so she would get along with everyone.

For mothers of daughters who grew up in White neighborhoods, the challenge was to help their daughters to feel good about their appearance because a White-oriented standard of beauty was often applied. One mother lamented, *"It was a challenge because you always had to talk to them and encourage them and keep them aware of who you are and accept that you are different. Your hair is different but so what? You are still a good-looking person, and your hair is still beautiful."*

Mothers also struggled to maintain an awareness of heritage. For example, one mother said, *"All the media and school books tend to be skewed, so the challenge was to find the balance and who she was so she knew she fit into those history books. She was always in situations where there were very few Black girls, so her friends were a mixture. She always felt comfortable being around the other few Black females in school. We tried to nurture her and exposed her to everything to make her feel good about herself."*

Concerns about finding a suitable husband also were present to some extent among the mothers. On the questionnaire, the mothers were asked, "If your daughter aspires to be married, to what extent do you worry that she will not be able to find a husband?" With the high number of African American women who are single, this issue is relevant for Black women regardless of their academic accomplishments. It also is reflected in the frequently heard concern about the lack of "eligible" African American men. Though it would not have been surprising for the mothers to express concern that the better educated and more accomplished their daughters became, the more distance they were putting between themselves and the pool of potential husbands, a great deal of worry was not expressed. Slightly more than half of the mothers (54 percent) replied that they do not worry at all, 32 percent expressed some worry, and 14 percent worried to a great extent.

These Parents' Emphases

We asked the mothers to indicate what they emphasized in raising their daughters. We wondered where they placed their priorities.[18] We learned that they placed the greatest emphasis on their daughters respecting adults (86 percent), communicating openly with their child (81 percent), not using illicit drugs (78 percent), and not using alcohol (71 percent). Spending time with the family, attending church, and not spending time with the "wrong crowd" were other developmental and child-rearing issues emphasized, though not to as great an extent.

We also asked about being raised as an African American and as a girl and a young woman. We wondered how frequently race and gender were talked about in the families. A heavy emphasis was placed on both these issues by half of the mothers, and an almost equal percentage replied that they placed "some emphasis" on the issues. Thus, these topics were discussed in almost every home.

Regarding academics, the mothers emphasized math and science to the same extent they emphasized English ("great emphasis" by 67 percent). The arts, playing sports, volunteering in the community, and sex education were emphasized to a lesser degree.

It is important to remember in terms of the mothers' responses that other people were usually involved in the daughters' lives. Fathers, siblings, cousins, teachers, preachers, and relatives often played a part. If the mother was focusing on one issue, it may be because she knew another significant person was focusing on another.

Concerns About the Future

We also attempted to gaze into the futures of the young women we studied. Mothers were asked what types of concerns they had regarding their daughters' futures, and, like most parents, they expressed concern to some extent about their daughters' relationships, work, and school. What the mothers reveal about the extent of their concerns related to race[19] is particularly interesting. Finding a job after graduation caused at least some worry among 30 percent of the mothers, while succeeding in graduate school was much less of a worry (14 percent). But when asked whether they thought their daughters might not be treated fairly in college because of race, 54 percent expressed at least some level of worry. This response reveals how deeply such concerns run, even among these families and even in relation to a university community to which the daughters have been recruited for a program specifically designed for African Americans and others interested in contributing to the African American community.

The level of concern about the post-graduate workplace was even higher. Worry about being treated fairly at work because of race was expressed by 68 percent of the mothers. As in other areas, the mothers prepared their children for the workplace, too. They also talked about competing and where to stay focused. One mother conveyed the following specific advice to her daughter.

"One of the things I tell my daughter about being an African American woman is, first of all, an African American woman speaks many languages and you, in that sense, have to relate to a lot of different people. One of the greatest things is when you walk in that door, your carriage actually tells a lot about you. The way you present yourself, the way you look, and how you sit back and talk about a range of subjects—not just your academic area—are extremely important as to whether you are going to be accepted for that job. An African American woman today needs to be multifaceted so that if the job market changes, she's qualified to go to another area."

Two other issues—spending time with the family after graduation and associating with the "wrong crowd"—were not seen as areas of concern by the mothers. Yet race remains a factor in the lives of these families even as the daughters consider entering the higher levels of academe and employment to which their talents have carried them.

Advice for Other Parents

We asked these mothers what kind of advice they have for other parents who want to raise an academically successful child? The mothers have five general suggestions: (1) *stay involved with your children*—get to know them in school and at home, go to the school, participate on school committees, and talk to their teachers regularly; (2) *support your children*—encourage them, tell them they can "do it," and communicate with them in an open and honest way; (3) *set high standards for your children*, communicate those standards to them, and help them do their best; (4) *involve your children and your family in church*—seek out the advice and help of other churchgoers and connect your children to church activities; and (5) *keep your eyes out for your children* and be prepared to assist them for many years in navigating through academic, social, and work environments that may not always be friendly to people of color.

More specifically, mothers suggested that parents (1) *read to their children and buy books* at every opportunity; (2) *give them chores* to make them feel a part of the family and to give them something constructive to do with their time; and (3) *expose them* to as many different activities and educational experiences as possible.

Summary and Conclusions

Peters writes that, "Black parents recognize that their children must be accepted in the Black community in order to have friends, and they must be accepted in the White community in order to survive."[20] Child-rearing patterns have thus developed as a result of the unique cultural and economic situations in which they live.[21] We have heard here the voices of mothers who have found a way of successfully navigating with their daughters through childhood and adolescence into young adulthood.

It has been easier for some mothers than for others. Some mothers seemed to encounter few problems as their daughters progressed on a straight path to success. For these mothers, the daughters' high achievement began early and continued into young adulthood with relatively little input from the mothers. But mothers who painted this picture may have been downplaying their own role. Their role may have been a subtle, quiet one— always there if needed yet rarely called upon. The mothers' consistent presence and how they have conducted their own lives have provided great support for their daughters and may have been experienced by the daughters as a foundation to which they feel they can return if the need arises (see Chapters 4, 5, and 6). The mothers have been communicating, providing love, and setting high expectations. As they have talked to their daughters, racial and gender identification has occurred. Limit-setting and discipline may not have been as necessary as they were for the other mothers, and there may not have been as much a reliance on the community. These families may have been more self-sufficient.

Other mothers, though, have been more active as problem-solvers in their daughters' lives. Key aspects of their daughters' lives may not always have come easily or gone smoothly. Struggles around academics and school placements may have occurred. Social, emotional, and developmental problems may have arisen that have required the mothers to take a firm stand and to provide vocal support within the home and advocacy outside the home. Community resources have been called upon to help the family navigate through difficult times. Strong limit-setting and discipline have had to be more actively employed. The focus has always remained on the child, and thorny issues have been discussed.

Not everything has been handled well. Parents in our study have made mistakes. And, significantly, their children have not always responded to good parenting. Some issues that arose have loomed large in the Black community for generations and cannot be easily resolved. Concerns about being treated fairly in college, even for those enrolled in a highly selective program, existed for many of these mothers. The sense that, as an African American, one must work harder to get ahead and always be vigilant about the way one is treated has remained a challenge. Fitting in socially as a young woman and sometimes being one of a handful of Blacks, or the only Black, in White environments also have posed challenges.

These mothers tried to prepare their daughters as much as they could for what lay ahead. They talked to their daughters about their heritage, being female, and being African American. In so doing, they strengthened the family tapestry. They enriched it as they passed on a part of themselves that their daughters, in turn, could pass on to others.

CHAPTER THREE

Fathers of Academically Successful Daughters
The Fathers' Voices

You know, the institutions were never receptive. If I were to go to school on matters concerning any of my children, it's almost like they looked behind me to see if my wife was with me, like they were asking, "Why are you here?" I wasn't amused. I was offended.

Later in the interview, this father told us, *"There was a situation that she brought to me about virginity. There was an immense amount of pressure in her circle, across economic-social boundaries, for her to give up her virginity in middle school. We are talking about young girls having babies. It was almost a badge of honor. And this was not an isolated incident. She was confronted by it and was very bothered by it.*

FATHER OF MEYERHOFF STUDENT

The greatest challenge was to have a daughter who was healthy, happy, and felt fulfilled by life and didn't have a lot of inner turmoil. And the challenge is to raise somebody who is healthy and happy in the bigger culture, which is predominantly White and racist. I don't mean racist in an obvious sense, but there are institutions that cater to the majority and are designed for lower expectations for Blacks. So we dealt with the challenge by trying to give her the most support we could as far as communication and having her prepared for any eventuality.

FATHER OF MEYERHOFF STUDENT

These two fathers' quotes encapsulate three central themes for African American fathers. The first reflects an experience common to many fathers, regardless of race—that a father's participation in child-rearing is not as important as a mother's. Fathers are often made to feel uncomfortable when they do express an interest. A second theme relates to the dangers in the community of associating with the "wrong crowd" and the pressure on these young women to become sexually active and have babies at a very young age. The second father speaks to the third theme, the challenges he sees his daughter facing as she grows up and tries to compete in an unjust world. This is a refrain that we heard throughout the interviews with the fathers.

This chapter presents the stories of the fathers. They are an important part of the tapestry that has produced their academically successful daughters. They have often been a counterweight to the mothers by offering education about the male world and by providing a male perspective. It is they who assume a protective stance (often along with mothers) as they warn about relations with men. And it is they, along with the mothers, who set the achievement bar high.

How did they learn the values they impart, and how do they help their daughters prepare for the future? We asked them what messages they received about education and about being Black when they grew up, and how these messages influenced their parenting style. We asked specifically about their daughters' abilities and interests in math and science. We were interested in who the fathers believed had been helpful to their daughters along the way. We particularly focused on adolescence and the thorny issues that arise regarding emotional and physical development, dating, and growing up Black. Finally, we asked for their wisdom—what do they recommend to other parents who want to engender academic excellence in their children?

The African American Father in Perspective

Many have a certain picture of the African American father, particularly those fathers who are poor.[1] Described by many as being a marginal force in the lives of their children, African American fathers have, over the past decade, increasingly drawn the attention of policy analysts, researchers, politicians, clergy, and educators. Their enhanced presence is being encouraged from all quarters, as statistics and stories about their participation in the family and the community have detailed the extent to which women have been left to care for their children. The Census Bureau reports that, in 1998, there were more female-headed Black families with children under the age of 18 (2,569,000) than those headed by married couples (2,055,000). Black families headed by single fathers accounted for another 370,000 families. In contrast, married White couples with children, of which there were 21,910,000, far outnumbered those headed by White single mothers (4,912,000) and those headed by White single fathers (1,514,000).[2] David

Blankenhorn notes that fathers in some predominantly African American neighborhoods are present in less than 10 percent of the homes.

These chilling statistics do not capture the extent to which fathers who are physically absent from the home may remain a significant force in raising their children. Some fathers drop out of sight after marginal involvement, or were never a presence in their children's lives. Others, though, while not being counted as living in the home, remain involved, visit from time to time, provide financial or material support, and track their children's progress through contact with the mother of the children or through their own mothers or fathers. To a large extent, it is difficult to characterize how "absent" the father is. In addition, if the father is not present, another male figure may be. Robert Hill[3] emphasizes in his work on the Black family that no family, whether female-headed, male-headed, or two-parent-headed, raises children alone. Because of the extended family network typically found in African American families, other relatives or "kin" are usually involved with the family in some way. They may be blood relatives, distant cousins, neighbors, or church members who have some tie to a family member. These men and women often play a part in the rearing of children. As such, while the biological father may not be present, it is difficult to conclude that children are being raised without a male presence. It is also possible to conclude that a father who is not an active presence in the life of one child may be an influence in the life of a child he has not fathered.

These issues need consideration in light of the role fathers play in families. It is not just Black fathers who are being called back to the family and encouraged by politicians, clergy, and educators to become more involved. It is all fathers. Fathers are seen as key to the healthy development of sons and daughters. While it is common wisdom that sons need fathers as male role models, it also is important for daughters to have ongoing contact with their fathers. Emotionally, daughters learn from their fathers about how to interact with men while also observing how their mothers interact with their fathers. But fathers can also provide another view of both the work world and the dating world. A few fathers we interviewed talked about giving their daughters "street smarts" and cautioning them about the intentions of young men they may be dating. In these ways, fathers form unique bonds with their daughters and help pave the daughters' way into young adulthood. The fathers we talked to are involved in their daughters' education and lives. Relationships between fathers and daughters have long been described as special. The daughter is "daddy's little girl." She has the ability to "twist her father around her little finger," a manipulation from which the mother is supposedly immune when the daughter is trying to extend her curfew or borrow the family car. When talking to these fathers, we gained the sense that, regardless of the nature of the father-daughter relationship, they held their daughters to a high standard. At some point when the daughters were young, these fathers came to expect great things from them. The fathers became wary of any distractions that kept their daughters from high achievement.

The African American father's role has not always been as it is today. Experts on the Black family have carefully traced the roots of the father's role both before and since slavery. Following the Civil War, couples with long-standing relationships, formalized by African rituals during slavery, attempted to "legalize" them as marriages. The goal was to gain recognition under U.S. law. During this time period, two-parent families were the norm.[4] With the great migration north, many families were separated as the men went ahead to find work. What they found, though, was often menial labor that did not relieve the economic pressure on the family to the extent many had hoped. Throughout the early part of the twentieth century, even as opportunities for Blacks increased, they were not sufficient to guarantee equality in employment or housing.[5]

William Allen and Michael Connor relate that after World War II the African American work force, due to lack of education and training and to continued discrimination in hiring, was not prepared for an increasingly service-oriented society. Eager workers were left unemployed or underemployed. African American women had greater success in finding entry-level employment in this changing economy. Roles became more flexible as both men and women took responsibility for childcare as well as finding employment. But, Allen and Connor write, "The net effect of decreasing male employment in predominantly blue-collar industries and increasing female participation in the service sector was increased pressure on African American families . . . and became a major cause of expanding unemployment, household disruption (e.g. divorce, single-parent households), and hopelessness."[6] Blue-collar employment opportunities continued to decline, leaving many men further behind. More recently, the workplace has become more open to the employment of African Americans at almost all levels.[7] Lack of education, though, continues to hold some back from many high-paying technology jobs.

Black Americans have always placed a high priority on educational attainment, according to Andrew Billingsley. Education was the "only way out" of poverty. But more recently, while high-school graduation rates of Blacks have equaled Whites, a disparity in the number of men going to college still exists. Whether one looks in the workplace or the schoolyard (as we hear below from the fathers we interviewed), the vestiges of American history remain. Black men are underemployed and undereducated when compared with Whites. Their involvement in their families suffers as a result. When considering the voices of these Black fathers and the ways they parent, these issues need remembering so we understand what they are attempting to do in raising their daughters.

The Fathers' Interviews

These twenty-seven fathers, like the mothers we focused on in Chapter 2, are more highly educated than is typical of African American men their age. With an average age around 50, the men typically graduated from high school in the 1960s or early 1970s, at which time between 21 percent (1960) and 30 percent (1970) of Black male high school graduates went on to college.[8] Two thirds of the fathers interviewed had at least a college degree, and about half of this group attended graduate school. Eleven percent had no education past high school. Some were completing their education at the same time their daughters were in school. Almost one quarter were employed in sales or as office workers, skilled workers, and unskilled laborers, while, at the other extreme, 15 percent were employed at the highest end of their professions.

All but one of the fathers interviewed had been married to their daughters' mother when the daughter was growing up, and 85 percent were married when we interviewed them. The vast majority of the fathers were raising two children, with about one quarter raising three and another few fathers raising four or more children. Clearly, the fathers' presence in the home adds to the stability of these families and is one factor in how their daughters have fared. The vast majority of the fathers we interviewed lived in the family home. We made a concerted effort to interview fathers who were not living with the daughters but had difficulty getting them to agree to participate. (In the chapters that follow, the voices of daughters who were raised in single-parent families, usually headed by the mother, are heard.) Thus, though according to census data the family situations here are not typical of Black family situations, the fathers' voices are important to hear because they share what they believe they and others have done to help their daughters succeed. In learning about these "best" and, in some cases, most privileged situations, we believe their stories can be instructive in showing the realm of possibilities about parenting.

We use the six components of parenting that we applied to the mothers in Chapter 2 as a way of thinking about the approaches these fathers took. These components include (1) child-focused love, (2) strong limit-setting, (3) continuously high expectations, (4) open, consistent, and strong communication, (5) racial and gender identity focus, and (6) use of community resources. These components refer to the manner in which the fathers raise their daughters and where they have focused their emphases.

The Fathers' Own Childhood: Messages About Education and Being Black

What were the messages these fathers received growing up? Over three quarters of the fathers were raised in homes where education was greatly encouraged, by either their parents or grandparents. This is not to say that those parents or grandparents were educated themselves—most were not. In fact, it was the lack of education and recognition of its importance that contributed to those adults spurring these fathers on to become educated.

One father who was college-educated recounted, *"My parents did not have that much education. Neither was a high school graduate. However, they both put a lot of emphasis on education, and they did what they could to make sure that I, being the youngest in the family, and all of my brothers and my one sister who were older than me, had the opportunities to at least get a high-school education."*

A similar set of circumstances is recounted by a different father who is also college-educated.

> *"My parents placed a high value on education because they were both laborers. My father worked in a steel mill and my mother cleaned homes for folks, so they emphasized to me that their jobs were not the best jobs that were out there. They really wanted me to do a lot better. They insisted I do well in school and get a good education and a good job. They made a direct correlation between my education and my work in the future."*

In some cases, the fathers give a sense that their own education was a family affair, with all pitching in.

"It was my parents, my grandparents, my aunts and uncles, everybody who was for me getting an education. They used to pool their money so I could go to school because they thought it important that I was the first one to go to college on either side of the family. Matter of fact, I think it was more important for them than for me because I didn't understand why everyone was making the fuss about my going to school and staying in school. My father did not think it as important as my mother because he couldn't see the immediate returns from it. I was the oldest of five in the family, and once he saw me bring home the first paycheck, he decided he was going to find a way to get the rest of the kids to college."

In families where education was not emphasized, it was usually replaced by a work ethic. In these families, a job brought immediate reinforcement with a payday. In others, continuing one's education was seen as being beyond a reasonable possibility.

One father describes this situation. *"I grew up in the projects. It was usually government-subsidized. In that surrounding, what you basically saw were people trying to get a job as quickly as possible, even if it meant dropping out of high school. The premium was on just getting a job. College was not a concept you even thought about. It was for the 'uppity.' You began [by] getting a paycheck and getting prestige from that."* He did eventually get a college education himself.

For other fathers, parents emphasized graduating from high school as the ultimate goal. But one father who finished college encountered resistance from his father who seemed intimidated by higher education.

"My father was a contractor and, while not illiterate, he never went beyond high school. My father made me go to the right schools, but most of my push came from me. I remember staying up until two in the morning studying French, Spanish, and Latin, and sometimes, if he thought I was staying up too late, he would take my light bulb. But I would get a candle and just study with that. I had friends, relatives, and neighbors who weren't going anywhere, but I also had some strong role models."

Messages About Growing Up Black

Growing up in the 1940s, '50s, and '60s, the fathers we studied were exposed to Jim Crow, the civil rights movement, and Black Power. We wondered what messages they received about being Black while growing up during these turbulent times, and how they passed on these messages to their daughters. We encountered a few fathers who said that race was not discussed at all. A few others said that race was discussed if some discriminatory incident occurred to someone in the family. That event then became a crucible within which issues would be raised. The bulk of the fathers said that their parents talked specifically about race and tried to prepare them for life in a White world. For this last group of fathers, the most commonly received message was that the father was going to have to work harder to succeed because he was Black.

One father, who grew up in Pennsylvania, told us about such a message.

"When we were growing up, our parents never told us about any distinctions [between the races]. We were just expected to do well. If I could say one thing about my parents on the whole issue of race, which was going around socially, it was that the issue was rarely discussed. We went to an integrated high school and lived in an integrated neighborhood. I understand racism and know what it is, but my parents never spoke negatively about another race. My father did tell me you have to be twice as smart and have twice the education to get the same job. He was valedictorian, and when he came out of the service, this White kid who ended up applying for the same job as he did, got the job, and this was a kid he helped through high school. I could see how hurt he was, so I knew I had to really excel. As far as being Black, we knew it, but it wasn't addressed the way it is today."

Another father (quoted earlier and interviewed in the same group as the previous speaker) was the son of two laborers. He offered the following perspective.

"My parents made a conscious effort to focus on the fact that you, as a Black person, were at a disadvantage right off the bat and that you had to do everything that you could to increase your opportunity for success. There was a lot of emphasis on the fact that you had to be better to be

equal, and that without an education, you do not stand a chance being a Black person in a White society."

Messages from parents were not always clear. If the parents thought they were clear, the fathers who received them found a great deal of ambiguity in how to live with the messages. The father whose quote begins this chapter told us about his parents being concerned for his well-being as a Black man, and about how that was conveyed in a way that left him unsure how to behave. He did not attend college.

"I got a message from my parents at the time. The position that my parents took was one that could have decided my health in terms of life and death. We were taught that we had a place to be in and if you wanted to stay healthy, that place was where you needed to be. That position, in its own way, has lasted all my life because it was one I resented and one that I also understood. It has been an adjustment not to allow that to affect my reasoning and believing that I am capable of anything. But because I experienced it so much as a child, that I had to limit my involvement in activities to avoid exposing myself to dangers, it wasn't very clear to me. If those activities aren't for us, then what is for us? And why am I here? Why are you forcing me to go to school and get an education if these things are not for me? Or be careful about how I use my intelligence because of the danger of how someone would perceive my confidence. It was always a conflict."

This father digested these messages from his youth and passed on a broader message to his daughter and other children.

"One thing I learned over the years is we serve no purpose by hiding facts. I've shared with them my life and said to them, 'Be conscious and aware of your circumstances and conditions but know who you are by your conviction to your value system.' If you keep a value system, all of the experiences we are confronted with, we can overcome."

A father raised in Baltimore City recounted how, during the Martin Luther King era, the messages from the civil rights leader conflicted, perhaps necessarily so, with what he received at home. This was not the only father who expressed this duality in his upbringing. Exciting civil rights changes were being fomented, but there was trepidation about getting on board. Baltimore, in fact, had a long history of holding Blacks back. Juan Williams, in his biography of Thurgood Marshall, who was raised in Baltimore, describes the city as having before the Civil War the largest population of free Blacks of any city in the United States. Yet, in the 1930s, the atmosphere was such that "Many stores on Pennsylvania [Avenue] did not let dark-skinned Blacks come in the door; others would sell to Blacks but refused to let them try on clothes. Marshall's mother and other Blacks had their credit accounts taken away at one point when store owners suddenly insisted that blacks pay up front."[9] This was the history that no doubt shaped the actions of the family members involved in this next father's story.

"Spirituality was very important, and we all went to church together and heard about the sit-ins. They would tell us that you are as good as anyone else, that Black and White are the same. Well, one time, a friend stopped by my house with two White girlfriends and asked if I wanted to go with them to McDonald's. Now, my grandfather wouldn't say anything when he was upset, he would just clear his throat. My mother worked nights and when they needed to get her up to go to work they would bang on the pipes and she would get up. Well, my grandfather was clearing his throat, and my grandmother hit the pipes, and my mother appeared and asked me what I was doing. I said I was going with my friend and these two girls to McDonald's. She said I couldn't go because people get hanged for doing that. So I laughed because the messages had been that all the races are going to get together. That was a strong message I got from them, that to survive you don't want to get into any foolishness.

"Now when I came into my stepdaughter's life, she had experiences at her private school where there was racism, and all I could do was remind her that this is the world she is going to live in, and it is not going to change just because it is wrong. . . . I told her that her best work would be her salvation."

A father who approached the issue of race with his daughter when a racial event occurred, in contrast to preparing her in advance (as his parents had tried to do) told us, *"We tried as little as possible to bring race and gender into the issue. We based it on, 'You are a person; you just happen to be a Black female. You do what you have to do to get ahead.' But then as she experienced racism, we began to discuss these issues with her."*

Others handled it by exploring and emphasizing culture.

"My parents didn't dwell on race, but dealt with it as it came up and then moved on. As far as my daughters are concerned, because I had been sensitized in college and gone through the whole experience, my wife and I were open to cultural differences. We made a special emphasis, though not overtly, by participating in a lot of cultural activities. I took them to the African American museum and festivals. We were sensitized to the fact that we were African Americans in a White culture and we had no misgivings about explaining to them that it might be rougher, and that they would have to prepare themselves to excel; but we did not dwell on it."

The tapestry that was woven by these fathers' families is one that often reflected an emphasis on education and getting ahead. The fathers, almost always raised by parents with little education, parents who were domestics, laborers, and occasionally teachers, were told that they were going to have to work harder to get ahead and that in order to compete they would have to "be better than." They conveyed this message to their daughters in a host of ways.

The most common refrain from the fathers to their daughters that derives from this upbringing was that they were as good as anyone else (the component of racial and gender identity), that they would have to work harder to get ahead (the component of continuous high expectations), and that the playing field was not always fair. This echoes what the fathers learned. With these messages they pushed their daughters to get ahead and never accept defeat. Some fathers (side-by-side with the mothers) delivered the messages before racially charged events occurred. Others responded to the issues as their daughters were confronted by them. For this second group of families, it was the events that set the agenda rather than the fathers purposefully initiating discussions.

Educational Attainment

To what extent is academic success the result of a person's genetic makeup (the "nature" of the person)? Or is success the result of the way a person was raised and the things to which she or he was exposed (the "nurture" side)? And, beyond the way one is raised, what impact does the broader social environment have on the individual? Specifically, does the way that women are treated or the way that African Americans are treated in their daily lives affect success? Measuring the impact of sexism and racism on academic performance has plagued researchers for years and is beyond the scope of this book, but these are questions we must consider (as we did in Chapter 2). Here we report on what the fathers' impressions are about their daughters' educational successes. We also ask how their daughters developed an interest in math and science, two areas that traditionally have been male bastions.

The fathers were asked their opinions on why they thought their daughters were so successful academically when so many African American youth struggle in this area. Their answers reflected to a large degree their belief that "family" and the values established in the home were at the core of the daughters' achievement (a reflection also of the parental component of child-focused love). Nearly 80 percent credited the home and family support. They described how this worked in a variety of ways.

One father said, "*The fact that my wife and I both went to college and we were able to pass that on—were things the children saw at home. A lot of stress was put on education and a lot of support was given by my ex-wife, who is a former teacher.*"

Another father credited the environment and the exposure to growth-promoting learning experiences. "*As early as I can remember, we began traveling when she was young. When she got older, whatever experience we could give her we did. She liked to eat so we usually gave her something to eat, as a memento to what she had done.*" This is an example of one of the parenting components—child-focused love, the dedication and time given to a child by the family.

Some fathers are not modest about the success of their daughters. "*I'm inclined to take credit for my child's success. Her success is due in great part to her understanding the expectations we placed on her. We established that communication in early childhood. Communication was a key factor of the success she may have.*" (Here is the parenting component of open and strong parent-child communication.)[10]

The fathers who did not immediately credit the home environment and familial expectations cited their daughters' own attributes. Daughters were described as naturally bright and highly motivated. These fathers credited their daughters with always having a knack for academics and were less inclined to link themselves to that success. A handful of fathers gave the credit to the mothers of the daughters (in one case the mother and father were divorced, and in another, the stepfather complimented his wife). The fathers described the mothers as role models and credited them with instilling good habits. Occasionally, the mothers were educators themselves. Finally, one father thanked prayer for the success his daughter achieved. The church community was mentioned occasionally by a few other fathers as a secondary or tertiary reason for their daughters' success.

Questionnaire Responses

We gathered information from the fathers about the specific roles they played in their daughters' academic achievements through a questionnaire (the same one the mothers completed.)[11] From the responses, we see a picture of involvement by the fathers that is similar to that of the mothers, in which involvement with school-related activities is highest in the elementary years and diminishes with time. In elementary and middle school, 63 percent of the fathers said they monitored the amount of time spent on homework, with the number lower in high school (52 percent). Monitoring the amount of time spent playing video games and watching television also fell from 54 percent in the younger grades to 44 percent in high school. Monitoring time spent with friends fell from middle school (52 percent) to high school (44 percent). This pattern makes sense as, ideally, children should become more independent with age and need less of a watchful eye. In all of these activities, mothers reported more active involvement than fathers in monitoring the daughters' behavior.

We also gained a sense of the fathers' involvement in their daughters' lives by asking them to compare themselves with other fathers in the neighborhood. Slightly more than half of the fathers believed they were more strict with their daughter than neighborhood fathers, and 58 percent said they believed they monitored their daughter's homework more closely.

These fathers were (and are) clearly very invested in their daughters' lives. Almost every father (96 percent) reported that he knew how his daughter was performing academically in school. Fathers (79 percent) also reported attending sporting events and other related activities in which their daughters participated, and having been frequent attendees (92 percent) at high-school programs aimed at parents. The academic life of the daughter was not the only endeavor that the fathers supported. Extracurricular activities were encouraged by 92 percent of the fathers. These fathers confirmed their daughters had a social life, too, at least as defined by their communication with friends. In fact, one quarter of the fathers were concerned that their daughters were spending too much time on the telephone. In sum, the daughters consumed a great deal of the fathers' energy, whether it was spent supporting a range of activities or fretting over their telephone use. Little that their daughters were involved in went unnoticed.

Developing an Interest in Math and Science

How did the daughters develop an interest in math and science, areas that traditionally have attracted many more men than women? The reasons varied a great deal. The most common answer from the fathers was that their daughters had a "natural inclination" for the subjects. These fathers took little credit for their daughters' interest in these academic areas, a similar presentation they made when asked about their daughters' academic success. Other fathers leaned more toward the belief that their strong personal interest matched the interest and inclination shown by their daughters. As one father put it, *"Math was my favorite subject, and I spent a lot of time with her on math. Plus, I think she has what people call a natural inclination."* Another father also connected his own interests with those of his daughter. *"I think she always had an interest in math because on all the aptitude tests she always scored high. She was a natural at it. I'm a computer systems manager, and my wife is an accountant. So I guess our careers were ones that, growing up, she looked at and gave her some inspiration in that direction."*

Other fathers credited external influences or chance. One said he and his wife pushed their daughter, and she found out she was good at it. Two fathers said their daughters "fell into it." Others said their daughters were influenced by older siblings or schoolteachers. For at least one, interest was spurred by a summer experience in a laboratory (this daughter likely expressed some interest in science prior to that).

What was striking was the variance in responses—some fathers thought their daughters' interests were derived internally or by chance while others held the belief that family and school-related opportunities were responsible. For the most part, there was consistency between the responses to the two questions on whom to credit for the educational attainment. Fathers who tended to credit the home with success were also more apt to credit the family with the interest their daughters developed in math and science. Fathers who said their daughters' natural abilities accounted for their success also tended to believe that their daughters had an inborn inclination toward math and science. Some fathers believe much more in the power and influence of the family in shaping success (nurture) than others who are inclined to look at their daughters' more innate abilities (nature).

We also wondered about the support systems that the fathers believe assisted in their daughters' academic success. Two thirds of the fathers mentioned some family member or extended family member first when asked about support systems. Those mentioned included aunts and uncles, grandparents, godparents, and "family" in general. Another third mentioned the church community and faith in God as being central. Teachers were mentioned next most frequently (some fathers mentioned more than one source of support), and friends and neighbors were cited occasionally. Only one father said that, outside of the immediate family, there was no support.

Specific Ways Fathers Helped Their Daughters

The fathers cited a number of actions they had taken that helped their daughters succeed. They are actions similar to those taken by the mothers. These are suggestions, not guarantees, for what parents can do if they want to enhance their child's chances for academic success. The ten most significant (also see Chapter 7) include the following:

1. **Promoting reading and phonics in the home at an early age.** Fathers described reading to their children when they were very young and often credited the mother with initiating this activity. One father said that to enhance his daughter's learning, he often pointed out connections between what they were reading and what they were doing.
2. **Restricting or monitoring television watching.** Fathers emphasized there should be a balance between schoolwork and television, and the less television the better.
3. **Enrolling the daughters in preschool.** Getting a jump on the daughters' education was seen as an important step toward their eventual success.
4. **Supporting the daughters in their extracurricular interests.** Whether it

was sports or art, the fathers encouraged and supported extracurricular activities.

5. **Monitoring course selection.** Fathers kept track of the courses their children were taking as a way of ensuring that they were availing themselves of the best opportunities.

6. **Resolving conflicts with the teachers.** Fathers worked proactively with teachers to iron out any differences in behavioral or educational expectations of their daughters.

7. **Exposing daughters to a wide range of experiences that enrich them academically.** Whether it was going to museums or science contests, the fathers reported taking their daughters to see and participate in a range of activities.

8. **Spending family time together.** Vacations, day trips, and doing things together were all emphasized as building a sense of family upon which values could be reinforced.

9. **Attending activities in which daughters participated.** Fathers placed great importance on "being there" when their daughters competed in athletics or performed in school functions.

10. **Emphasizing the importance of educational and work achievements.** Like their own parents, many fathers talked to their daughters about the need to excel both academically and at a job.

The fathers kept a watchful eye over the daughters while often leaving the "nitty gritty" of childcare to the mothers. We are left with the impression that fathers tend to encourage their daughters on the one hand while, as we see in the next section, protecting them on the other. The mothers tend to push them a little more while also supporting them. This is often a balancing act in a family. If the mother is going to be the supportive one, the father will observe this and have the freedom to assume a slightly different role. However this balance is struck, there was a sense from the fathers that the mothers were playing a key role with the daughters—the pronoun "we" was often used.

Support and Handling Emotional and Developmental Issues

Although it is frequently assumed that high academic achievers have their lives in order, this is not always the case. Helping their daughters academically is just one part of these fathers' responsibilities. They also help them emotionally and with their development. They serve as disciplinarians, role models, and guides. They educate them about the world of work as well as the world of men. These fathers attempt to prepare their daughters for the normal struggles of adolescence and young adulthood. In other words, their involvement is not just about academics.

Teenagers today have to cope with both internal and external pressures. Internally, they are developing at a sporadic and unpredictable pace as they progress through puberty. Their friends may be ahead of or behind them in physical maturation. Wherever they are developmentally, they are apt to be out of sync with one of their peers. Appearance takes on extreme importance as a way of being accepted and as a key to self-definition. Academic achievement, especially for good students, becomes part of this self-definition.

Simultaneously, external pressures interlock with internal ones. Peer pressure, positive or negative, can catapult a youth in a variety of directions. Pressures on "attractive" or "unattractive" girls may be different, but they are still pressures. Pressure to conform with peers can separate a young girl from family and support systems, or further reinforce their importance. Growth and development are inevitable. The challenge is to cope and adapt successfully with everything that is happening, with both the body and the social circle. Parents play a vital role in helping with this process by being supportive, lending guidance, and negotiating age-appropriate parent-child separation.

We asked the fathers, "Girls face many developmental challenges growing up, especially in the teen years. What types of challenges or experiences did your daughter face, and how did you help her deal with them?" This question elicited a range of answers that both reflects the difficulties in raising teens today and provides insight into the kinds of roles that fathers play in the child-rearing process.

A few fathers described their daughters' struggles with physical appearance. They told of daughters who matured physically after or before their peers. In both cases, the daughters felt uncomfortable. As one father stated, *"I can recall very vividly, probably during freshman year in high school, that she didn't think she was attractive because there were other people around her who were starting to develop and she hadn't started yet. My daughter has always been small, and so she wasn't as big as everyone else, and was also younger than her classmates. That was a problem. Basically, I just encour-*

aged her. I always told her she was beautiful. I think she went to her mother more than me for those kinds of things, while I did the sports things."

Issues concerning appearance were mentioned much more often by mothers, as the father just quoted can attest. The girls went to their mothers with those issues, and the daughters may have felt more comfortable initiating discussions about appearance with their mothers. Yet this is not to imply that fathers were not involved in this area of development. The following statement from one father provides the depth of awareness on his part of his daughter's struggles.

"Daughters see themselves developing physically and use that consciousness in their social realm. It's a test of will to help them to understand that the physical being is not as important as the spiritual or conscious state of how you perceive yourself. Because I feel it is such a dangerous time in their lives because of all the possibilities they could explore, you have to approach it realistically with them."

Our interviewer then asked this father, "In many households the mother is left to explain sexuality and development. How important is it that a father play a role in this from a male perspective?" The father responded, *"My involvement has been positive for my child because she is a lot more comfortable with her being. The idea that these issues should only be addressed by a female is a misrepresentation of reality because, at some point, who you are is based on building a healthy relationship with the opposite sex. I was blessed with the opportunity to raise three daughters. I had to take care of them when they were children. We had conversations about certain things you can and should do. I felt, who better to assist my daughters, aid them from a male's perspective without physically or emotionally getting involved, than myself?"*

The concerns about appearance and development are linked in many ways to the area of dating. In general, the more physically attractive the young women are, the more they are going to draw the interest of others who are interested in socializing. Sometimes, appearances aside, the young women can send the message through the way they spend their time (studying, extracurricular activities, etc.) and the way they carry themselves that they are not interested in dating. Overall, the girls were not active on the dating scene, according to the fathers. As one father stated, *"She was never really chasing boys and they weren't chasing her, because she was too much into activities."* Essentially, these young women's focus on academics and activities left them with less time to socialize. It also gave them a way to define themselves in areas that did not involve dating. When they were interested in dating, they encountered opposition from their fathers, as we heard from this father. *"Eventually the day comes when she starts to date, and I wanted to stay in there and handpick anybody she went out with. You hate to say it, but there isn't anyone good enough for my daughter."* Other fathers also admitted to being overprotective.

One father, who raised his daughter by himself, shed light on a number of difficult parenting issues when he described how he learned by accident what appeared to be his daughter's first serious relationship.

> *"When I walked past her room one night I heard those four dreaded words, 'I love you, too.' And I went, 'Oh, God no.' She was fifteen or sixteen, and I thought that with this relationship would come distraction from academics. Being a single parent, I didn't know how to deal with it because this little knot-head, whoever he was, was not going to even think about hurting my daughter emotionally and, God forbid, physically. He doesn't know who he is dealing with, I thought. Our relationship was coming together and, I'll admit selfishly, I didn't want someone to come between us. I get a sense I may have sheltered her from some things, wanting to give her the opportunity to focus on school. When she did finally get more freedom, she went a little wild, so I had to call on some other resources. That's what it takes—a whole village to raise a child. I began to understand my own limitations as a parent, as a person, and as a man."*

From this story we gain a sense of the father-daughter bond and the threats to it that arise. We also get a sense of the protectiveness that arises that may have been felt most acutely by this single father. (This is also an example of the parenting component of child-focused love.)

The protectiveness demonstrated by this father extended to concerns about pregnancy. We heard this concern from many sources. One father remarked, *"We pray every day because we hear so many horror stories about girls getting pregnant and dropping out of school. We didn't want that to happen to her. So it was a challenge to really keep her focused. Her grades slipped in her junior year, though she still got her A, but it was all a challenge."* Fathers worried that their "jewel," the child they had put so much into and who had so much to offer, would get derailed by teen pregnancy and other social issues.

Fathers often left discussions about sexuality to the mothers. If they took the issues on, they preached abstinence or the value of education about human sexuality. Some fathers believed in teaching specifically about the world of men, an area they did not think their wives could teach. The messages came in different forms. One father, for example, recounted, *"I always tell the girls, 'All men are stupid, including your father. They will deceive you. They will dump you and keep going. They don't care.' And that is true. Men, by nature, always look for something to conquer and then wonder what is next."* Fathers took the responsibility for educating their daughters about these issues seriously. They believed it was their job to provide this type of instruction.

The approaches took two forms—one approach was to prepare the daughters from a very young age. Fathers (and mothers) would talk to their children, educate, and instruct them about what to do if situations came up that involved sex. These messages also came to include discussions about drugs and crime. The fathers in this group took a preventive approach that was meant to establish a groundwork from which a value-laden series of decisions could be made by their daughters.

The other approach (and the two are not mutually exclusive) was to talk to the daughter as issues came up. For example, one father said they would read the newspaper or watch television together and discuss the topics as they arose. This was using news items or story themes as "teachable opportunities."

A few examples follow of the first approach.

"We found a church that had a strong Sunday school program. They got into a lot of discussion on crime and drugs, but my daughter was never in trouble. She has a good sense of morality. For sex, my ex-wife, I think at a too early an age, from the time they were five or six, gave the full lecture. Starting with the body parts and where nobody is allowed to touch you. By the time they were thirteen, I said we needed to have a talk and they just laughed. They asked, 'Where you been, Dad?' The message was that if you do this you are never going to get to your goals. And if you want to get to your goals, you can't do drugs or be involved in crimes, and you certainly can't have a baby. I showed them a videotape on sex-

ual awareness and sexually transmitted diseases. I made all her friends sit down and watch it, too."

Another father took a similar approach.

"My emphasis early on was on abstinence and avoidance. I associated consequences with behavior. This is what happens if you do this. As she got older, I have emphasized drugs, alcohol, and sex more because I expect young adults to experiment with sex as they experiment with drugs and alcohol. My emphasis in sex was on understanding what you are doing first, and protecting yourself in the process. So I focused on educating her rather than setting a moral standard. On alcohol and drugs, I have focused on avoiding them because of being unsure what the consequences were. Every year I have an update with them on what they understand and what questions they might have."

A third father also used an explicit approach to prepare his daughter for the world of men.

"We explained sex to her at a very young age. I did anyway. As she got older, about ten or eleven, I said, 'Most young men have a three "F" theory: Find them, blank them, forget them. Now if you want to be part of that syndrome, I cannot stop you. It's the choice you make. I would prefer that you not have it until you feel ready, but that is between you and your God.' Whenever she came and asked me something, I did not hide it. I explained whatever questions she asked. And then I would go back to her later and say, 'Did you have a specific reason for asking that question?'"

Mothers were also key instructors, as we hear from this father.

"Sex was something her mother talked to her about. Her mother talked about premarital sex, and my daughter enjoyed talking to her about that part of her life. It let her know where her mother stood."

Concerning drugs, at least one father used his own personal struggle with drug abuse as a jumping-off point for educating about its evils.

"With the drug thing and my being in recovery, it came to the point

where they saw the [drug-addicted] behavior. Whether I realized they saw it or not, I let them know from a drug standpoint that what I suffer from could be passed on to them through heredity. I know they both have at least experimented. I didn't want to see that but all I could do was tell them what is possibly in their genes. There are things that I will not allow in the house."

The daughters faced other difficult social issues. One had to do with race. Girls were called race-related names. They were also placed in lower-level academic courses, below where they should have been placed, an action that fathers believed was race-based. In one case, a father told us, *"There were teachers in school who weren't particularly supportive of Blacks, and that was a challenge for her. We tried to make things as safe as possible. In other cases programs that were available were not made known to her. These things go back to race."*

It is not always the teachers or White students who bring up race-related issues. One father complained that the Black students at his daughter's school were calling her a nerd because she was academically focused. Another said that his daughter went to a predominantly White school that her friends (who attended a predominantly Black school) referred to as a nerd school.

A few other developmental issues were mentioned by fathers. Grades slipped during middle school or the early years of high school in some cases, and the father or mother had to confront the daughter. This was a frightening time for a few families. If the daughter did not have enough years of success under her belt or if the parents believed their own achievements as adults were tenuous, it raised the specter of losing hard-earned gains. By being persistent in the pursuit of excellence, the families together overcame these bumps in the road as is evidenced by the daughters' success. A different issue had to do with how difficult the early teen years, 13 to 15, were in general as daughters refused to communicate or sulked around the house. Many daughters were described as stubborn at this stage. The use (or overuse) of the telephone became another battleground for families.

Not all the fathers said their daughters struggled. A handful said there had been no major problems that they observed in the teen years, and no substantial discipline problems at all.

These are the ways that fathers, often with the assistance of the mothers, confront these thorny emotional and developmental challenges. Without sound guidance and monitoring, it is hard to predict what may have happened to many daughters' academic pursuits.

Special Challenges Raising African American Women

While many of these issues are central for all parents raising teens, there are unique challenges that parents of high achieving Black women face. They have to prepare their daughters not only for young female adulthood, but also for being Black women who are talented academically. How do they prepare their daughters for a challenging world where certain doors may be open to them, while other doors may be closed because of the color of their skin and their gender?

In the following story, one father exquisitely and painfully sums up the part of the challenge having to do with race.

> *"One time in a grocery store I saw some kids playing. There were some White kids and some Black kids. The White kids were running all around the store. Their mother said, 'Come back here,' and they kept running. The Black kids were relatively close to the shopping cart, usually within arms' reach. They weren't too far away. What I took from the moment was, as these children grow, the White kids are going to see and feel they can go anywhere because they always have. On the other hand, the Black kids can't go that far. And that's what I see as my concern. I want my daughter to understand the world is hers. But will she really see the world as hers to explore?"*

This theme was echoed by many other parents in various ways. Some parents think Whites have a "pipeline," to use one father's term, to success. The pipeline is more difficult for Blacks to get through. Others speak more specifically about the racism that they believe their daughters will encounter.

> *"For the White, everything is there. For the Black you have to work one hundred and twenty percent more. If you and a White were hired for a job today, same intelligence, same everything, when you get to that job, the leadership will go to the White. You have to prove yourself twice as much to get the assignment."*

Fathers describe how their daughters' academic achievement was also affected because of race. One father felt that the predominantly White school in which his daughter was enrolled did not support her efforts to become the first African American valedictorian. Another reported having to fight for advanced placement courses for his daughter, and having the feeling that the teachers expected her to fail.

Appearance, discussed earlier, was an issue that the fathers raised when we asked about special challenges.

"One of the biggest challenges early on was to get her to believe she was as pretty as the little White girls in school with the long hair. That's not the way you're supposed to look. What you have is just as good."

Fathers sometimes attempted to boost their daughters' self-esteem with reassurances about their beauty. But they also tried to be supportive by emphasizing and teaching about their African heritage. By providing a cultural context, they gave their daughters a message that they were part of something larger and that their beauty was linked to their culture.

It is difficult to separate out the meaning for the fathers of raising a Black female from that of raising a female or a child who is Black. The two are intimately intertwined in society. As we discussed in *Beating the Odds*, race and gender are connected when issues about African American men arise. We make the same claim for the young women. We have described some of the issues that arose that were linked to race. But let us not forget that fathers, over time, have often been puzzled by women. Their daughters are no exception. In fact, a number of fathers were not sure they understood what raising a daughter meant, as evidenced by this father who has, apparently, learned a great deal from the experience.

"I was raised as the oldest of nine and, coming up, I never identified with female agendas. When it came time to raise a daughter, everything was new and I was expecting to have a son. I was a little apprehensive, but she has given me such pleasure. I remember wishing my second one, who was a son, had also been a daughter.

"The challenge for me as a father of a daughter was understanding the interests that females have. She seemed to be a little more aggressive than I feel males are. Males tend to be more laid back. I was thinking of hang-

ing out with a son and watching a game. But she took me to a different level. She was into dance and for me to sit through all the recitals was a cultural experience. But it was a joyful experience. The challenge was in staying with her every step. With sons it was, 'Let them sow their wild oats, and boys will be boys.' With her, it is making sure she has her needs met and being protective. When she was in her teens, I was aware of who she was dating and was protective, though not with my sons. With her wanting to go into engineering, a traditional male career, I found I had to give her a perspective about male roles. With a son, I wouldn't have done that. That's the gender piece that I put together."

This father struggled with many of the issues that the other fathers went through. Here was a bright, motivated female who was entering what many considered a male profession. The fathers saw their job as one of preparing their daughters for that traditionally male world, while also trying to figure out for themselves what raising a daughter could mean for their own lives (including fewer sports discussions and more dance recitals).

The issue of protection which this father raises is a recurring theme in the stories we heard. In at least one case, protection included supporting a daughter when there was evidence of sexism.

"We attended a White Baptist church, from when she was five to age fourteen or fifteen. One activity they had was when the boys played football or basketball, and the girls made quilts. She came home one day and said that she was getting tired of that, and there was sexism there. We had seen it also because the only woman in the pulpit was the pastor's wife or a soloist. But when she saw the evidence, we changed to another church."

Another recurring theme throughout this chapter is the preparation that fathers give to their daughters as they enter historically male professions. Whether it is engineering or other sciences, fathers were keenly aware of where their daughters were heading professionally and the lack of potential support. We heard from one father, *"For a Black girl to be in physics, there is not a lot of precedent. There are not a lot of network or support structures there."* The vestige of this feeling can be seen in top-rated departments. MIT acknowledged in the late 1990s that female faculty had not received the types of mentoring and support that male faculty had received.

Despite the obstacles, the fathers acknowledged that much has changed.

More opportunities exist today for Black women than when the fathers were growing up. These opportunities allow a father greater latitude in guiding a daughter. One father specifically commented on this.

"When my sister was growing up, there weren't any Black role models for her. We have an opportunity now to let our daughters know that positive role models from a Black female perspective are out there. They see in the media not just actresses or sports figures, but corporate Black female executives. As the father of a female, I was brought up as the male protector. But there comes a time when we have to let them walk their own course. That was hard because a father hates to see his daughter cry. The role models are there for them, though, and they weren't before."

A few fathers commented on the difficulties raising daughters in contrast to raising sons. This gave us insight into how they viewed the challenges they experienced with their daughters. Some fathers saw sons as being easier to raise, in part because they understand males better. As one father put it in lamenting his lack of control, *"They are easier to talk to than daughters. They have sports and TV, and you can talk to them about those things. With daughters, they get on the phone and you don't know who they are talking to."* A corollary of this is that daughters provide more social challenges. A number of fathers spoke specifically of having to protect their daughters from males and early sexual experiences. They were less concerned about such situations for their sons. Sons, it was believed, would, and perhaps should, sow wild oats. Such behavior was not acceptable when exhibited by daughters.

Other fathers saw sons as more difficult. They spoke of concerns about violence and trouble in the street that males were more apt to encounter than females. As one father stated, *"We did have discipline problems with my son. You know, lying, cheating, stealing, disrespect. He grew up when they were breakdancing, doing graffiti and all that. We had problems. But our daughter was the complete opposite. I had to spank my son, but with her we never had a problem."*

These Parents' Emphases

The fathers were asked on the questionnaire to rate the extent to which they emphasized various child-rearing issues in raising their daughters. They were offered a choice of responses, including "great emphasis," "some emphasis," and "little emphasis." The greatest emphasis in child-rearing was placed on "respecting adults" (81 percent placed great emphasis on this), on "communicating openly between parent and child" (79 percent), and on not using illicit drugs (71 percent) and alcohol (67 percent). "Attending church" (62 percent), "spending time with family" (58 percent), "not spending time with the 'wrong crowd'" (54 percent), and "being African American" (54 percent) were also emphasized, though to lesser degrees.

In terms of school-related endeavors, the fathers emphasized, though to a lesser extent than those mentioned above, math, science, and English. These received greater attention than the arts, sex education, playing sports, and volunteering in the community.

In looking at these responses, it must be remembered that there were often other important adults in these young women's lives. As such, while the father may have emphasized one thing, the mother or another significant adult may have emphasized something else. This complementariness could provide a balance of influences. For example, if the mother is emphasizing the arts, the father may focus on sciences as a counterbalance.

Concerns About the Future

Fathers also had the chance to rate the extent to which they had concerns about their daughters' future progress, both personally and professionally. Concerns about finding a husband were not expressed as paramount. Three quarters did not worry at all about their daughters finding a husband. Given the dearth of eligible African American men and the perception that highly educated Black women have a particularly hard time finding mates, this finding about the daughters' prospects was surprising. Other issues were of greater concern to the fathers.[12] For example, almost two thirds (62 percent) expressed at least some worry about their daughters being treated fairly in college because of race. Given the Meyerhoff Program's mission, this percentage appears quite high. It shows that even when special programs are created for underrepresented minorities, there may still be doubts about a college's treatment of its students. This may be reflective of such programs residing in a larger university context where African Americans historically have had to be on guard. A slightly higher number (65 percent) worried that their daughters would not be treated fairly at work because of race. Perhaps this also reflects a historical concern about the treatment of African Americans in the work force. Even if a worker is highly trained, concerns can arise about how just the job climate will be. Forty-two percent of the fathers expressed at least some worry about their daughters finding a job after graduation. Less concern (though still a significant amount) was expressed about their daughters' academic abilities. Slightly over one third (35 percent) worried that their daughters would not succeed in graduate school.

The fathers' worries do not end there. One third indicated they had at least some worry about their daughters associating with the "wrong crowd." A handful were concerned that their daughters would not spend enough time with the family after graduation. While some of these worries or concerns are typical of all parents of daughters, it is interesting to note that even among parents of high-achieving daughters, concerns remain. To what extent should fathers be immune from these concerns by virtue of their daughters' talents and achievements? Clearly, from the fathers' responses to a number of questions, high achievement by the child does not prevent the parent from having a number of concerns about the child's future.

Concerns of Fathers versus Mothers

Do fathers worry about their daughters more than mothers? Both sets of parents expressed similar levels of concern about the impact of race on their daughters' college and work lives. Fathers, though, have markedly greater concerns than the mothers in relation to their daughters finding a job after graduation and succeeding in graduate school. This could be interpreted a number of ways. It could be that the fathers have less faith in their daughters' specific abilities, or less faith in women generally to succeed in graduate school and the workplace. The mothers may have a better assessment of their daughters' capabilities or a rosier assessment. Another interpretation is that the fathers have an accurate assessment of the workplace that awaits their daughters, and are being appropriately cautious about the future. As Black men have historically encountered great resistance in employment settings, they may anticipate a similar fate awaiting their daughters. Mothers, with their history of success, may be more realistic.

When we make comparisons based on the questionnaire responses, we see that, in almost every area, the mothers described a greater degree of involvement with their daughters. Whether it was monitoring homework, monitoring time with friends, or having concerns about various developmental issues, the mothers were more involved in or absorbed by the issue. This is not to say that the fathers were not involved—they were simply less involved than mothers. As noted, these fathers were highly committed to their daughters and saw themselves as more involved than their male neighbors. They attended sporting events and programs for parents, monitored their daughters' schoolwork, and taught them the importance of showing respect to adults. The fathers' involvement could reflect solely their personal conviction and commitment regarding its importance. It could also be linked to the positive relationships that the fathers in the group we studied (the majority of whom are living with the mothers) have with their wives. Research suggests in relation to children that "high paternal involvement appears far more grounded in good marital relationships than in poor ones."[13] In other words, fathers are more apt to be so highly involved when their home lives and marital relationships are fulfilling. The reverse could also be true—that committed fathers are more apt to have fulfilling marital relationships.

We do sense from the fathers a slightly more protective air in their responses during our interviews. Though it is subtle, the fathers seemed to talk a great deal about teaching their daughters about men and about work. The mothers emphasized excellence a little more and seemed to push their daughters to succeed more than the fathers did. The mothers were more the nurturers and the ones who engaged in the difficult discussions about sexuality and womanhood. The fathers were more the guides to the outside world, the mothers to the internal world and to the female legacy.

Advice to Other Parents

The fathers have a number of suggestions, both specific and general, for what parents can do to improve their children's chances of succeeding academically: (1) become involved with your child's education; (2) learn about the schools your child attends, the programs of study they offer, their extracurricular activities, including opportunities for athletics; (3) attend parents' nights; (4) read to your children at an early age and encourage them to read; (5) expose them to as many and varied educational experiences as possible; (6) take them to museums, ice skating, on hikes, and so on; (7) involve them in after-school and weekend activities; (8) turn off the television; (9) spend time together as a family; (10) work to find a balance between your own career and the needs of your children; (11) have a spiritual family; (12) teach your children to be honest and to have respect for others; (13) help them to strive for excellence; (14) be clear about expectations and consistent with discipline; (15) communicate with them; (16) advocate for them with the schools; (17) tell them that you love them; and (18) be there for them.

Conclusions

The seventy-three fathers and mothers who are the focus of this and the previous chapter affirm the importance of committed and involved parenting. The six components of parenting—child-focused love, strong limit-setting and discipline, setting continuously high expectations, fostering open and strong communication, focusing on racial and gender identity, and using community resources—provide a framework for understanding the approaches the parents in our study took in raising successful daughters. Many parents came from financially impoverished backgrounds; many also came from homes where they were nurtured and attended to. The messages from their parents, the grandparents of the young women who are the focus of this book, were clear. Work hard, and you can succeed. These messages have been handed down to the young women as strong strands in the family tapestry.

In the next three chapters, we move further into the emerging tapestry, and we hear from the young women and learn how the tapestry is being woven for current and future generations. It is fitting to conclude this chapter with a statement from the father whose quote began the chapter, and who has faced many struggles in raising his daughter. His advice underscores the basic tenets of good parent-child relationships—communication. *"Communication is essential. Nurturing, constantly changing, building on communication is essential. As much as young people or most of us think that we know everything, we don't. So it is a constant nurturing of that communication that is encouraging to children because it reflects a caring."*

A Diversity of Family Contexts
The Daughters' Voices

My mother grew up in Mississippi. She had to pick cotton when she was lit-
tle. Her mother had to do it, and her grandmother, born thirteen years after
slavery, had to do it. . . . [One time] I was riding past, and a man said, 'Pick
that cotton.' Little stuff like that happens to you. I love being Black, though. I
wouldn't choose to be anything else.

MEYERHOFF STUDENT

I don't think it is a White thing to be successful. I don't think it is a White
thing to be smart. I don't think it is a White thing to want to learn about
things that you've never done before. . . .

MEYERHOFF STUDENT

You walk into the interviewer's office, he is going to see that you are Black.
You can't change that. That is just what they see. I feel like I am straining
myself more than anybody else, to make them overlook that. I'm not saying it
can't be done, it can. But it's like I have to work doubly hard to do that.

MEYERHOFF STUDENT

In this first of three chapters focused on the daughters, we examine the challenges they faced and why they think they succeeded
where so many other young African American women have struggled. Their
messages, while similar in many ways to those we heard from the parents,
have a different resonance and emphasis. The daughters provide new perspectives about the challenges they faced and the factors that have led to
their success—factors that the parents either were not aware of or did not
think were particularly important.

This chapter highlights the varied nature of the family, the challenges facing each daughter in school and the neighborhood, and the factors that
helped the daughters succeed. In the two preceding chapters, commonalities across the families were often emphasized. We are now ready to explore
in more detail some of the differences across families.

Previous research on adolescent female African Americans has tended to focus on their deficits, including their social, academic, and behavioral problems.[1] A recent body of research, however, focuses on the strengths, resilience, and empowerment of Black youth. The literature regarding strengths emphasizes the positive resources young people bring to bear in coping with difficult lives and hazardous environments.[2] For instance, involvement in activity that draws upon latent skills and talents (e.g., leadership skills or artistic talent) has been found to be related to positive development among urban youth.[3] The literature on resilience focuses on high-risk youth who succeed in life despite unfavorable odds.[4] One key factor that leads to their success is the support they receive from at least one primary adult—whether inside the family or in the larger community.[5] Finally, empowerment-related research examines ways in which youth can develop an inner sense of competence and an enhanced sense of power in order to achieve significant personal goals in the face of environmental obstacles. One model suggests that it is especially important to provide young people with a positive, inspiring belief system that focuses beyond the self and emphasizes developing capabilities, contributing to others, and a strong support system.[6]

In this chapter, we focus first on four different groups of daughters who took part in our study in order to portray as clearly as possible the varying life- and family-related contexts in which the daughters were raised. Readers wishing to know more about distinct challenges faced by specific family types will be interested in the different experiences reported by the four groups of daughters. The groups differ based on family structure (single-parent vs. two-parent) and parents' education (college-educated vs. not college-educated). These groups reflect basic demographic differences that may pose distinct challenges (and opportunities) in raising African American daughters.

Significantly, none of these challenges represents an insurmountable barrier. Thus, consistent with previous research, we found that parents, whether single or married, college-educated or not college-educated, can provide the kind of positive family influence and parental supports that empower their daughters to succeed.[7] Each set of families mobilizes and engenders child-focused love, strong limit-setting, high expectations, strong communication, and positive racial and gender identification, and effectively draws upon community resources. Thus, they embody the six components of effective parenting discussed in Chapters 2 and 3 and also utilize a common set of education-related parenting practices that all four groups of daughters report contributed to their high levels of academic success.

In considering the different groups of daughters, the marital status of the parents is significant because daughters who live with a parent who has been divorced or has never married will likely face challenges different from those faced by daughters in two-parent families.[8] When, for example, the father is absent from a household, the mother is likely to bear special burdens and responsibilities that combine the roles of mother and father. Also, the daughter is likely to lack the male perspective in the home (although a number of daughters learn from other adult males' involvement with the family) and, in many cases of divorce, to suffer a substantial loss of connection with the father. A divorce would also expose her to other potential emotional problems. Slightly more than half of the daughters we spoke to (52 percent) lived with only one parent for some or all of their upbringing. As noted in Chapter 1, in the mid-1990s, two thirds of African American children in the United States were being raised in single-parent (mostly female-headed) households.

The parents' educational level is significant in a different way. Parents without a college education will likely bring to their daughters' upbringing fewer academic and economic resources than those with a college education.[9] Furthermore, they are less able to serve as a role model of someone achieving a successful academic or professional career (although, as we see below, many were very effective in personally supporting their daughters and serving as models of hard work).[10] Slightly more than one third (36 percent) of the young women we spoke with grew up in families in which neither parent had a college degree.

The number of parents in the household and the parents' educational level also affect family income, what kind of neighborhood the family lives in, and the quality of the schools the children attend.[11] Daughters whose parents, for instance, are not married and lack a college education will more regularly be confronted with negative peer models and less academic support, because they are more likely to live in less advantaged neighborhoods and to attend poorly funded schools.[12] Overall, about one third (32 percent) of the young women we interviewed lived in urban or rural neighborhoods rather than suburban communities.

In this chapter, then, we present four sets of home- and family-related contexts in which these academically successful daughters grew up. The first set includes thirteen daughters who grew up, for all or part of their upbringing, in single-parent homes in which the parent was not college-educated. These daughters, especially those growing up in inner-city or poor rural neighborhoods, are among those facing the least favorable odds.

Yet, as the reader will see, the mothers display tremendous strengths, and the daughters themselves are a very impressive group. One key question here is how these youth stayed focused on high levels of academic success, given all the factors potentially leading to distraction and deviation, including very high pregnancy rates among female peers.

Next, we look at girls growing up in single-parent homes, where one or both of the parents are college-educated. This group of twenty-one daughters, it turns out, included a number of youth who faced significant challenges during their early teenage years, most often related to peer influence and peer culture. In some cases, the challenges were related to family dynamics (e.g., divorce, strained relationships with fathers). Both the mothers and the daughters in this group displayed great commitment and persistence. A key question is how the girls' parents helped them negotiate the difficulties of early adolescence when significant adjustment problems emerged. And for those parents in this group whose daughters did not face as difficult a time during this period, what made the difference?

The third group of daughters is from two-parent homes in which neither parent is college-educated. These eleven young women varied in terms of the challenges they faced, depending, for example, on whether their parents worked the night shift, were in the military, or lived in an urban or suburban neighborhood. Here, we see considerable variation in the nature of family ties, and for the first time in the chapter, we consistently hear reports of fathers playing a significant role in the youths' development. An interesting question here is to what extent did having a father in the home offset risk factors associated with the parents' lack of college education?

Finally, the young women in the fourth group have a number of potential advantages: both mother and father are in the home, and one or both parents are college-educated. These twenty-one youth grew up in middle-class suburbs for the most part, and their academic peers at school, and in many cases their neighborhood peers as well, were primarily White—factors that resulted in special racial and cultural challenges for many.[13] An interesting question here is to what extent, and in what ways, did college-educated parents serve as a bridge among the cultures of home, school, and community?

Although we focus on the prominent experiences of each group of daughters, this does not mean that daughters in other groupings did not, at least to some extent, have similar experiences. We are attempting, though, to highlight the differences; we do so primarily in descriptive fashion (larger sample sizes are necessary for more rigorous comparative analyses). In discussing each group, we draw out particularly salient themes, and do not include other themes that were less consistently emphasized.

Also, within each of the four groups of students, important differences emerge for each daughter in terms of the details of their lives and the combination of factors that led to their success. No two stories are exactly alike. Although the groupings help us to distinguish among sets of daughters, each young woman presents us with a unique tapestry.

We are now ready for our journey through the varied lives of these academically successful young women. We turn first to those who likely have faced the greatest odds—girls growing up primarily with one parent (most often the mother) in the home, and who lack the model of a college-educated parent. How did these youth succeed, overcoming these enormous odds?

Those at Greatest Risk: Girls Raised in Non-College-Educated, Single-Parent Households

One-fifth of the daughters we spoke with were raised by a single parent, in most cases the mother, who did not have more than a high-school education. The vast majority of these youth spent their formative years in poor urban or rural neighborhoods—where, by their own accounts, they were exposed to drug use, crime, high rates of pregnancy, and an antiacademic peer environment. Yet, in the face of such obstacles, these young women stayed focused and achieved at the highest levels. Let's listen as the daughters discuss the substantial challenges that beset them, and the parenting and community and personal resources that led them to where they are today.

The Challenges

The daughters describe a variety of challenges they faced growing up, putting a human voice to what we read about in newspaper accounts and in social science research. The first daughter, Shantay, grew up in inner-city Baltimore.

> *"In my neighborhood, there were drive-bys. I have seen people get shot when I was younger. My father's side of the family has seventy cousins,*

alone, in Baltimore. A lot of them had children at fourteen and fifteen years old. A lot of my cousins either used drugs or sold drugs."

The next daughter, Tanya, faced comparable neighborhood challenges in government-subsidized, public housing, in a very poor, mostly Black neighborhood in rural Maryland.

"People in despair—that's what I saw in my own neighborhood. We had drug dealers on the corner. People got shot. My friends went to jail. Half of my friends are still in the same [neighborhood] situation that their parents were in. That feeling of hopelessness, that things can't get better—not knowing how to make them better."

Leanna moved from her mother's house in an extremely dangerous neighborhood to a more stable area to live with her father and stepmother, but then in escaping that dangerous environment faced major challenges related to her new family situation.

"We lived in my mother's house, on the worst street for a number of years. It was in the paper that it was the most dangerous street in Baltimore City. My sister and I later moved with my father into a good neighborhood, mainly for financial reasons, because my mother had eight kids, but six were from her first marriage. It made much more sense for us to go live with our father because he was getting married again. You get a new mother, and I was still young, clingy to mother. For years, I used to cry every night, and my dad just never ever knew. And I never ever let him know about it."

Patricia, like a number of other daughters in this group, describes a family legacy of teen pregnancy that she had to overcome.

"There haven't been too many young people who have gone to college in my family. For the longest time, it seemed like my sisters and I were the only ones really into school, and really doing well. My cousins were waiting for me to slip up, to mess up. I really didn't appreciate that. I'm the only woman in my family without a baby. That's the legacy I've had to try to break away from."

Strong Maternal Influence

How did these daughters succeed in the face of such odds? First, and foremost in the view of most of the daughters, was the powerful and positive influence of their mothers. Uniformly, they report that their mothers had high academic expectations and a strong focus on the importance of education. The daughters also generally report having a positive and open relationship (though not without some conflict) with their mothers and deeply respecting them. In addition, many of the daughters express an appreciation for the hard work and ongoing effort their mothers made to contribute to the family's financial stability. A number of these themes are reflected in the following four quotes.

> *"A lot had to do with my mother, and the fact that she had the expectation that we were going to do well. She taught me to expect it from myself. Of course, if I needed something, she was there. She was supportive and she was encouraging. I could talk to my mom about anything. She trusted me, and I recognized that. She just set the expectations, and I just did it. My mom set a Christian example. Everything else falls in line after that. I always had the utmost respect for her."*

> *"When I was very young, my mother would always read to me, and encourage me to read, and things like that. She started me out so early that I was pretty accelerated in school. My mom really encouraged me to come home from school and do my homework as soon as I got home— after awhile, it just became a habit for me, choosing to come home and do my homework instead of hanging out with my friends or watching TV."*

> *"My mother always worked hard to support us, to make sure we were doing well. She still really couldn't support us, but she was trying her hardest. That always made me want to try my hardest at everything. . . . There aren't many people I look up to besides my mom. I guess I always wanted to make sure I could give my children what she gave us, plus more."*

> *"My mother always wanted me to be at the top. If I didn't do well, then I got in trouble. I remember one time in high school I came home with*

three ninety-nines, a ninety-six, and a ninety, and she asked me why my ninety was so low."

The Role of Fathers

In contrast to their consistently positive relationships with their mothers, the daughters' relationships with their fathers varied considerably in nature. Some of the daughters noted a positive paternal influence. In these cases, fathers imposed high academic expectations and sometimes offered hands-on academic help, especially during periods when the daughter was living with the father. For some daughters, however, fathers were not present at all, and in a few cases, daughters reported the negative influence of alcoholic fathers.

Shantay reports that her father, a high-school dropout whom she lived with most of the time following her parents' divorce when she was six years old, had a strongly positive influence. While emphasizing academics, he particularly helped her to understand men.

"My father always worked with me when I was in kindergarten. When everybody was first learning to print, my father had already taught me to print, and I was writing cursive. When I would come home from school, even though my cousins were outside playing, I always had to do my homework first, and then read a book. For him, doing well was doing my best. . . . Growing up in the city, being female, we talked less about academics and more about being a female. Not getting involved with certain groups of people. Watching out for guys, not getting pregnant—there were no ifs and buts about it with my father. It was just 'don't do it.' When I was living with my father, I never did anything [bad]. I respected my father a whole lot."

Another daughter, Evelyn, similarly reports her father's strong focus on education and strict limits prior to her parents' divorce when she was ten. She also notes that her father's involvement increased again when she was in eighth grade.

"When I was young, my father used to check my homework. Before I went to bed, my homework had to be correct. From fourth grade to sev-

enth grade, there wasn't a lot of involvement, because they were sepa-rated [in ninth grade, they divorced]. My father wasn't around. The eighth-grade year, my father got involved, to get to know my teachers. In fact, a lot of my teachers were, 'Well, I talked with your father this morn-ing.' He was talking to them, pretty much to get me on the right track. My father told me stories about how he didn't make the best use of his high school education. From middle school on, there was no doubt about that I was going to college. And he would tell me we don't have any money, so you need to get a scholarship, and you need to have good grades."

The next two daughters, in contrast, had very negative and difficult rela-tionships with their fathers. Tracey's father was violent.

"I had a rough childhood. I don't really have any positive memories of my father, just painful ones. He was not involved in my education at all. I don't want to be mean [though] because my father is a different person now than he was when I was growing up."

Tanya's father was alcoholic.

"I didn't really have a relationship with my father. I was just too angry with him. He was an alcoholic. He was kind of in and out. My whole perception was, 'Why can't you just act right, why can't you do right?' I loved him, but I didn't like him. I had a hard time respecting him. I am not sure we ever had a conversation that lasted more than ten minutes. He died [from drinking] about two years ago. My father taught me a lot about what I didn't want to be. I guess it helped me to strive to do what is best, and what is right and what is good."

Teachers

Beyond mothers (and fathers in some cases), teachers are reported to have been important, positive sources of support and influence. Most of the daughters report at least one teacher who played a pivotal role, and those in magnet programs or schools report extremely favorable experiences. In a few instances, though, there are reports of racist or sexist practices.

The first two young women, Leah and Michelle, discuss the general supportiveness of teachers.

> *"My teachers always supported me. They always rewarded us for doing well, which made us want to do well. Since I was in special programs, we were always able to get the special attention we needed. I think a lot of teachers expected more from say the Asian students, or the Caucasian students, but they didn't necessarily have low expectations of me just because they expected them to do well."*

> *"From the beginning, teachers play a very important role. Once they see that you have the ability to do well, they push you to do more. My third-grade teacher put me up against a fourth-grader, doing multiplication tables. I think I did pretty well against that person. My teachers had such high expectations for me."*

The teacher described by Evelyn helped her during a very difficult period.

> *"My parents separated. I had problems, and it reached a point during my sixth-grade year, where I didn't want to do anything. I didn't want to participate. My teacher sat down with me, and he talked to me. He made me feel better, and at that point, school was like a highlight. I wanted to go to school because I wanted to get away from problems, and I had someone to talk to."*

The final daughter, Sheila, from a rural area of Maryland, had a very traumatic and negative experience with a racist second-grade teacher, but then reports a positive turning point at the end of third grade.

> *"There was a point where I could have really fallen by the wayside. In the second grade, I had a teacher who had a problem with teaching minority students. I guess I was slowly being brainwashed by this woman. Everything I did was wrong. Even after my mother went to the school board, I still felt, at every opportunity, she was calling me a stupid child. I went to third grade with the attitude that school wasn't important—why should I pay attention if everything I do is going to be wrong.*

"My patient third-grade teacher put up with pretty much a year of this from me. Near the end of the year, I was playing with some of my friends in class, and being a little rowdy and smart-mouthed. All my friends got to go to recess except for me. The teacher was like, 'Wait a minute, I need to talk to you.' She told me, 'You are very academically gifted. I'm taking this chance with you. I've enrolled you for next year into the gifted-and-talented program. I have faith that you can turn this around, but you just can't go with this attitude.' I was completely sobbing, because I had this wonderful teacher, and I felt like I treated her so bad all year. This woman really cared. From that point on, things started being different. That was a big deal for me, to be going to that program. I had the summer to cool off, think about it with my mother's help, and go back to school with a positive attitude. The program turned out to be really fun, and really interesting to me. That was the big turning point academically."

Peer Support and Coping with Two Worlds

Many of the daughters in this group discuss the importance of support from peers who shared their academic goals, and the challenges of coping with peers (often from their neighborhoods) who did not. Leah describes how she coped with negative reactions from peers when she was young.

"Growing up, the kids who weren't doing well always teased you because you were doing well. I guess little kids are cruel. But I would always say, 'Where will I be in a few years, and where will you be?'"

The next two daughters, Carol and Shantay, discuss the positive influence of peers.

"One of the most important experiences that really contributed to my success was having good friendships with people who had the same interests, ideals, and goals that I had. Growing up in the inner city, it's very easy to get involved with different people. I mean, there are young women—their aspirations may be to have babies—and then there are other groups whose aspirations may just be something like nursing assis-

tants or bus drivers. From an early age, all my friends—we have always done well in school, we have always been academically inclined, and we have always had goals for ourselves."

"From pre-K to fifth grade, I went to different elementary schools every year. My parents moved so much. Then I had the opportunity to go to a citywide middle school. You had to apply to get into the school, so most of my friends were on the same level. In my neighborhood, in the beginning, even though I was still cool, there was a lot of negative feedback. It was, 'Oh, you know, she's the smart one.' But I guess I could switch from being the smart one, to being the neighborhood girl. Now, when I do well, they say, 'Congratulations.' When I do bad, it's like, 'Oh, what's the problem?'"

Special Sources of Motivation

Significantly, many of the daughters in this group report a special, deep-rooted motivation to succeed based on the difficult life situations they and their families faced. Here, we listen to a number of young women who described such motivations. First, we hear the voices of two daughters, Tanya and Leah, whose desire to succeed stems, at least in part, from wanting to help their mothers move out of their current economic and neighborhood situations.

"We were poor. We struggled. My mom raised three kids on less than $10,000 a year. To see her go through that and give so much, and not live the life that I thought she deserved to live—I think that had the biggest impact on me. I decided that I was going to do whatever I needed to do, to make life better for myself and for my mom. I just always had that voice inside me that said, 'This is temporary and you are going to do what you have to do to make it better.' The voice was probably planted there by my mom, who always made me feel like my future was brighter. It was a struggle. It was really hard."

"Ever since I was little, I always wanted to get out of that neighborhood. I always said to myself, when I'm older, I'm going to do better than how

my mom was doing, and live in a neighborhood where people are more successful. I always wanted to be able to buy my mom a house somewhere else. In order to be successful economically, I have always felt that I had to be successful academically. I knew that from the early stage of my life, and so from then on, I tried to do well. My only way to get out was to succeed at school."

Patricia emphasizes wanting to overcome a family legacy of teen pregnancy.

"One day, I sat down and did the math. I figured out my mother had me when she was seventeen. I was looking at pictures, seeing my mother and father going to their prom, and sitting in the background was my grandmother. They never really talked to me about it, but I started thinking about it. And later on, I learned that my mother was really bright in school, and so was my father, but neither one of them went to college. It kind of made me think I want to make them proud. I want to do the things they couldn't do, probably because they had to take care of me. Later I learned it wasn't because they had me. They just had different goals, different plans."

Some of the young women note a special obligation resulting from the fact that they have done so well, and so many others in their situation, including siblings, did not, as indicated in the quote from Leanna below.

"I didn't have a social life in high school. I went to school, and I worked. Two of my sisters have had children out of wedlock. My brothers have been arrested, and two of them are in jail serving long sentences. Why am I the one who is doing so well and received these opportunities? I feel like, there was a reason, it was a blessing, it was intended for me and I'm supposed to do something with it. I want to become a true public servant."

The deeper motivations of the final two daughters, Tracey and Wendy, stem from unique family situations—a harsh family life, in one case, and the death of a grandmother, a key academic support, in the other.

"For me, school was a way to escape from hard work in a dysfunctional family. I would wake up at five o'clock in the morning and take care of my younger siblings. That was my day, and I was very resentful of that. . . . I never, ever want to feel under the whim of anybody. Just looking at my dad's violence towards my mom, I always wanted to be self-sufficient. The things that I went through as a child made me a stronger adult. My childhood taught me about perseverance. Going to college was freedom, the only way to leave the house. That's the quick escape I saw."

"I can remember the death of my grandmother when I was in ninth grade. That impacted me greatly. My mother, she hasn't lived with me since I was five or six, but my grandmother, my father's mother, somewhat played that role. And she was also one of the main people who stressed going to school, getting good grades, doing your homework before anything else. I can remember her last few days, because she was terminally ill, the last few days she just told me basically to keep going—'I know you will do well in life'—and that kind of impacted me, because it made me keep going. I am not only doing this for myself, but for her."

Summary

The daughters in this group are impressive. Most faced poverty and difficult neighborhoods in which sex, drugs, and violence were prominent during their childhood. For many, these experiences served as a direct source of academic motivation—if they were going to build a better life for themselves and one day for their children, they knew that academic success was the only means to do so. Most were highly motivated to succeed from a young age, and they demonstrated early on a strong academic potential. High levels of parental support, expectation, and structure provided fertile ground for their talents and motivation to flower.

These daughters' lives, in most cases, were never easy—their internal drive, and the various strands of the tapestry of support noted above, led them to stay the course and achieve at the very highest levels. Although no two stories, or pathways, were quite the same, the result was an astounding resilience, and marked success against the greatest odds.

Special Challenges Facing College-Educated, Single-Parent Households

Parents with a college (or graduate or professional) degree carry with them a major resource for their daughters' academic success. The parents can serve as strong academic role models and guides to success in education. There is also generally a strong relationship between the levels of parents' education and household income. Thus, they are also less likely to be raising their daughters in the most dangerous neighborhoods or sending them to weaker schools.

The advantages of having a college-educated parent in the home, however, do not ensure that the young women will not encounter the various obstacles facing many young, female African Americans in our society. This may be especially true when the daughters have low self-esteem, when their neighborhood peers are disengaged from school, when a father is not present in the daughter's life, or when the transition to middle school or high school is problematic.

Academic and Social Challenges

We begin with the voices of several daughters who reported academic or social difficulties during the late middle-school or early high-school years.[14] For the first daughter, Mia, academic difficulty occurred at the time of transition to a highly competitive high school and involved, in part, the negative influence of neighborhood friends.

> *"My first semester in the ninth grade, I got like a 2.7 [grade point average], the first time I didn't make honor roll. That was a wake-up call because I was going to a challenging, very competitive program. Part of the problem was that the people I was growing up with were all of a sudden doing drugs and drinking. Everyone I knew would say, 'Come on, just try.' I would see people who dropped out of school, girls getting pregnant—people I grew up with, who when younger were all good kids."*

A second young woman, Shani, faced problems in the area of self-acceptance and relationships with peers.

"In middle school, my schoolmates avoided me, because I was smart. 'You're smart, you're a nerd, stay away from me, you're not cool.' And I got teased for being too tall. And they didn't like the fact that I had a perm. Many people were like, 'You want to be White.' I wasn't very popular. I wanted to have friends just like all the people in the regular program. I started to downplay being smart, so that I could get along with them. I started stealing stuff, talking in class, writing notes, not paying attention to the teacher. I wasn't performing at my real level. It did work to an extent, because I had a lot of friends in eighth grade."

Janice, like Mia, also faced difficulties in ninth grade.

"My grades were not that great in ninth grade, maybe because I just tried to skate by. Maybe I wasn't going in the right direction. Maybe I didn't see that I had to do what I had to do, to have discipline and to really do my work."

Another important challenge reported by some of the daughters involved difficult situations with fathers, as reflected in the case of Racquel.

"The reason my parents divorced was because my dad became somewhat abusive to my mother. Mom says she never wanted to stay in a relationship like that. Also, he was having an affair. I was angry at my dad for a long time, just for not being there. I didn't forgive him. Why would somebody have children, and not want them?"

The final daughter, Aisha, was one of several who, at least for some part of their upbringing, lived in dangerous neighborhoods.

"It wasn't safe playing outside where I grew up. There were drug dealers on the corner. When we were in elementary school, the middle-school kids were pulling out guns. And we were like, woooh, we got to go inside. That kind of thing was hard to deal with. My mom and I lived near the corner, and it was pretty scary coming home at night. We really wanted to get out of that area because it wasn't helping me at all."

These varied challenges could have led to negative outcomes for the daughters. However, due to a combination of supports and resources, including internal ones, the young women not only survived them, but flourished. As with the first set of daughters, mothers are viewed as the critical, positive influence, although the specific nature of the influence differs for these daughters in some important ways.

The Importance of Mothers

For the majority of daughters in this group, it was their mothers who played the central role in their lives. In most cases, strong mother-daughter bonds developed. Academically, the mothers were very involved. In terms of limit-setting, the mothers were strict. And, when dealing with social and academic problems, the mothers were supportive and resourceful. The academic, limit-setting, and problem-solving domains of influence of mothers are portrayed below.

Academics

The academic involvement of mothers in this group was generally more direct and hands-on than it was in the first group. It also often involved different types of guidance and modeling than for daughters in the first group. The five stories below reflect these varied aspects of the academic influence of the mothers. First we hear from Shani and Gladys.

> *"I came from a single-parent home. My sister and I were the only two in my family, and my mom had always pushed so that we could survive on our own. She was very into our academics. She was involved in our school; she knew what was going on. She knew when we had homework—she would actually sit with us, and make sure we understood. If we had any questions, she would help us out. Basically, she cut off all outside interaction while we were doing our homework so that we could keep focused. . . . My mom was the first one in her family to go to college. So 'no college' wasn't even in the vocabulary. My mom never allowed me to fall short. If I was struggling in class, she would stress the class and I would do more exercises. We had a computer, so she would get computer programs. She gave us supplemental materials."*

"One thing my mom did with all of us—I have two sisters and one brother, we've all been very successful students—she always said to us, 'I just want you to do your best.' So, I don't remember any occasion when I was scolded on a grade. It was always, 'What happened? Did you do your best?' She was always encouraging, always helping, not being critical of us. She's just such a remarkable person. Even when we came home late some nights, she'd bring dinner up to our rooms. She'd make us hot chocolate and bring it to us because she knew we were going to be up. Or she would tell us to go to bed, and she'd wake us up the next morning at five a.m. to finish. People always say, 'Well, I don't understand how your mom got so lucky. All four of you are good in school and good kids.' I don't think it was luck. She put in the time as a parent. She did the right things."

Cherita focuses on her mother's active involvement, and advocacy, within the school.

"My mother was very involved with teachers and school. I remember moving to a predominantly White county for high school. And when my mom went to set up my schedule for ninth grade, they saw a little, short Black woman walking in. They said they didn't think I should be in Algebra II. 'Maybe you want to put her back in Algebra I.' My mother looked at that man, and said, 'If my daughter is not in Algebra II the first day of class I will come down here and you will remember my face, and you will remember my name.' The first day of class I was in Algebra II. No problem. My mother has always been that way."

The next daughter, Melinda, emphasizes her mother's influence as a role model.

"I use my mother as a role model. She has her doctorate degree, and I want mine too. She has set an example for me, and so that motivated me to do better, to achieve."

The final daughter, Benita, sees herself as part of a larger, intergenerational evolution and lineage. This heritage is echoed in the chapter on parents where parents, too, discuss the sense of history and development, from one generation to the next.

"There weren't very many opportunities open to my grandmother. She would get As in school, but she would get beat up for her As. For my grandmother, arithmetic was the level of math that she encountered. . . . My mother's philosophy was, 'I might not be the prettiest or the smartest, but I can be different.' And there are a lot of things that she did as a part of being stubborn. Like, she went to Smith College. Her advisor told her that she wouldn't be able to go there, she wouldn't get accepted, and that motivated her—'I'm going to apply and that's where I'm going.' My grandfather told her that women shouldn't be professionals. . . . I see myself in a point of evolution, from my grandmother and my mother."

Limit-Setting

As a group, the young women in this section emphasize the strong limits and discipline they experienced. Janice and Celeste discuss several aspects of this important form of parental influence.

"I wasn't the type of kid who got grounded—I was disciplined hands-on. My mom didn't send me to my room. She didn't let me get away with stuff. I was an only child; she was the only one who was there. I was scared my mom would find out if I did something, so I just didn't do it. No behaviors to hide, because I can't hide from her. She always finds out, I don't know how."

"My mom didn't really let me out into the city neighborhood much. . . . She always followed me around, with a magnifying glass over top of me, like making sure I wasn't doing anything. I was raised with a strong Christian background. My mother's father is a Presbyterian minister. So, sex, drugs, anything like that was a strict no. There wasn't even, if you are going to do it, maybe you should use protection. It was just you are not going to do it. And I would get on punishment a lot, for a really long time, for breaking the house rules, like getting caught with food in my room. I would get angry because I had friends who were having sex, or doing drugs, and something would happen and they would never even get in trouble."

Coping with Difficult Problem Situations

Beyond academic support and strict discipline, the mothers played a key role as well in helping daughters cope with difficult challenges in growing up, including dealing with changing peer, family, and school environments. Mia describes her mother's role in helping her cope with her parents' divorce, and also discusses the support provided when she did poorly academically upon entering a very competitive high school.

"When our parents got divorced, my dad ended up taking a lot less of a role in the parenting. I think a lot of my brother's [behavior problems] came from the lack of having a father around, supporting him. I have a really tight bond with my mother, so I think that is what helped me through these things, knowing that I have her there for me. . . . In ninth grade, I realized I had let my mother down. . . . In response she took an active role, but it wasn't necessarily in my face. She would sometimes just ask, 'How is this going?' Or, 'How is that going?' It was never a thing where she was putting me down or putting a lot of pressure on me. . . . My mom, she's just supported me, no matter what I have done. She doesn't let me feel bad about myself. Just her example has been good for me."

Janice also experienced a very difficult year in ninth grade, not trying very hard. Thanks to a very active intervention by her mother—having her enter ROTC—the situation turned around in tenth grade.

"My mother put me in ROTC, in tenth grade. When I got into ROTC, I kind of woke up. It was like a realization: I am not going to get As or get the kind of grades I want if I don't do [all] my homework. My ROTC instructors were the only teachers I ever had who really cared about me. All of my academic teachers were White. The ROTC instructors wanted to see me succeed, and they did everything they could to help me."

Spirituality and Religion

Spirituality and religion are emphasized by most of the daughters in this group. In the case of some daughters, they became especially important when the young women were coping with difficult personal or life situations. For others, spirituality and religion were an ongoing source of support. Overall, 84 percent of the daughters in this group indicated their families attended church regularly, almost twice as many as the 45 percent of the young women in the first group.

Shani talks about the importance of spirituality in her struggle with low self-esteem during her middle-school and high-school years.

> *"Self-worth has come from God because I had probably the lowest self-esteem of any person you know. That was something I struggled with throughout all my life. I guess that's why I struggled for other people's acceptance. I didn't feel pretty. I didn't feel accepted. But, God has shown me my unique traits. . . . As long as you keep your priorities straight, and make God first, nothing, nobody, can keep you down."*

The next two young women, Janice and Mia, describe the ongoing role of religion and spirituality in their development.

> *"The motto of my church is, 'The church where love is in action,' and it really is. Most people in my church knew my mother before I was even born, so I have people coming up to me I don't even know. And they just show me so much love. A lot of stuff I didn't do because I knew it was wrong. My mother has raised me Christian. She was Christian all her life. She does not drink or smoke. My religion set a lot of morals into place, like the premarital-sex thing.*
>
> *My mother is encouraging. I have learned from her I 'can do all things, through Christ, who strengthens me.' She's just always telling the positive side of everything."*

> *"The kids my age at church, the few of us who were doing well, they always supported us. A lot of times they would announce your GPA at service, and things like that. Spirituality definitely has pushed me through a lot of obstacles in life. There were just some things that were very hard, and no one else could understand. But I could pray and I could read the Bible, and that would give me the strength to keep on going and do what I needed to."*

The final quote is from a daughter, Aisha, who lived in a dangerous neighborhood. Her religious faith was an important source of her longer-term motivation.

"I was always taught that God was there to support me. I had to work hard, and then God would help me out. That's how I was taught. I had faith in the fact that God would make my life better later on, because I was working hard now."

The Role of Fathers

When the young women discuss the role of fathers in their lives, it is most often in terms of their academic influence. The college-educated fathers in the group communicated high expectations of academic success to their children. Furthermore, some of the fathers provided hands-on influence, especially when the daughters were younger. Others, however, had little direct influence. The variation in the specific nature and extent of paternal influence is revealed in the following set of quotes.

"My father is a science teacher. He was very gung-ho about my education. He started teaching me to read when I was four. He used to go over his lesson plans with me. I have just always liked math and science from that point on. I always said that I wanted to be a doctor. And when I was ten or eleven, I really did want to be a doctor."

"My dad always made sure that he knew what my grades were. I always brought a copy whenever I went to visit him. As long as I was doing well, he was always happy with me, and encouraged me. If I did poorly, I needed to work harder, stay after school, see my teacher, get tutored. He would give me advice on how to do better."

"My dad completed college, and he was never struggling. My mother dropped out of college, and she married my dad, and she was struggling. After the divorce, my dad wasn't involved with school or teachers. He's the financial person. He'll say, 'I'll write the checks; that's what I'll do.'"

"My father wants to be involved in my life, but I don't let him. He's done some things. The reason my parents got divorced was because he was abusive to her. He calls, he tried to be an influence in my academics or social life, but I pretty much don't let him."

Peers and Extracurricular Activities

Additional sources of support and influence emphasized by many of the daughters were peers and involvement in extracurricular activities. The first two young women, Mia and Melinda, briefly comment on the importance of positive, academically oriented peers.

"Before, I just chose to stay around people who were fun, or who were popular. I realized it is kind of a change in lifestyle. You need to be around positive people, and do positive things to be successful. I started making more friends who were doing well in school, and more friends who could be beneficial to me in terms of helping me with my work."

"We would just study together, and push each other to do well. Having expectations that we're all going to do well encouraged us to do better."

High levels of involvement in extracurricular activities marked the lives of many of the young women in this group. Shani and Sonya portray the positive importance of these involvements.

"I loved basketball. My high-school basketball coach and I were really close, because I had been with her for all four years. I really loved her. She was really cool. Basketball gave me more confidence, and that reflected in my schoolwork. Because there was a schedule I had to keep for basketball, it made me be more scheduled in my class work. I feel like I do the best when I have a lot of things to do."

"I played the piano for a long time. When I would get tired of practicing, my mom always encouraged me. Playing the piano taught me discipline, just being able to sit down and practice for two or three hours at a time."

Summary

The daughters in this group clearly benefited in distinct ways from having a college-educated parent. The distinct and empowering influence of mothers, together with that of teachers, religion, peers, and extracurricular activities, helped daughters to develop self-confidence and a belief in themselves and their capabilities. The mother-daughter bond is consistently described as a very strong one, with mothers playing helping, guiding, and modeling roles. The college-educated fathers in the group appear to have high expectations of academic success for their children, which appears to have contributed to their daughter's motivation. Rarely, however, were both mother and father central strands in their lives, a situation which is markedly different in the two-parent families to which we now turn.

Mother and Father Combined:
Two-Parent, Non-College-Educated Households

In contrast to the preceding group of daughters, in which it is rare to see both mother and father as important strands in the tapestries of their lives, strong parenting roles for both mother and father characterize many of the families in this group. Overall, these families reflect the positive strengths traditionally associated with blue-collar or working-class families: a focus on structure, rules, discipline, hard work, and respect. Questionnaire responses indicate that in these families, in contrast to families with college-educated parents, there is less social-political discussion, less focus on learning "new and different things," less attendance at cultural events, and less discussion of racial obstacles to success. Overall, these working-class families provide structure and support for these young women, serving to anchor them against the challenges they confront, including dangerous urban neighborhoods, a sense of needing to fit in, pervasive teen pregnancy among peers, and, in many cases, difficult family legacies that these daughters were strongly motivated to leave behind.

The Challenges

Deanna grew up in an urban neighborhood.

"I lived on the east side of the city. . . . I guess it was a typical environment, like you see all the Black guys hanging on the corner, just standing there doing nothing. I saw a lot of bad things. A lot of people would fall off, and end up just not doing anything with their lives. My best friend in high school had a baby. I swear ninety percent of the people I know from my high school have children now, or had children in high school."

The next daughter, Carmen, reflects on the limitations stemming from her family's socioeconomic status, and also comments on difficulties faced by relatives.

"My sister and I wanted to play some instruments in elementary school, but my parents couldn't afford lessons, so we never really started. I couldn't buy the kind of clothes peers could buy. It hurt me sometimes. In middle school, I was always in the gifted-and-talented classes and didn't relate to the people in my classes. Most of them were high middle-class, and my friends were more toward the low middle-class. I just wanted to be with my friends. Also, with my parents' families, there are a lot of them who have done time, or been on drugs."

The final young woman, Tamara, notes the challenge of teen pregnancy within her Black, middle-class neighborhood and, again, a legacy of social problems among various members of her extended family.

"I lived in an all-Black neighborhood. Middle-class, lots of family, lots of kids around to play with. It was a pretty good neighborhood to grow up in, I think. There wasn't much crime. Teen pregnancy was an issue. I had friends who got pregnant in high school. . . . Also, my uncles were involved with drugs. My aunts' husbands, one died, another was put in jail, another was in rehab. Along the same lines, my grandfather was an alcoholic."

Combined Parental Focus on Education

Their parents' combined emphasis on academic success helped these young women succeed and stay on track in the face of a variety of challenges. The parents sent strong messages about the importance of education. They emphasized homework and had high expectations for their daughters' academic success. Three representative quotes follow.

"It was always, 'You need to study, education is important. You can't get anywhere without it.' There were always times when I would come home, and it would be, 'Did you do your homework? Well, did you study?' 'How are things going in school?' And I think that sort of mind-set, that sort of habit, developed when I was younger. As I got older, they weren't over my shoulder all the time, but the habit and the mind-set were still there."

"A lot of it was support from my family. I was told from the very beginning that I could do anything that I set my mind to. There was a push to do well. I think it was just family support, a lot."

"Neither of my parents went to college, so they were really big on getting an education, and working your hardest in everything you do. There were seven children. When we received our report cards each of us would be called into my parents' bedroom, and we would sit down and talk about our grades. I can remember when I didn't get good grades, it was always, 'Well, last semester you got a B and this semester you have a C. What is the problem here? Life is not a game—you should always be improving.' My parents have always been there for me. When I said I was going to be President of the United States, my parents said 'Great, we're proud of you. You can invite us to the White House.' They've always been, 'Whatever you say, you can do it.' And I've always been grateful for that."

A number of the daughters discussed how other Black young women they knew did not stay on track, in part due to lower levels of parental involvement and less focus on education. Carmen highlights what can happen when parental support and high expectations are not present, in this case regarding a best friend.

"My best friend, we were at the same level in elementary school. It's like they accidentally put her in a lower class in seventh grade, and she stayed there. I knew she shouldn't have, I know she is smart. She's not even in school now. She might have been convinced that it would be easier if she stayed in those lower classes. Judging from things my friend said, maybe her mother had a little bit to do with that. Her mother was at work most of the time. Her father wasn't there. I don't think her mother had enough time to help her with her homework, or give her encouragement like my parents did. I think that probably made a difference."

Although daughters consistently reported high expectations and a strong emphasis on the importance of education from their parents, actual levels of parental hands-on involvement varied tremendously. This is in contrast to the previous group of daughters, for whom the vast majority of parents were consistently engaged in a hands-on fashion. The variability in this group is reflected in the following two quotes. Deanna portrays a relatively lower level of hands-on parental involvement, and Eva a high level.

"I did my homework in my room, and I did it on my own. Nobody told me to do it. Nobody helped me with it, but when I did come back with a good grade, everybody was happy. They didn't pressure me. I knew they expected me to do well, because after a couple of times of bringing home all As, you just can't come back without that. Other than that, my parents were basically not involved in-depth with my education. For example, I was in a program at Johns Hopkins when I was in middle school. It was during the summer. You could accept to go; my counselor just put me down as accepted to go. My parents found out after the fact."

"My mom was so involved in elementary school, the principal and she butted heads on several occasions. I mean he didn't like me because he knew who my mom was. It kind of made me feel good because my mom cares, my parents care about what is going on in my academic life. I knew that I just couldn't do anything—you know, bring home some mediocre grades, because here my mom is going head-to-head with this man on a weekly basis. I think being involved was the most important thing. When your parents are not involved, it relays a sense to you, they don't really care, so why should I care."

Relationships with Mothers and with Fathers

Whereas daughters in the previous group were likely to be more satisfied with their relationships with their mothers than with their fathers, those in the current grouping report, in response to the same survey item, had comparable levels of satisfaction with their mothers and fathers. Not surprisingly, though, the specific nature of daughters' relationships with dads and moms differed. The young women generally share more of their lives with their mothers, as reflected in this quote from Tamara.

"My parents and I are close. I am closer to my mom in the sense that, I can talk about everything with her. Not as comfortable with my father."

Eva emphasizes her mother's support and acceptance, and provides a concrete example which demonstrates varying responses of her mother and father.

"My mom calls me her last hope. So, she is anxious to do anything to shelter me from any sort of bad influence or any interference. Whatever I did in school was always accepted; whether I did well or didn't, I was still loved and accepted. . . . My dad used to say to my mom, 'Why is she playing Atari in the morning or Nintendo, she should be eating her breakfast, or whatever.' I remember my mom would say, particularly on days when I had standardized achievement tests or something, 'It's good for her, it gives her coordination, and it relaxes her.' So I would play."

Fathers are more likely to focus on task-oriented than interpersonal topics, as revealed in the case of Valerie.

"With my dad, it is more business-like. I would go to him if I needed funds for certain things—if I really needed transportation, if there is a place where we need him to be. With my mother, it is more of the social interaction."

The next daughter, Wanda, reports similar differences, and also is one of several young women reporting periods of conflict with their fathers—in this case, ultimately involving a very negative outcome, school suspension.

"My dad and I really deal with the business side of things, which I think may be the case for a lot of Black men. It is very difficult for them to get into the emotional part of things. My dad is, 'Well, that's life, so deal with it, don't gripe about it.' My father and I have had rough times, but it is because we are so much alike. I mean we are both stubborn, and we are both temperamental. The first time I started was about thirteen. Everything up to that point that Daddy said, went, it didn't matter how right or wrong it was. It was his house, his rules. He is the head of the house. I got tired of things eating at me. I challenged him all the time. I would anger him so much because he couldn't take my being as strong-willed as him. Then, I went through this stage, when I got to high school, I was dying inside because I just felt like all of these things that everybody else was experiencing, I couldn't."

During her first year of high school, Wanda became involved in a negative, gang-like peer group. This involvement included skipping school regularly and engaging in fights with groups from other neighborhoods. She was full of anger and hostility during this period, but she hid her negative activities from her parents.

"I was the master of deception during that time. I still came home, still did my homework, still went to work, still helped my sisters. Then, I got suspended. My parents were just like, 'I cannot believe this.' It wasn't until later, after I had safely gone to college, before I started telling them some of the things I did."

After the suspension, her parents moved to a new neighborhood. In part due to the influence of involvement in a church in the new neighborhood, her life turned around (as described in the following section).

Religion

Interestingly, religion is not as consistently important a factor for these daughters as for those in the previous group. For example, whereas slightly more than half of the daughters in this group indicate that their spiritual/religious background was very important to their academic success, more than four fifths of the daughters in the previous group indicate this to be the case. Similarly, slightly more than one third report regular church attendance within their family, compared with 83 percent in the previous group, and 90 percent in the two-parent, college-educated group (the greater the parents' educational level, the greater the church involvement).

Religion, however, was important for some of the daughters, and was especially critical at a key juncture in Wanda's life detailed just above.

"My sophomore year in high school, I started going to church. We moved to this new neighborhood—first time in my life that I had been in a house. I started going to this church. I was the only one in my house who was going to church. Everything that I was upset about started coming out. Rather than fight it, I just went to church. I got to a point where I looked forward to Sunday morning. I was in church four or five times a week doing different things. That was my release, that was my getaway. That was the only place where I felt like people understood what I was going through. That is when the fighting stopped."

Peers and Teachers

Two additional supportive resources emphasized by the daughters were peers and teachers. Tamara underscores the increasing educational influence of friends, relative to parents, in the high-school years.

"My parents were important in the earlier years. When I got to high school, it was a group of friends, in the Science and Tech program. We all helped each other out. A little bit was competing against each other. I ran track, and I did student government—leadership stuff. And the mock-trial team, my best friend was the president. Another one of my best friends was secretary."

Finding like-minded peers, however, often involved for these daughters an active process of separating themselves from prior social networks. This separation process is emphasized in the next set of quotes.

"For a long time, there were two different entities to me, until I started becoming friends with the people who were smart too. Usually [before]

my friends were not in my class, they were not the smart ones too. After a while, all my friends were just like me."

"The kids around my neighborhood were real bad. I had to separate myself from them after a while. After middle school, I only hung out with my best friend, who lived right up the street. Just us two, we never really hung out with the neighborhood kids, because they were just going downhill."

"People that I was friends with in middle school kind of fell back into drugs and alcohol, and we kind of lost contact. I had to realize that in order to do well I had to stay by myself and choose my friends more wisely. It's just a decision on what was more important—learning and continuing my education or hanging out. I chose to stay on the school track."

"In elementary school, my friends took school seriously, as I did. There was no problem, everything was positive. That changed—my very best friend, about eighth grade, she found popularity more important, it seems. We kind of separated. When I got to high school, I was in mostly honors classes. There may have been two other Black girls, and separation from the other people in regular classes was really evident."

The final two quotes focus on the importance of key school personnel. Juanita remembers an influential classroom teacher, and Valerie the importance of a middle-school homeroom teacher.

"Through elementary school I wasn't that great a student, until I got into fourth grade. Then, I had this teacher who I really liked, so I guess that's when I decided to start working at school. He really made learning fun and interesting. I kind of had a crush on him, I guess, and I wanted to impress him. I wanted to be smart, and so I think I worked harder. And then after that, it was just kind of a habit. . . . And in middle and high school, I've just been so lucky with science and math teachers. All have been great, excited people."

"In middle school, I had a sixth-grade homeroom teacher who just seemed to take a special interest in me. She really, really encouraged me,

and continued to do so throughout seventh and eighth grade. So, every time I saw her, she always wanted to know what I was doing, what I was thinking, what I wanted to be. I think that really helped to encourage me, to pursue something more, since I knew that someone else was rooting for me, really hoping that I would be a success."

Special Sources of Motivation

Some of the distinct motivational themes articulated by daughters are consonant with those expressed by daughters in the earlier groups, and some are unique to the specific life-circumstances of a given daughter or family. Interestingly, only for this group of daughters was "having a dream" selected by the majority (63 percent) on the survey questionnaire as one of the three most important reasons for their success (parental support and hard work were the second and third reasons selected). The importance of "having a dream" is clear in the first quote, from Carmen, and reflects the hope and optimism present in this group of young women.

"Nobody on our side of the family had ever graduated, and so I felt that would be something special if I was the first one to graduate from college. Since being smart was what was special about me, I had to fulfill my destiny. It had a lot to do with feeling like I had a legacy to fulfill with the family. Plus being a role model for my younger sisters and brothers."

Three other examples of motivational stories, Deanna, Laura, and Juanita, add further to our understanding of these young women's pathways to success.

"I have really bad asthma, so I missed a lot of school. As a result, my mother had to take care of me. She did a good job because I never had to stay overnight in the hospital. My father used to be the one who took care of us during the day, because my mother worked nights, until they switched, and he worked at night, and she worked during the day. She missed a lot of work, the same days that I missed school. I thank my parents for keeping me alive."

"I wanted to be the best, you know, even in kindergarten, from day one. From the very beginning there was that drive."

"We're a very close family. And my sister was this great track star, and it was through my grades I could show them that they did something right. Yes, I wanted my parents to be proud of me, so I worked hard to make them proud of me."

Summary

The daughters in this group grew up in a variety of environments, ranging from inner-city to middle-class neighborhoods. Regardless of the type of neighborhood, the family provides a structure that binds these daughters in a positive sense, keeping them focused on academic achievement. The strength of bonding to parents is not emphasized as consistently and strongly by these daughters as by the young women in the other three groups. Nonetheless, as noted above, the daughters indicate that support from parents was one of the three primary factors leading to their success. This factor, together with hard work and strong personal aspirations linked to a desire to transcend family and neighborhood legacies, represent critical strands in the tapestry of their success.

A Bridge Between Cultures: College-Educated, Two-Parent Households in a Predominantly White World

The final group of daughters is from two-parent families in which at least one, and in many cases both, of the parents are college-educated. Almost every one of these daughters grew up in a middle-class suburban neighborhood, with the majority attending special math/science magnet programs in high school. And, in almost all of the families, both the mother and father were very engaged and very influential in their daughters' academic development. Nonetheless, these daughters faced special challenges, most often linked to coping with White and Black peers in predominantly White school programs, and for a number of the youths, in predominantly White school systems and communities.

Challenges

Aimee and Araba had negative experiences in predominantly White schools.

"I went to a predominantly White elementary school. I was the only Black person in my class who was doing well. You kind of get picked on for doing well, especially if you're a Black person and doing well. It was like you weren't really accepted by the White people because you were Black, and you weren't really accepted by the Black people because you were smart. They defined you as trying to be White. It was difficult. . . . I had like a bully, in third grade. I hid it from my parents for a while, but eventually they found out. I started really not wanting to go to school and feeling sick every time they woke me up to go to school."

"When I moved [to a predominantly White county] in seventh grade, it was very difficult, just adjusting. Before I had been all straight As, now I was getting Cs. The social adjustment was very difficult for me, being in an arena where I was the only Black person, people looking at you because you are Black. People treated me ridiculously. And then in high school, you start to have doubts. Why aren't there any people who look like me in these [math and science] classes? You wonder about The Bell Curve, *that came out when I was in high school. Of course, it was ridiculous, you hated the idea of it, but then you look around."*

A number of the daughters grew up in a predominantly Black suburb or county outside of Washington, D.C., but nonetheless faced the problem of negotiating two-peer cultures—magnet-program classes were primarily White, and most other African American students were in the regular classes. This difficulty is described by Allison and Leanne.

"There were no Black males in the gifted-and-talented classes, and by the time I got to high school, I was the only Black person in these classes—in a high school that was 97 percent Black. I wasn't very outgoing then, so whatever group I was put with, that's the group I stayed with. So you could see me with the White kids—the Black kids would say, oh, she thinks that she's White. I didn't know how to deal with that. It was really, really hard for me."

"In high school there was a struggle trying to find a balance, because the people you spend all day in class with and have fun with are White, but you also identify with the Black students. They went, 'Well, you're a nerd and a snob, and you think you're better because you hang out with the White kids.'"

The daughters in this group surmounted the challenges noted above and achieved at very high levels academically. Next, we turn to some of the factors these daughters view as contributing to their success.

Special Parental Resources

These young women emphasize a number of the benefits of growing up in two-parent, college-educated families. These parents have very high expectations that their children will excel academically and go on to college, as they did; the daughters appear very sensitive to these parental expectations and do not want to disappoint their parents. Almost two thirds of the young women indicated on a survey item that "family members are compared with each other in terms of school and work," in contrast to one third of the daughters in the other three groups. The parents are consistently supportive and encouraging of their daughters and their academic pursuits.

In most cases, parents are extensively involved in a hands-on manner in all aspects of the academic enterprise. They monitor and help with homework, spend time in the schools and get to know teachers, arrange optimal educational placements and entrance into summer academic programs, and so on. And, significantly, the parents are able to provide relatively safe neighborhoods and good public school systems for their daughters. Finally, they are likely to take advantage of academic and community resources outside of school. For instance, more than four fifths of the daughters report that family members often go to the library, compared with two fifths of the daughters in each of the two previous groups.

Given the special resources and opportunities available to them, the daughters in the two-parent, college-educated homes appear to be strongly motivated and extremely well prepared to succeed academically, as indicated in this quote from Araba.

"I think it's a matter of opportunity and circumstance. A lot of people don't have resources available to them. I always grew up around certain

things—human resources, financial and academic resources. My father is an internist; I grew up around science and reading. I saw a lot of Black people around me who were very well educated, and they were all professionals. My mother was always really involved, and going to see the teachers, and going to school. There was always someone there when you got home—that helped a big deal. My parents instilled in me that I had the ability to be anything, that I could do anything—they were really serious about that. My parents are very encouraging people. Just the moral and verbal support with everything, in all aspects of life, athletic, academic, social. You can't help but to be driven by their support."

Several of the students went to private schools for a segment of their education, as described by Cynthia.

"I attribute my success a lot to my parents. They prepared me for any of the challenges I might come across. I've just been lucky. I went to private schools the majority of my life, and then I went to public school for high school. My private-school foundation was so great that anything I came across afterward, I was able to do in terms of academics. My parents were very supportive. They would have done probably anything to help me academically. My dad had done math in college, so he was always helping me with math. Just knowing that you can go home and ask for help is a big incentive to do what you have to do. My mom was into English, and she would help me with papers. I took the test for the magnet program in high school—I missed by half a percentile, or something like that. My mom didn't go for that; she only had to question it, and that was it."

The final daughter, Brenda, touches on another important resource emphasized by a number of the students—the summer as a period for academic learning. This quote also makes explicit the importance of highly educated parents as academic role models.

"My parents would always push, and always expose us to new and different things. During the summertime, my mom would give us all these books that we had to read. And we had to give her book reports, and she would sit there and she'd grade them, and read them, and tell us to rewrite them. Since the fifth grade, I always had something academic in

the summer. Either it'd be space camp or a medical camp, or you'd volunteer at a hospital. So I knew about different things before other kids did. My parents were role models and mentors. My mom had a master's degree, and my dad had his Pharm.D. I'm like, okay, that's what I'm doing, I'm going to get some type of graduate degree."

Strict Rules

Interestingly, more than 90 percent of the daughters in this group indicated they could not "get away with" much in their families, compared with less than one third of the daughters in the previous groups. On a related survey item, 90 percent indicated there was a heavy emphasis on following rules in the family, a much greater percentage than the one half to three fourths of the daughters who reported this in the other three groups. The interview comments support these survey findings—the vast majority of the young women described their parents as extremely strict, in both the academic and social realms. Leanne, Brenda, and Chanel focus on the academic realm.

"In my house, academic success wasn't an option. If you got anything lower than a B, you knew that you were in trouble. There was a certain amount of discipline that came with that. My parents were very, very strict."

"If my grades slipped, they were really harsh. No TV, no whatever, like they weren't used to seeing a B. 'This is not what we expect from you.'"

"I did a lot of back-talking around that puberty stage in middle school. I got in trouble at school, back-talking a teacher. My punishment from my parents was a beating—I think that was my last beating. My back-talking at home was leaking into school—that was the turning point for me, to say this has got to stop. My parents always disciplined immediately after we made mistakes. They definitely instilled fear, to respect them, to honor them as my parents."

In the important realms of sexual relations and dating, nearly nine in ten of the daughters report that their parents emphasized the importance of abstaining from sexual intercourse until adulthood or marriage. This compares with two in three of the daughters in the previous group.

Vera and Tyra, like many in the current group, describe their parents as "overprotective"—providing very tight restraints on social behavior, dating, and sexual relations.

"My parents are not my friends. They have made this very clear—they are my parents. They are very overprotective. My friends were running the streets and stuff—and of course I wanted to run the streets. But, no, I wasn't running the streets. If I wanted to run the streets, I had to move out. A lot of stuff like that. One of my girlfriends got pregnant. My mother was, like, 'We know that will never happen to you, because you wouldn't be stupid enough to do something like that, would you?' 'No, mommy, no, not me, not ever.'"

"Dating was out of the question, until I was eighteen, no discussion, that was it. When I was younger, I got spankings, most often for talking back. The worst time of all was when I was thirteen. I was really mouthy, I was just trying to assert myself, trying to be more like my friends who I thought had more freedom. I couldn't hang at the mall with them. I couldn't go out with them on weekends. We had a lot of fights about that—it probably lasted two years, until I just found more things [school-based activities] to do. I decided not to talk about it anymore, because I knew I was going to get a 'no' anyway."

In many cases the parents' strictness was rooted in their strong religious beliefs, as indicated by Vanessa and Brenda.

"We were raised in the church, we go to church, we're Christians. My parents never had to say anything about drugs, teen pregnancy, sex. It was just, you don't. There was never a question in my mind."

"My parents are devout Catholics, and premarital sex is just 'no.' It wasn't like, 'Let's talk.' It was just, 'Guys will deceive you; guys are going to do this. You don't need them right now. You're not dating, period. Boys will ruin your life.'"

Distinctive Roles of Mothers and Fathers

Both mothers and fathers are very important to these daughters. Some daughters report they are closer to their mothers and can reveal more details of their lives to them. Although fathers sometimes take on this confidant role, they are more likely to focus on academics and sports. More than three quarters of the fathers were very involved in their daughters' schooling in the primary school years, somewhat higher than the two thirds of the fathers in the previous group. A number of representative quotes are presented below. First, we hear from Jeannette and Kira.

"My mother and I have a very open and honest relationship. She's just always there. You can tell her anything. My father, he's more basically, 'You have to do well in school and succeed.' He doesn't really get into the nonacademic aspect of our lives."

"My mother and I are very, very close. I'm much closer to her than my father. I can just talk to my mother easier than I can to my father. My father and I, our relationship has grown around sports—because he was my track coach and my basketball coach. We talk about basketball, football, whatever. And he was always encouraging me."

For Jana and Allison, their fathers played an especially significant role.

"My father played the biggest role. He kind of pushed me to do well in both areas [academics and athletics]. He was always the supporter of the athletics—he drove me to come back to playing soccer [after a major injury]. He carted me to and from [physical] therapy—he made a lot of sacrifices for me at the time. Also, that summer, when I was going through therapy, he was working at Georgetown University Hospital. He got me a research position under a scientist at the medical school. I was able to have my first experience in the lab. That helped a lot."

"My father is a software engineer. He deals a lot with math and science. So, when I was younger, even though I would get frustrated, he would always make me do it over and make sure I got it right. If I didn't get a problem right, he would let me struggle with it for hours. It would really upset me, but that's the only way I learned it, because he would continu-

ally say, go back and look at it again. By the time I got to middle school, I was staying up very late, just doing my homework. Also, I probably would have gotten into more mischief if it hadn't been for the fact that my father was there. Not just because of his bellowing voice, very intimidating, but because I've always had a great admiration and respect for him. It was like I never wanted to disappoint him. I was Daddy's little girl."

Extracurricular Activities and Religion

Similar to the daughters in the second group, a large number of daughters emphasized the importance of extracurricular activities and religion. Almost all of the young women were involved in one or more extracurricular activities, ranging from sports to dance to academic clubs. This helped them to structure their time constructively, and also provided various social and psychological benefits, including friendships, discipline, and confidence. The first two quotes, from Vera and Teresa, reflect varied aspects of the young women's involvement in extracurricular activities, and the positive impact they experienced.

"I really did not have time to get in trouble. It was crazy—I had marching-band practice at seven o'clock in the morning. Then I was at school until 4:30, and then I would stay after school. I'd get home after seven. When I got home, it was too late to go outside. So I got home, and I just had to stay in the house. I didn't really go outside in the neighborhood any more. I had a girlfriend who lived down the street, and I spent a lot of time at her house because we were involved in the same activities."

"Running track really made me feel good about myself, being able to compete against someone and being able to see improvement, being able to stick to something and see improvement. When you first start, you don't feel like you are getting anywhere, and when you start competing and you start beating people, and you have pressure on you and you perform, that's a really good feeling. It disciplined me a lot, because I had to manage my time for real. It added to my confidence level, it made me feel you really can do what you put your mind to."

In addition, religion is extremely important in these households. Four fifths of the families attend church regularly, in contrast to less than two fifths of those in the two-parent, non-college-educated households. Two thirds of these daughters indicated that religion has played a very important part in their academic success, in contrast to about two fifths of those in the previous group. The following two quotes, from Chanel and Janine, capture some important aspects of religion in the daughters' lives.

"The most important thing my parents have done was introduce me to God. I think that has been the focus that has kept me aware that I can't do this by myself, and that there is a higher being that is watching over me. And church people encouraged me to be successful."

"My church was a great church, a great environment for children. My father was very spiritual and very religious. We began doing devotions, and reading through the Bible—we would read through it in a year. It taught me dedication and devotion and judgment. If I hadn't had that spiritual, religious background, there may have been a question as to whether I wanted to do something. The question didn't present itself. It was very important in directing me, I think, in the right direction, in the right way."

Helping Daughters to Deal with the White World

This group of daughters more consistently interacted with the White world than any other. The vast majority lived in racially mixed or primarily White neighborhoods and attended racially mixed or primarily White schools. Their parents are more likely to teach them about racism than those in the previous group, and the young women strongly emphasize the importance of such teaching—more than two-thirds of the daughters in this grouping indicate such an emphasis, versus one-third in the previous group.[15] Three-quarters feel strongly that society is not fair to Blacks, and, interestingly, more than two-fifths feel strongly that racism even bothers children who are younger than five. The feelings of the young women in the previous groups about these issues are not as strong.

The daughters in this group consistently heard from their parents about the necessity of having to work harder than White youth due to stereotypes and discrimination. Significantly, the parents serve as immediate, in-the-flesh embodiments of the reality that African Americans can overcome stereotypes, discrimination, and negative peer influence and forge highly rewarding paths toward personal, academic, and career success. The following three quotes, from Vera, Jana, and Aimee, reflect some of the messages communicated to the daughters from their parents.

"My parents grew up in the sixties. My dad went to University of Virginia, when there were sixty Black people there, and I think before they even had women there. He had a White roommate—the White roommate walked in and saw him there, and moved out. I learned from my dad, 'People are going to talk about you. They are going to have opinions about you. You just have to be comfortable with who you are.'"

"I would have to work a lot harder. But they didn't want me to see it as a limit to what I could do. They always encouraged me to set my goals high, and to realize that I had to work one hundred and ten percent if everybody else was working one hundred percent."

"My father said, when it comes down to it, it's still a racial thing and you have to just watch yourself and be cautious. . . . It comes blatantly, it comes subtly. You just have to work and succeed regardless of it."

Special Appreciation of Family

For the most part, these families are highly cohesive, with the daughters likely to report a priority on time spent together, availability of family members, and commitment. More than 90 percent report that family members put a lot of energy into "what we do" at home, compared with one third to one half of those in the three previous groups. Similarly, 90 percent of the daughters report that family members frequently volunteer when something has to be done at home, compared with between one quarter and one half in the other groups. The young women report less conflict than those in the previous group, and they are more likely to report that family members "really care about each other." Finally, more than three quarters of the daughters indicate that there is plenty of time and attention for everyone in the family, compared with less than two thirds of those in the previous group, and approximately half of those in the two single-parent-household groups. An illustrative quote is provided by Aimee.

"We are the type of family who would go on vacations every year. And we would take day trips all the time. Whether it is just to the museum, an exhibit, or just going out to eat, we always try to get the family to do things like that. Sometimes, my dad would just say, come on, and we would hop in the car, and we would just drive. I mean just anything to create bonding in the family. We would just hop in the car, drive around, get lost, and find our way back and go home. We would even get in a little family war, like play-fighting and stuff. We were a really close family."

One quarter of the young women in this group had parents who immigrated to the United States from either Africa or the Caribbean. Special cultural pride is expressed by many of these daughters. The next two daughters, Araba, whose parents were from Ghana, and Cynthia, whose parents were from the West Indies, discuss aspects of their cultural heritage.

"When they had us kids, my parents decided they didn't want to give us English names; they wanted us to have Ghanian names. That was like the first stone was set, in terms of knowing who you are. Because of the position my parents had in my community, we used to have a lot of parties at the house, and I was always surrounded by the culture. Ashantis are very proud people. They passed that on to me. My parents are proud people, and they respect themselves, and they have always shown that—both of them."

"I feel my West Indian heritage very strongly, and I attribute a lot of who I am to that. My parents instilled such a great work ethic, so that whatever you got, you worked for it, and it's not something owed. And the fact that education is important—that in itself is a West Indian ethic."

Summary

These young women have many familial and socioeconomic advantages, and yet still face difficult challenges as talented African American women. Due to their parents' persistent support and engagement, and to resources including good schools, safe neighborhoods, religion, and internal motivation, they have successfully negotiated the challenges they faced. Their families helped them to bridge effectively the African American and mainstream American cultures, a necessary part of the journey for these daughters who, more so than the young women in the other groups, consistently interacted with the mainstream culture in their neighborhood, schools, and the larger community.

Overall Observations

We have highlighted a number of distinctive features of the four groups. Daughters who grew up in households with single parents who did not have a college degree faced great challenges. These young women credit their mothers with consistently communicating high expectations, providing support, working hard, and sacrificing for them, and they emphasize the importance of their own motivation to escape from difficult financial and neighborhood situations through education. Daughters growing up in households with a single parent with a college degree consistently highlighted the importance of close bonding with their mothers,[16] their mothers serving as successful role models, the centrality of religion, and, in some cases, the difficulty of school and peer-group transitions. Among daughters growing up with both parents, neither of whom had a college degree, distinctive themes included the simultaneous influence and support of mother and father and holding fast to one's dream in the face of challenges related to the neighborhood, family, and school life. Finally, daughters from college-educated, two-parent families emphasized distinctive family educational and social resources, family cohesion and support, parental strictness, and having to cope with mixed-race or primarily White schools and neighborhoods.

The tapestries of the young women's lives are quite diverse in terms of the specific combinations of challenges they faced and the particular sets of factors that contributed to their ability to meet the challenges and overcome the odds. No two daughters faced exactly the same circumstances or succeeded due to the exact same combination of factors. The marital status of the parents and their level of college education helped to differentiate among groups of daughters in terms of the challenges they faced and the parenting and community resources available to help them overcome these challenges. Within each group, the unique qualities of the young women and parents, together with the distinctive aspects of the daughters' living situations, produced different patterns of coping and success. No two life tapestries are exactly the same. On the other hand, woven within these different patterns is a set of common textures, colors, and markings.

Having emphasized the differences between the groups, we can now turn to some of the common factors the daughters describe in their parents' behavior that contributed to their academic success. We learn from the young women what worked.

Common Factors Leading to Success: The Daughters' Perspectives

We wanted to know about the specific actions parents took to help their daughters succeed academically. It turns out that these actions cut across parents' marital status, level of education, and geographic locale. The daughters' most consistent interview themes and their most frequent responses to questionnaire items are the material from which we develop this portrait of common factors contributing to high levels of academic success. Many of these themes were articulated by the daughters' mothers and fathers in earlier chapters, though with somewhat different emphases and from somewhat different points of view. We believe an awareness of these commonalities can serve as a guide for parents and educators in helping African American children achieve their fullest potential.

A Focus on Reading

Parents' focus on and involvement in reading began early in the daughters' lives. Ninety percent of the students indicated that their mothers read to them when they were young, with slightly more than half reporting that their fathers did so. Three quarters of the young women indicated that reading was more important than television-watching in their family. Moreover, 53 percent of the parents placed great emphasis on reading for pleasure, and another 36 percent placed some emphasis on it. Reading's positive contribution to cognitive development and the negative contribution of watching too much television have been well documented.[17]

Three brief quotes are included below.

"As a child, my parents read to me every night. I remember sitting on my Dad's lap and either he would read to me or I would read to him."

"We couldn't watch TV when I was growing up, during the week. My house was close enough to walk to the library, so I walked to the library a lot, and read a lot of things."

"I honestly think teaching me to read at an early age was their most important academic contribution. Not just teaching me to read, but to love reading. If you can instill the love of reading in a child, basically you have won the battle. If a child loves to read, the whole world is open to them."

Learning and School Achievement as Family Priorities

Every single daughter indicated that her parents viewed education as both necessary and valuable, and as one of the most important aspects of one's life. Furthermore, almost every daughter reported that her parents expected and encouraged her to do well academically, at every level of her education, and to attend college. The overriding message was abundantly clear: education is extremely important.[18] Consistent praise for academic efforts, as well as consistent encouragement to do one's best, generated high levels of motivation, and during times of uncertainty or difficulty helped the young women to maintain a persistent and positive focus.

The following brief quotes encompass several of these facets of parental emphasis on the importance of education.

"Education was always stressed in our house. No ifs, ands, or buts about it."

"Education was important to my mother, so she put that into me. A big part of it is that she went to college. She didn't come from a rich family, she had to struggle, but she got through. Mom went to college—we never talked about me not going."

"My parents have never told me that I was anything less than great—they have always emphasized my potential."

"My parents expected me to do well. It wasn't an option. It didn't matter how good my grades were. If it wasn't my best, then it just wasn't good enough."

Homework: Parental Interest and Monitoring

One of the concrete ways parents channeled their determination that their children would succeed academically—and a way that sends the clearest message about the importance of school and learning—was to show a consistent interest in homework and schoolwork, and to monitor the time their daughters spent on homework.[19] Through all levels of school, according to the daughters, their parents focused on the importance of homework: 75 percent in elementary school showed "quite a bit" of interest in their daughters' homework, while 58 percent in middle school and 43 percent in high school continued to show this level of interest. Four fifths of the parents, according to the daughters, monitored the amount of time they spent studying in elementary school, one half did so in middle school, and one third of the parents still did so in high school.[20] In addition to parental interest and monitoring, assistance with homework was provided by 75 percent of the mothers and 50 percent of the fathers, and it was highly emphasized by the young women. Finally, three quarters of the daughters talked about their schoolwork with their parents either once or twice weekly (32 percent) or daily (43 percent). These responses are similar to those we heard from the parents in Chapters 2 and 3.

The following quotes are representative of what we heard from many of the young women.

"My mother came home from work and she checked my homework. We redid the homework most of the time. She checked it every night until I

guess I was in the fourth grade, until she thought I was grown up to do it for myself."

"In elementary school and in middle school, I had to do my homework before I went outside, as soon as I got home."

"When I was younger, I had to take my homework to them every night. We would go through it. They would make sure that I had written my stuff neatly, and that I had answered the questions the way I was supposed to."

Parental Involvement in the Schools

The parents, according to the daughters, did not limit their involvement in education to activities in the home. They actively engaged in activities in the school as well.[21] One primary form of parental involvement was contact with the classroom teacher. More than three quarters of the mothers and two fifths of the fathers are reported to have made it a point to know their daughters' teachers. Two thirds of the parents had "quite a bit" of contact with elementary schoolteachers, with two fifths maintaining this level of contact in middle school. Three-quarters of the young women reported that during their senior year of high school, their parents had phone contact with a teacher, counselor, or principal, and half reported their parents were involved in school-based volunteer work, including fundraising, Also important from the daughters' perspective throughout their schooling were parents' efforts to ensure appropriate placement in special programs and schools. The critical importance of parental contact and involvement in the school to academic success cannot be overstated.[22] Two quotes which indicate the special efforts parents sometimes had to make are included below.

"My mother would come to school and help out, not only in my class but in some other classrooms in the school. My parents would go to PTA meetings. . . . I remember back in sixth grade, I got a D on the first quiz in math class. I think that a lot of kids, they might get a D on a quiz, but number one, are they going to tell their parents, number two, are the parents going to ask? But both of my parents were right up there at the

school and spoke to the teacher. Those types of things are what really made a difference."

"My parents always came to parent-teacher conferences and open houses. And if I ever had problems with teachers, they were always right in there defending me, no matter what it was. . . . I remember one time I was in a gifted program called Probe, and we had a video-production class. I was the only Black person, and my face came out really, really dark on the video. One of the kids commented, 'Oh, you can't even see her.' I felt really uncomfortable, so I went home and told my mom. She was right in there, telling the teacher that the school needed to have better video equipment, equipped to videotape people of color. They were just always in there supporting me. No matter what it was, I knew I could go home to my parents, and they would be on the ball defending me."

Extracurricular Activities

From the daughters' perspective, parental encouragement and support for involvement in extracurricular activities was one of the most important contributions parents made to their success. Over three quarters of the young women indicated that their parents always supported their involvement in these extracurricular activities. The daughters noted that participating in these activities helped them to develop positive traits and habits, and simultaneously helped keep their attention and time meaningfully focused during non-school hours. During their high-school years, almost nine in ten participated in community-service activities; slightly more than two thirds of the daughters participated on a school-based or community-based athletic team; slightly less than two thirds participated in church activities; three fifths participated in ethnic activities; slightly less than half participated in dance or chorus; two fifths held a leadership position in student government, participated in a math or science club, were involved in church-based activities, or participated in a foreign-exchange experience; and, finally, one third participated on a debating team The following two daughters' comments illustrate some of the benefits reported from extracurricular involvements.

"I started taking piano when I was six. I was always into extracurricular activities—sports, band, softball, Black Person's Club, Science

Bowls. In high school, they just helped me manage my time better, knowing that I had these other things to do. I had to get my work done, but also have a release from academics."

"My mom started me out dancing when I was five. I did competitions. Dancing has helped me with discipline. Sometimes you have to hold a stretch that really hurts, and you just have to persevere, and hold it for a little longer. Just like in academics, when you are ready to pass out during finals, you have to just keep on going."

Arranging for Optimal Academic Environments

A number of students emphasized the importance of their parents' arranging optimal academic environments and placements. Such involvements ranged from gaining access to a valued summer program to entrance into a competitive science-and-technology high school. In some cases, special parental efforts, with either the daughter or the schools, were necessary, as was the case for the next two young women.

"I didn't do well on the test to get into the gifted-and-talented program. My parents went to the school, and the gifted-and-talented teacher was Black, and they talked to her and she let me into the class."

"Probably one of the most important things was that my mom didn't let me go to my neighborhood high school. I went to a math-science magnet school instead, so I got exposed to a lot of different things—math up to Calc II, all these AP classes, drafting—a lot of stuff I never would have done had I gone to the local school. . . . My mother put her foot down about this."

The young women we spoke to credited many factors for their academic success, including positive neighborhood or school environments, self, and religion. However, parental support was by far the most frequently cited factor, selected as one of the three most important factors by 80 percent of the daughters (the next most frequently selected factor was "hard work," chosen by 42 percent of the daughters). Many social science research studies have linked greater levels of parental involvement in education to higher educational achievement. Here, we find that for African American girls, in particular, parents put forth substantial effort to help ensure that their daughters would successfully overcome the barriers and temptations that have tragically undermined and derailed the academic focus of so many other capable Black youth.

Significantly, the daughters' stories are very similar to those of the parents in emphasizing the six general components of parenting, discussed in Chapters 2 and 3. The tapestries of success described by the daughters are woven throughout with strong strands of (1) child-focused love,[23] (2) strict limit setting,[24] (3) consistently high expectations,[25] (4) open and honest communication, (5) drawing upon varied community resources,[26] including church,[27] schools, teachers,[28] peers,[29] extracurricular activities,[30] and extended family,[31] and (6) strong ethnic and gender identification.[32]

The similarities between parents' and daughters' impressions about effective parenting are striking. To some extent, this may be due to the passage of time—families may communicate about and develop shared, common interpretations of what has occurred during the course of child-rearing, and why. For the most part, however, we see the general convergence of the accounts of daughters and parents as confirmation of the general validity of the information provided. This is certainly not true in all areas— parents' and daughters' accounts of the extent of the daughters' deviance from family (and societal) rules, for instance, certainly vary in some cases, as one might expect. Overall, though, we view the overlapping perspectives of the daughters and parents as confirmation that the components of parenting we have presented substantially reflect the actual child-rearing experiences of these successful, female African Americans.[33]

One very special and important facet of these daughters' academic achievement that we have not yet examined in depth is their achievement and interest in mathematics and the sciences. In the next chapter, we focus explicitly on how parents and others helped prepare these young women for success in the math and science disciplines.

CHAPTER FIVE

Parenting and Educating
for Success in Math and Science
Early Childhood through College

While the young women we focus on in this book have been successful in general in their schooling, they have achieved at the highest levels, in particular, in mathematics and science. Indeed, strong course work and high grades in mathematics and science courses in high school, along with high SAT scores in math, were among the primary criteria used to admit them to the Meyerhoff Scholars Program. As discussed in the first chapter, education and careers in math and science grow increasingly important in our technologically focused society, and African Americans, particularly African American women, are extremely underrepresented in these fields. To help increase the representation of Black women in math and science careers, it is useful to identify the factors which contribute strongly to academic success in these fields. In so doing, we hope to provide insights that will contribute to the success of future generations of African Americans in these disciplines.

In Chapters 2 and 3, the mothers and fathers described a number of ways in which they helped support and encourage their daughters' academic success, including approaches focused specifically on math and science. In Chapter 4, the daughters described the many ways in which their parents had been helpful and supportive in their academic endeavors overall. In this chapter, we listen as the daughters tell us, in their own voices, tell about those factors that helped them to be successful particularly in math and science.

The first section, "The Pre-College Years," focuses on the initial development and longer-term maintenance of the daughters' interests in math and science, and the critical roles parents, teachers, and others played. In the second section, "Voices from the Community," we hear directly from a number of people from the community who have had contact with some of the daughters during their pre-college years. The young women identified these educators, church members, and other community members as playing a significant mentoring role in their lives. These mentors share with us their experiences related to the pre-college math and science pursuits of the young women, as well as other Meyerhoff students, and African American youth more generally. The third section, "The College Years," describes the daughters' experiences as they progressed through math, science, and engineering majors in college, including their experiences in the Meyerhoff Program. We conclude with a look at their future plans and a summary of the most salient factors leading to success in math and science.

The Pre-College Years

Although gains have been made in recent years, many female and ethnic minority students have typically not enjoyed success in math and science at the elementary- , middle- , and high-school levels. Even when these students are successful in math and science in the early years, positive attitudes, confidence, and interest often decline later on.[1] Reasons for the lack of either initial or enduring interest in the sciences among girls and African Americans in the pre-college years include (1) teachers' low expectations for success and related differential treatment; (2) perpetuation of the myth by teachers, parents, and peers that math and science are "White-male" areas, (3) inability of girls and African American students to see themselves as future scientists based on a lack of exposure to role models, advanced courses, and career opportunities, (4) overall lack of encouragement to succeed in the sciences from parents and teachers, and (5) doubts about their ability to succeed at higher levels in math and science.[2] One study found that female African American eighth-graders were less likely to express interest in science and aspire to science careers, even though they were performing at or above the level of their male counterparts.[3]

Given all the possible barriers that could have prevented the daughters we interviewed from developing or pursuing interests in the sciences, we were curious about how such interests were developed and subsequently maintained. We also asked the young women to describe the math- and science-related challenges they faced in the pre-college years as they progressed through elementary, middle, and high school.

Developing an Interest

In the interviews, the students were asked specifically about how and when their interests initially developed in math and science. The responses were reminiscent of the "nature" versus "nurture" issue discussed in the parents' chapters. There, we wondered about the relative influence of being born with certain interests and aptitudes (nature) versus that of one's environment in bringing out those interests and aptitudes (nurture). Regarding the origin of the students' interests, some described being encouraged (and in a few cases pushed) by their parents, from a young age, to pursue science or math because of a parent's profession or personal interests. For example, one daughter stated that her father, a science teacher, started reviewing his lesson plans with her at age four. Below, we hear two students describe how their parents were instrumental in igniting their interests in math and science.

"I think initially it was my father. He never graduated from high school, but while he was in high school, math was his favorite subject. And starting in first grade . . . [I was] able to do my multiplication tables ahead of everybody else and stuff. My father saw that in me, and he would practice with me more. My father used to always make it so that I could understand how [math] applied in real life. I think that helped even more than just learning."

"I guess my mom has always encouraged me. I wouldn't say she forced me, but she has always strongly influenced me to be in the sciences. Ever since I was little, she would tell me, 'You know, you're going to be a scientist. What kind of scientist do you want to be?' So it really got ingrained in my head. And not only did she do that, but she paid for me to have lessons at the Museum of Science and Discovery, and all kinds of advanced science courses and extra tutoring. She really focused on the sciences."

In contrast, other daughters described their initial interests in math and science as growing solely out of a natural inclination or ability. Some discovered at a young age that math was easier than other subjects, or was more appealing because it was *"objective, concrete, and straightforward."* Others were not aware of their proclivity toward math and science until middle school or high school. From one daughter's perspective, *"people tend to do well at things that they like.*" Several other students explain how their interests in math and science developed naturally.

> "*Compared to the social sciences, like history and English, I think it was the 'hands-on' thing. I enjoy experiments and mixing chemicals. That was something that I just could not get from the social sciences. Not saying that I did poorly in the social sciences, but I just never really put my focus on those things. I always had my focus on the sciences.*"

> "*I liked math and science from kindergarten. I remember my mom bought me a ruler that had the multiplication table on the back, and I went over that every day. It was just something that came to me and I liked it. So I pursued it a lot from kindergarten up to now.*"

> "*I personally don't do any better in math and science than in any of my other classes. But I always liked science. There's always something I really enjoyed about having a problem and sitting down with the formula, like in a math problem.*"

> "*I mean you have an answer, you know that that's the answer. In English, it's more abstract, so it wasn't as interesting to me. In high school, I wasn't even really that good in math, but I liked it so I worked harder at it and tried to be better at it.*"

Finally, a number of daughters noted that it was the combination of their natural interests with encouragement from parents or other family members that sparked their initial interest in the area. For these daughters, the impact of both "nature" and "nurture" was such that neither factor was given more weight than the other. These young women commonly described being influenced by one or both parents or other family members in a math- or science-related field, while also having a natural curiosity or interest in the area. Below, one daughter provides us with an account of how her parents' influence and her natural affinity, together, contributed to the development of her interest in math and science.

> "*I guess my parents encouraged me to do well in everything in school, and I think I just took a liking to math and science. My dad used to be a math teacher. I don't think there is anything genetic with that. But I mean he would always help me with math, and I just sort of liked science*

and took to it. They always encouraged me, and when they found that was what I liked, they always supported and encouraged that. And I guess that just made all the difference."

Maintaining an Interest

Whether or not parents played a role in the development of their daughters' initial interests, most played a key role in helping them maintain those interests, through both verbal encouragement and their involvement in numerous ways. A number of students described their parents helping them with science projects and homework, especially when they were young. Others noted that their parents helped to ensure that they went to special math/science schools and/or summer programs. Purchases of educational aids—from a ruler with multiplication tables on the back to a junior chemistry set to a computer for the home—were also mentioned as helpful in developing their interests. A few daughters described incidents in which their parents argued with administrators to ensure that they were placed in the correct class or were able to take advantage of a special opportunity in math or science. In other instances, when daughters were struggling in a particular subject area, parents sought special tutors or found computer aids. Two daughters provide us with a sampling of the ways parents actively encouraged the girls' math and science pursuits.

"[My parents played the role of] coach, cheerleader, and teammate. They have always just been encouraging and telling me that I am smart. . . . My dad was a scientist, and my mother was a teacher. I guess I was just sort of edged towards the sciences. . . . We lived at the Air and Space Museum when I was younger and the IMAX theater. My parents were big on museums and that sort of thing."

"I had to choose a high school, but my parents didn't let me choose. I lived in [X] county, so you can go to a science school or some type of college prep school. I wanted to go to my neighborhood school, which doesn't exactly have a program. And my mother said, 'No, you're not going there, end of discussion.' I was upset, and I actually cried awhile, because I hadn't gone to my neighborhood school forever, and I really wanted to go with all my friends. But she just told me I wasn't going,

and the first day of school, I got on the bus to go to that [science] school. There was nothing else to be said. It wasn't worth arguing."

Parents and other family members in math-and-science occupations supported several daughters' interests in the field by discussing their jobs, introducing them to coworkers, and/or taking them to the workplace. In addition to extended family, church members were also noted by some as being particularly supportive. Other daughters stated that their interests were stimulated by famous role models such as Dr. Benjamin Carson (an African American neurosurgeon at Johns Hopkins Hospital, in Baltimore) or Mae Jemison (the first female African American astronaut). Others were influenced by role models whom they knew personally, including mentors from summer or school-based programs, and, in one case, a treating physician. Below, two daughters describe the influence of their "personal" role models. The first daughter describes how her goal of becoming a doctor, decided at an early age, was greatly influenced by her own physician.

"When I was young, I was really, really sick. . . . After a surgery I had, all the problems and symptoms went away. . . . One doctor who had performed the surgery saw me afterwards until I was sixteen. He was a very big role model to me. I looked up to him—I don't know if he knows it. Just the fact that someone who was just doing their job, a surgeon, basically did save my life. That inspired me to do something great myself."

The second daughter describes how both her mother and her mother's tutor became role models.

"My mother went back to school. She took some math classes, and she had this tutor. He was like a genius. I wish he was still around. He knew math; he was just great. You could call him a mentor, I guess. The fact that my mother went back to school and took math classes—after all those years of not taking math, she went back and just did it—that was encouraging."

Teachers also were mentioned frequently as playing a critical role in helping the young women maintain and further develop their interests in math and science. The daughters mentioned that there were specific teachers who encouraged them to do their best and told them about special math and/or science opportunities. Others described having teachers who were influential because they made the material "fun" and "interesting." They used innovative teaching strategies, offered hands-on experiments, or demonstrated real-life applications. Two daughters describe the important ways in which teachers helped them maintain their interests in math and science.

"I think the best role model that I had was a teacher who had graduated herself from my [high school]. She came back to teach. I took her genetics class. It was very good to see someone else, similar to me, doing things that I wanted to do. When she [had been a student at the school], there was a certain teacher who had told her, 'I don't think you want to go into science, you know that is not really for you.'... Yet, she went on to do well anyway, and she came back to help the rest of us who were there. It was just her enthusiasm and her knowledge that she tried to share with us. And her aim was not so much to teach above us, but she wanted us to understand what was going on. She wanted us to get something out of the class, and not just be sitting there taking up space."

"My second-grade teacher played math games with us. I liked her a lot. She managed to make it fun. I had enthusiastic teachers, and I think that makes a big difference. When the teachers are excited about what they are doing, it makes you more interested in what they do. . . . My Algebra II-Trigonometry teacher in high school, I think she took a special interest in me as an African American student. Although it wasn't anything overt, I think she [went] out of her way to make me comfortable in the class. The last time I talked to her, she was still very supportive and interested in what I was doing."

The research literature indicates that a number of factors influence interest and skill development in math and science, including parents, teachers, curricula, special programs, cultural beliefs, and a student's natural aptitude and interests.[4] In the case of these daughters, we found each of these factors to be important.

Pre-College Challenges in Math and Science

As discussed above, a number of factors, including low expectations held by teachers, stereotypes about science as a "White-male" area, and discouragement from parents, teachers, and even peers, are potential barriers to success in math and science, even when a student has well-developed interests. Despite the presence of supportive parents and encouraging teachers, several of the daughters described facing obstacles in elementary, middle, and high school as they pursued their interests in math and science. Specific challenges included being placed incorrectly in lower-level classes and having to change schools or travel long distances to attend special math/science high schools. In addition, the daughters described negative experiences with peers who thought they were "acting White" and with teachers whom they perceived to be discriminating against them because they were Black and/or female. Other challenges mentioned included becoming temporarily sidetracked with social activities, having illnesses that decreased school attendance and impaired concentration, and being persuaded by a family member to take "practical" courses (e.g., typing) instead of math and science.

Several daughters also described periods when they struggled academically in a particular math or science course. For some, receiving a poor grade for the first time was particularly difficult. Strategies used to overcome academic obstacles included working extra hard, seeking help from peers, accepting that they could not be at the "top" of all courses, asking teachers for extra help, and reducing involvement in or quitting athletics or other activities. The next two daughters describe their academic challenges and the help they received in overcoming them.

"I didn't really experience hardships until my senior year [of high school]. In calculus and chemistry, things didn't come as needed, and I had to study. I turned to my peers and my teachers. [My parents] went out and got the study books and [found] a study group for calculus on the Internet. They really didn't know themselves, so they just tried other resources."

"I was in the tenth or eleventh grade, and I was doing calculus. I was pretty much goofing off in class and not turning in any work. I was just not really being myself, but I had a teacher who did not put up with it. She didn't accept it from me, and told me that the choices I was making did not only just affect this one class, but affected my whole life. She pretty much treated me like I was her child, and said, 'It's not acceptable, I will not accept this from you.' And she went on to even point out

people who she had this conversation with before, and who didn't listen, and how their lives had gone since then. . . . I listened to that."

Voices from the Community

Throughout the book, parents have consistently been described as having the primary influence in most areas of the daughters' lives. In the section above, the daughters continued to mention their parents as critical in helping them to develop and maintain their interests in math and science. Others, however, including extended family members, teachers, and church members, were also cited as having influenced their math and science pursuits in the pre-college years. We thought it was important to interview some of those who played an instrumental role in the lives of the young women.

Each daughter was asked to identify at least one community member who had been important to her academic success as she pursued her interests in math and science. We also asked the Meyerhoff Program staff to identify individuals who had referred students to the Meyerhoff Program over the years. From these lists, we invited more than eighty individuals to participate in group interviews. Twenty-five individuals participated (two were interviewed over the telephone). The results, below, reflect the insights of three high-school principals, ten high-school teachers, three high-school guidance counselors, one middle-school teacher, three staff members from summer math/science programs, four church members, and one basketball coach. The majority of these individuals personally knew at least one of the young women we interviewed. The remainder knew other Meyerhoff students personally. Below, we listen to the community members discuss challenges that the students faced in math and science, and how they helped the daughters and others through such challenges. The section ends with suggestions from our "experts" within the community on how to help Black female youth with interests in math and science achieve success.

Common Challenges

When asked about challenges in math and science, the community members responded in a variety of ways. They frequently mentioned the lack of opportunities available to young Black women to achieve success in math and science. In particular, the majority believed that despite the gains made by these students in math and science, stereotypes and negative perceptions persist about their presumed lack of ability in the sciences. Because of such preconceived notions, young Black girls with promise are often overlooked for specialized school programs or other opportunities. A teacher provides insight into this compelling issue.

> *"One of the things that young Black females are faced with is the lack of opportunity. Sometimes it's not that they are not gifted or not intelligent, but they face roadblocks put before them. Sometimes it's not having knowledge of certain programs that exist. Minority students don't get a chance to participate [in special science programs] because, for some reason, the information doesn't get out to those schools. . . . Sometimes no one helps them to explore their options and alternatives as they relate to getting the best possible training."*

Even when Black girls are afforded the opportunity to take specialized math and science classes or enroll in certain programs, they encounter other serious obstacles—the expectation that they will not be able to succeed academically and the perception they are not as capable as White students. One of the community educators expands on these impediments in the following comment.

> *"Contrary to popular belief, there still are for young women in general, and African American young women specifically, a lot of gender-equity issues, most specifically in terms of placement in math and science classes. That's where we see a very small sample of African American women; we'll see a higher number of [Black] women than men, but still, overall, it's not at the percentage it should be. . . . Within the classroom, in higher-level math and science classes, girls are not expected to achieve at those levels. They are not called on as frequently. They are not asked as in-depth questions."*

Relatedly, some felt that society, in general, discourages women from entering math and science disciplines. Likewise, they observed that the media rarely promote the positive gains of Black women in these important fields. One community member stated, *"I have to agree that I see a lot of negative socialization and historical [i.e., dated] views of women in the sciences.*

The guy is supposed to be smarter, and if the girl is smarter, you see them playing down their intelligence and flirting."

Another frequently mentioned challenge was peer pressure. Through their observations and direct experiences with the daughters and others, the group cited peer pressure as a difficulty for young Black women in math and science. On the one hand, young Black girls are often the only Black student (or one of a few Black students) in their math and science classes. They not only feel isolated and alienated, but they also experience pressure from fellow Black students in the larger school environment not to "act White" or be "too smart." Our community representatives also observed that young African American girls not only want to fit in with their peers generally, but simultaneously they must deal with pressures to be found attractive by their male counterparts. Two educators shed light on the issue of peer influence.

"Peer pressure is a real big problem. I do find that because we have a few more African American females in higher-level courses, they do at least have a few more of each other to bond with and find support with, so it's not as bad [as it was]. . . . But they are still suffering from the age-old problem of trying to impress boys, especially at this time in their development. So, often times, they don't want to appear too smart. That's a major obstacle that we are combating constantly."

"In my experience, for African American females, in high school, the issue of fitting in is very difficult. That's a challenge because they are a minority within a minority sometimes in the average American high school. They have always excelled in the class, but that isolated them a great deal, sometimes from African American young men who excelled athletically, but had a different perspective about academics. The girls felt isolated from that experience and wanted to be a part of the world of the young men, but the two [worlds were] very difficult to mesh. I think there was some loneliness from the fact that they spent a lot of time studying, and a lot of time excelling, but they were still kids."

Other challenges noted were at the personal or familial levels. Specifically, unexpected tragedies such as the death of a loved one or difficult circumstances such as poverty or having family members on drugs were mentioned as interfering with the academic aspirations of Black youth. One guidance counselor recounted how teen pregnancy can also be a barrier for promising African American female students. A church member, who also taught Sunday school, describes the complex set of personal and familial challenges faced by one of the daughters interviewed.

> *"She has one brother who was unsuccessful in college. She felt that her parents expected too much of her, that they were comparing her, without saying so, with her brother. . . . She was in her teens and going places, even out of the country, but they still saw her as a child, so she [also] had to cope with that. She would be angry and she used to mull things over in her mind rather than sharing them with someone. And this had to be overcome, to express what she was feeling. Another thing was just expecting too much of herself. . . . In helping her go through all of these phases, I taught her she wasn't responsible for what had happened in her family's past, what her parents had done, what her brother had done. She was responsible for only her life."*

This Sunday school teacher also stated how she was able to help the daughter overcome these multiple challenges by teaching her the importance of prayer and how to believe in herself. Similarly, other community representatives stated that they had helped the students overcome their academic, personal, and familial challenges by providing encouragement, nurturance, and support. Within the academic setting, in particular, the educators added that they had very high expectations for their students, regardless of their backgrounds. The following statement, from a basketball coach of one of the daughters, serves as a powerful example of the types of encouragement provided during times of challenge.

> *"She called and said, 'Coach, some of my Black friends said I'm trying to act White because I'm going to [X] high school.' She played three or four sports and carried a 3.9 average, too. I said 'If acting White is carrying that big average and making the honor roll and doing everything right, you be as White as the sheet you are sleeping on at night. Send those kids to me and let me get them straight. They don't want you to succeed.'"*

Recommendations for Parents, Educators, and the Community

One of the primary benefits of interviewing the community "experts" is the opportunity to elicit practical recommendations for parents and others. These recommendations are similar to those offered in the literature, including (1) increasing the number of minority-focused and female-focused programs in math and science, (2) promoting teachers' awareness of needing to foster female and minority students' confidence in their math and science abilities; (3) encouraging parents to support their children actively in pursuing their interests in math and science through participation in relevant activities, and (4) increasing the number of female and minority role models in the sciences.[5] Our group of educators and community members offered suggestions both about parenting and about how educators and others in the community can become more involved in helping African American girls succeed, both in the sciences and more generally.

Regarding parenting, all agreed that active parental involvement is critical to the students' success. Parents are advised to do the following while their children are young: (1) read to them regularly, (2) let them see you reading, not watching television; (3) play educational games and puzzles with them, (4) encourage them to ask questions; (5) teach them not to be afraid to make mistakes; and (6) limit their television-watching. Specific recommendations regarding the academic setting included: (1) participate in the students' math and science activities and programs if a parental component exists, (2) seek out information about special courses or opportunities in the sciences, and (3) tap into their interests early in order to communicate and provide support. Below, a school principal, speaking from both his personal and professional experiences, summarizes several key action steps he believes parents should take.

> "*They have to monitor the young ladies. They have to demand a rigorous academic performance. They have to hold the school accountable. They have to make sure they get in the proper courses. They have to make sure that they have the proper teachers and the proper support. It's the parents' responsibility to hold those individuals who aren't giving [proper support] to them accountable. My parents didn't do that because they weren't educated enough to do it.*"

The educators and community members also encouraged parents to be particularly active both in helping to build their daughters' self-esteem and in disciplining them. One individual, for example, stated that parents must instill self-confidence and *"remain as fanatical a parent as possible until they are twenty-one."* Parents and other adults also were encouraged to spend time listening, in a nonjudgmental manner, and supporting the youth as they develop into adults. Regarding discipline, it was suggested that parents not only set clear expectations, but also establish clear consequences when those expectations are not met. One educator cautioned parents to strike a delicate balance between disciplining and instilling self-esteem.

> *"African American women want to be told, 'You are gorgeous, you are pretty, you are smart, you are loved.' I think a lot of times parents are so busy disciplining that they don't recognize that they need that positive boost. . . . Most young ladies are very smart; what's keeping them from achieving is the way they feel about themselves."*

In addition to parents, the educators and community members provided advice for others in roles similar to their own. The majority believed that serving as mentors and role models for young African American women is extremely important, as is the need to expose the young women to a range of settings and career options, especially in the sciences. A former teacher of one of the daughters interviewed describes what she believes to be a school, parental, and community responsibility.

> *"I think that very early on, little African American girls have to be introduced to science, the joy of science, the wonders of science, and the discoveries of science. They have to be introduced to it at a time when they can do anything, when they are anxious to learn."*

Another educator provides a mandate for the community and outlines some specific responsibilities for mentors.

> *"I think, as a community, we need to try to put together a resource listing or a resource base of persons of color who are in various career fields. We need to look at those people who are local and try to encourage them to do some mentoring to reach out to kids—to mentor one-on-one or to*

provide opportunities for these students to have internships or to shadow them, just to expose them to the work setting."

While the following ten recommendations offered for other educators and community members vary in focus, reflecting the wide-ranging experiences of the individuals we interviewed, there was agreement that "it takes a community effort to raise a child," and that the church, community, and school must support and reemphasize practices and values that, ideally, should be taught at home.

1. Be mindful to give as much attention to the girls as the boys, because the tendency is to believe the girls will be "okay," in contrast to the challenges faced by African American men.
2. Take more responsibility for helping parents and working with them to give their children the best education possible.
3. Offer small-group peer tutoring and coaching classes for students.
4. Maintain high expectations for students and "raise the bar" for what is currently expected of students.
5. Help African American children understand that math and science fields are a microcosm of American society, where they will be the minority and may not have a nurturing environment.
6. Encourage them to do their best and to "understand and appreciate themselves and their own talents."
7. Create an environment where students can express themselves without ridicule.
8. Encourage more attention on values and "character education" in the schools.
9. Provide positive, alternative academic or career options, rather than simply telling youth what they cannot do.
10. Enforce academic requirements in order for students to be eligible to participate in extracurricular activities (e.g., maintaining a B average for interscholastic sports eligibility).

The College Years

As the daughters graduated from high school, leaving the familiar surroundings and comforts of home, school, and community to pursue math, science, and engineering majors, their challenges continued.[6] Largely as a result of these challenges, every year large numbers of African American students with high SAT scores, impressive high-school GPAs, and a history of success in high-school honors math and science courses transfer out of these majors. In addition, many studies have reported that SAT scores are less predictive of academic performance in college for Black students than for White students.[7] African American students with respectable SAT scores who underperform provide evidence that factors other than pre-collegiate preparation and native ability work to depress minority achievement and persistence. These factors may include (1) academic and social isolation, (2) motivational and performance vulnerability in the face of negative stereotypes and low expectations for performance, (3) peers not supportive of academic success, and (4) perceived and actual discrimination.[8] A number of the factors related to success reported in the research literature are briefly addressed below, before we move on to discuss the experiences of the daughters in the Meyerhoff Program.

Academic and Social Integration

Academic and social integration appears critical to the success of African American science majors, including those who are highly able. Black students have a higher probability of becoming academically and socially isolated on predominantly White campuses and in science majors than do White or Asian students.[9] Research suggests that contact with faculty outside the classroom, and the development of mentoring relationships, including with minority faculty, can decrease academic isolation and contribute to positive outcomes.[10] Furthermore, increasing the number of like-minded, highly able Black student peers can substantially enhance peer academic and social support, reduce perceptions of racism, and increase cultural comfort in science classes—contributing to academic persistence and success in science.[11]

Knowledge and Skill Development

Developing knowledge and skill represents a second important focus for efforts to enhance the success of African American science majors. Involvement in peer study groups, for example, consistent with Uri Treisman's pioneering work, has been shown to produce enhanced mastery of technical knowledge and higher performance in courses by minority students in science.[12] Furthermore, strong study habits, time-management skills, and analytic problem-solving capacity, and the willingness to use available departmental and university resources, have been linked to positive academic outcomes.[13]

Support and Motivation

Support and motivation represent a third set of factors linked to high levels of success among science majors. Financial aid continues to be one of the cornerstones of support for African American students[14] and, in the case of scholarships to study science, can be made contingent on high levels of performance in science courses. However, due to the difficult nature of introductory and advanced science and mathematics courses, and the attractiveness of other majors, various other sources of support and motivational influence appear necessary as well to enhance minority students' performance and persistence in science. These include (1) high faculty expectations for African American students' success, (2) hands-on research experience, (3) academically supportive friendship networks, (4) involvement with faculty, (5) tutoring, and (6) emotional support during times of stress and difficulty.[15]

Monitoring and Advising

Monitoring and advising, if available on a frequent basis, can help students make wise academic decisions in selecting coursework, position themselves for graduate study, and prevent or limit the influence of emerging academic or personal problems. Consistent monitoring can help to ensure regular assessment of a student's academic and social situation and to identify early warning signs of academic or personal problems. Advising and feedback, including but extending beyond discussion of important academic requirements, can provide students with valuable input about their strengths, weaknesses, options, and the potential consequences of various strategic plans of action. Taken together, personalized monitoring and advising can help to ensure that no student leaves or is unable to succeed in a science major because that student was not offered appropriate academic, psychological, and social resources and advice.[16]

The daughters we interviewed mentioned various academic difficulties, including experiences of race and gender discrimination in math and science at the college level. In addition, some faced additional challenges to their success in math and science, such as trying to balance social interests with academic pursuits and adjusting to unlimited freedom. As in the pre-college years, the daughters described their parents as being supportive and encouraging. Professors and teaching assistants also provided assistance when needed. Especially critical to the daughters' success in science, however, were the peers, staff, and mentors associated with the Meyerhoff Scholars Program.

The Meyerhoff Scholars Program

As noted earlier, the Meyerhoff Scholars Program at UMBC was developed in response to the lack of success of well-qualified African American science majors on that campus. The program's creators sought to incorporate multiple components addressing the broad range of factors linked in the research literature to minority student success: (1) academic and social integration, (2) knowledge and skill development, (3) support and motivation, and (4) advising and monitoring. The program was launched as a collaboration between philanthropists Robert and Jane Meyerhoff and the University of Maryland, Baltimore County, in 1988. Currently, between forty and sixty Meyerhoff freshmen are selected each year from over 1400 nominations and applications from across the nation. Beyond strong grades and SAT scores, preference is given to those who have taken advanced placement courses in math and science, have research experience, and provide strong references from science or math instructors. Additional criteria include a commitment to stay in the sciences and a desire to "give back" to the communities from which they came. (The program's web site is: http://www.umbc.edu/meyerhoff.)

In 1996, the Meyerhoff Scholars Program was recognized nationally with the Presidential Award for Excellence in Science, Math and Engineering Mentoring administered by the National Science Foundation. The program incorporates fourteen different components, briefly described below.

1. **Recruitment.** The top 100–150 applicants and their families attend one of two recruitment weekends on the campus. These weekends provide opportunities for faculty, university administrators, program staff, and current students to meet with the applicants both formally and informally and to give prospective incoming students chances to interact with student-peers, faculty, and staff.

2. **Financial Aid.** The Meyerhoff Program provides students with a comprehensive financial package including tuition, books, and room and board. This support is contingent upon students maintaining a B average in a science or engineering major.

3. **Summer Bridge Program.** Once selected for the program, Meyerhoff students attend a mandatory pre-freshman Summer Bridge Program and take courses in math, science, and African American studies. They also attend social and cultural events. The purposes of the Summer Bridge Program include preparing students for the new expectations and requirements of college courses and providing opportunities for interacting with peers, faculty, and staff.

4. **Study-Groups.** Group study is strongly encouraged by the program staff because it is viewed as a critically important ingredient in students' success in science and engineering majors. Study-groups promote academic support and create opportunities for social support and interaction.

5. **Program Values.** Strongly emphasized values include high academic achievement, seeking academic and personal support from a variety of sources, peer interaction, setting high academic goals (with emphasis on earning the Ph.D. and pursuing research careers), and giving back to the community. Beginning in the program's recruitment phase, the shortage of African American Ph.D.s in science is discussed, and the importance of achieving a research-based Ph.D. is emphasized. As a program objective, earning an M.D. degree is not emphasized, given the program's focus on producing Ph.D.-level researchers (and students know this).

6. **Program Community.** The Meyerhoff program provides a family-like academic and social support system for students. Students live in the same residence hall during their first year and are required to live on campus during subsequent years. In addition to peer connectedness, students are in continual contact with program staff, who are highly accessible and involved in student life. Meyerhoff students and staff meet in large "family" meetings on a regular basis.

7. **Personal Advising and Counseling.** The program employs full-time academic advisors and other staff members who monitor and advise students on a regular basis. When students do poorly in a key science course, program staff strongly encourage them to retake the course. Counselors are concerned not only with academic planning and performance, but also with any personal problems students may have.

8. **Tutoring.** Program staff members strongly encourage Meyerhoff students either to tutor others or to avail themselves of tutoring in order to maximize academic achievement. Tutors are regularly identified from within and outside the program.

9. **Summer Research Internships.** All students participate in substantive research experiences during the summer. These internships provide students with hands-on experiences that contribute to developing knowledge and skills, create opportunities for relationships with mentors, and stimulate students' interest in scientific research careers.

10. **Faculty Involvement.** Key faculty and department chairs in science and engineering are involved in the recruitment and selection phases of the program. They also interact with the Meyerhoff students by participating in academic presentations and discussions. There also are opportunities for social interaction. Most important, perhaps, a number of faculty work with the students in their laboratories, serving as mentors.

11. **Administrative Involvement and Public Support.** The Meyerhoff Program is supported at all levels of the university, including ardent support from the President (the program's cofounder). Over the years, the program has attracted considerable national attention and generated substantial financial support from public, private, and nonprofit sources.

12. **Mentors.** Each student is paired with a mentor who works as a professional in an area of science or engineering. These relationships often create excitement and provide practical insights for students about pursuing research careers.

13. **Community Service.** All students are strongly encouraged to engage in a community-service activity, often involving volunteer work with at-risk Baltimore youth. This component reinforces the program value of "giving back" to the larger community.

14. **Family Involvement.** Parents are kept advised of their children's progress and are included in social events. They created and maintain the Meyerhoff Family Association, which serves as a mutual-support program.

Student Success in the Program

The evidence to date reflects dramatic success for students in the Meyerhoff Program. Research indicates that more than three quarters of entering Meyerhoff students matriculate into science, engineering, or mathematics graduate programs, or professional school. Fully 83 percent of entering Meyerhoff students maintain a science major and a GPA in science courses of 3.0 or higher (with a composite GPA of 3.3). When Meyerhoff students are compared with various groups of equally talented students, we find that the Meyerhoff students are much more likely to succeed in science. For instance, among students who were accepted into the program, but who declined the offer and attended another university instead, less than half (46 percent) of those who started off in science majors successfully completed the major (many switched into nonscience majors). Furthermore, in the past, talented African American students at UMBC achieved science GPAs substantially below those of their comparably talented White and Asian counterparts. Today, in dramatic contrast, the Meyerhoff students achieve science GPAs slightly higher than those of their contemporary, equally talented White and Asian counterparts.

The evidence to date thus indicates that the program is generally effective in achieving its goal of helping students achieve at the highest levels in science, persist and succeed in science majors, and matriculate into graduate or professional programs in science, mathematics, or engineering. From the student's perspective, next we hear why this is the case.

The Student Perspective on the Meyerhoff Program: Sustaining the Success

We administered questionnaires regularly over the years to the Meyerhoff students, focusing on their experience both in the program and at the university. We also conducted interviews regularly with different subsets of students over the years, including the daughters we interviewed for this book.[17] The surveys and interviews revealed that the students viewed a number of programmatic factors as especially critical: (1) program community, (2) financial support, (3) program staff, (4) research internships and mentors, and (5) campus academic environment. We now turn to a brief discussion of each of these factors.

Program Community

The survey item, "being part of the Meyerhoff Program Community," has been consistently rated as a primary contributor to academic success over the years. Additional survey items related to academic and social aspects of the program community, including "academic activities with Meyerhoff students," "study groups," "Summer Bridge Program," and "social interactions with Meyerhoff students," received similarly high ratings. These results have been strongly supported by the interview findings, as students interviewed consistently cited both academic and social facets of program community as among the most helpful aspects of the program.

In terms of the academic aspect of program community, for instance, Meyerhoff peers were described as being "role models" and as providing encouragement, support, and positive competition. Meyerhoff peers are turned to when students experience difficulties in their math and science courses, and they provide assistance through individual tutoring or through study groups. The three quotes which follow illustrate the academic aspect of program community.

"Number one in my book is the support. Having other smart, talented African Americans around you at all times is an asset. In high school, I didn't have that. I could count on one hand the number of smart, intelligent Black people that I could come to and say, 'I'm having problems in this class. . . . Maybe you can help me out, direct me to someone I can speak to.' Coming into the program, I was really, really impressed because there were so many Black people that wanted to major in science and math. They are so smart. It is really encouraging to be around that type of population."

"Without the program, initially it would be much more difficult, at least academically. I would be much more alone going to classes. You know that there is a sort of net under you in case you fall."

"That feeling of family when everybody came together in the Family [program-wide] meetings. . . . I learned that all of these people are doing so well. Those things were an inspiration to me. I think that made me do so well my freshman year, and made me continue on to doing well."

Other students emphasize the social, family-like nature of the program community and the importance of friendship networks, as illustrated in the next three quotes.

"It would have taken me a while to become social with people. But in my first year of college, I knew about thirty people [Meyerhoff peers], so it was easy. I had friends. I didn't feel like an outcast."

"The Meyerhoff Program is like a family, and that adds a lot of support. There is a lot of help. You don't have to assume all the responsibility yourself at once."

"I think just being with the other Meyerhoff students was such a blessing. I made lots of good friends there. After I left, I went off on my own to graduate school, a predominantly White school—leaving this environment, where I was surrounded by so many, really talented, smart, funny, diverse, Black people, it was just hard to go back to the [same] environment that I was in at high school."

The final two quotes focus on responsibility and pride associated with membership in the program community.

"I feel that it is my obligation to give something back, whether it be some test notes or class notes or solutions, things like that, to help out my little [Meyerhoff] brothers and sisters."

"When you go out in public, you're not only representing yourself, but you are representing the program. So you carry yourself with a little more pride, and a little more dignity."

Taken together, the interview excerpts illustrate how a critical mass of talented minority students can positively affect students' academic achievement. Clearly, having a critical mass of like-minded peers on a campus serves to enhance African American students' academic and social integration into the university environment, one of the key factors linked to academic success, as noted earlier.

Financial Support

The financial assistance provided by the program was described as an extremely helpful aspect of the program by the students in both their survey responses and interviews. Financial aid was described as liberating for the students and their families. It also was perceived as a strong incentive for "paying back" the community and avoiding failure. Specifically, several daughters indicated that the assistance from the program lifted a financial burden "off the shoulders" of their parents. For some, college would not have been an option without the Meyerhoff Program's financial support. Two representative quotes follow.

> *"The financial support is a whole other aspect because you don't have to worry about a whole lot of things . . . having to get a job if you couldn't afford college, or putting that burden on your parents. . . . So, that's [a lot of stress] off your mind."*

> *"You don't have to worry about money, like a lot of other students who have to take a job to get through school. The Meyerhoff Program, you just do your work and everything is taken care of for you, so you can concentrate completely on academics."*

Program Staff

Program staff members were consistently identified by students as central to their academic success. Staff contributions were consistently and highly rated in survey responses, as reflected in items assessing program-wide ("family") meetings and cultural activities, and personal counseling and academic advising. In the interviews, students characterized the program staff as encouraging and supportive, in terms of the students' personal as well as academic lives. Staff monitoring of student academic progress was perceived as motivational. Staff members' knowledge of university resources guided students through, and lessened the impact of, personal, academic, and financial problems. Interview responses also indicate that staff members are viewed as strongly promoting and contributing to the "family-type" environment that characterizes the program community. Staff encourage students to respect and care for one another as they would members of their own families, and are often in a parental role as they provide advice, support, and discipline.

The daughters speak of continual nurturing and support in reference to the Meyerhoff Program. One daughter stated, "It's like your family away from home." The following, additional comments reflect diverse aspects of the staff's role.

> *"[The Meyerhoff staff] are definitely committed to us. They want to make sure we're staying involved with our academics . . . staying in touch with other students in the program. They want to make sure that we're networking and that we're basically getting the most that we can get out of being here. They're constantly calling us or saying here's this activity or here's an internship I think you would be great for. That type of thing."*

> *"The Meyerhoff staff really push you. You know they believe in you, and that helps you even more."*

> *"Meyerhoff Program staff will tell you if you're not doing well. . . . They are really helpful in the sense that if you have a problem, they will listen to it. They'll push you to get good grades, and if you get good grades, you will be rewarded."*

> *"The staff are people who wanted you to do well. They accepted your successes and failures, and they still loved you despite them. That's why I feel like I can still call today and speak to them, and they know exactly who I am. I think other reasons they were valuable is that they didn't limit themselves strictly to your academics. They looked at you as a whole."*

Research Internships and Mentors

Summer research internships were another program component rated by students as important contributors to their success. These internship opportunities were mentioned enthusiastically by a number of the students interviewed. The internships provide hands-on, meaningful research that gives students a realistic look at what scientists do. For many Meyerhoff students, these experiences have helped them confirm their desire to pursue the Ph.D. In fact, many of these students have published articles with mentors in referred scientific journals (e.g., *Science*, the *Journal of Molecular Biology*) or presented academic papers at professional conferences. In addition to research internships, students are paired with mentors who are part of a group of Baltimore and Washington area scientists and engineers who volunteer their time to work in this role. Two students describe some of the benefits derived from research experiences and working with mentors.

> *"The research experiences have been very valuable. I worked with Dr. T. my first year, and he set a basis for everything that I was going to be using later on. Then I worked with Dr. F., and I presented at three difference conferences on the research that I did with him about myoglobin. Then I worked with Dr. I. He works in neuroscience, and his work was pretty interesting too. . . . Most valuable has been the thinking process, how you go about trying to solve a problem, and all the different techniques you can use to get around problems—that, and all the contacts."*

> *"Every summer I worked, I did research. My first year, I worked with Dr. N. He is an African American, and one of the mentors for our program. We did basic stuff to help me along. When I did my research the next year, I found it really did help. The next year, I worked with Dr. S. He took an interest in me. He really kind of molded me, and he guided me a lot. He actually helped me to apply to Harvard. Then Dr. B., this year—he's a real big name at Hopkins, so it was good working with him and with his graduate students."*

Some student responses suggested the special importance of a mentor who was African American, or, in the case of female students, who was of the same gender.

> *"I was lucky enough last year to get an internship in a Black professor's lab. I feel like I got to know him pretty well. We just talked sometimes, just about the future and stuff like that, ways that I could do things in the future, different directions I could take."*

> *"My mentor and I talk about research, and about being a minority in*

science and being a woman, things like that. We've developed a good relationship, and I've received a lot of emotional support."

Campus Academic Environment

Although not a component of the program per se, and not assessed directly in the surveys, a number of the students interviewed spontaneously identified facets of the campus academic environment as important factors contributing to their success. Science faculty on campus are generally very knowledgeable about the Meyerhoff Program, and, in addition to teaching relevant courses, some of the faculty take part in special academic and social events related to the program. In their interviews, students emphasized that as Meyerhoff students, they benefited from the high expectations faculty had for them and from enhanced access to faculty, as revealed in the following four quotes.

"After faculty figure out that you're a Meyerhoff, I guess there's this underlying assumption that you're going to do well . . . there's a little more motivation in that class when they know that I'm a Meyerhoff."

"It seems like everybody thinks that if you are a Meyerhoff, then you must be smart. I get that from teachers and people who just work here. It's nice attention. They seem to admire you a lot and they seem to have a genuine sense of caring for your education."

"An advantage [of being a Meyerhoff student] is that we get to meet faculty members and they get to know us personally. So, if we have any problems we feel comfortable going up and talking to them and asking them questions."

"A lot of the professors were very, very personable. I know I would not have gotten that type of student/professor relationship anywhere else."

Negative Aspects of the Program Experience

Both the survey and the interview results underscore the positive contribution of the Meyerhoff Program to students' academic success. However, after noting positive facets of the program in the interviews, some students noted a few negative ones as well. The next three students focus on the difficulties involved in coping with high expectations and close scrutiny.

"Because the program is so popular . . . the faculty members recognize us more. When we get in their classes, they may know us before we know them, and they may expect more from us because they know we're Meyerhoff students, so that can be a disadvantage."

"I do kind of feel like I'm always being watched, and sometimes I would like not having everyone looking to see how I do. There's just . . . no freedom."

"Sometimes, teachers will expect more from you than other people, plus, everyone in the program will know your grades, test scores, and so forth. That's okay, that's part of the support system, but at times it can be real trying."

The final student quoted discusses alienation from other students on campus following the Summer Bridge experience.

"The downside of it sometimes is that you feel alienated when the fall begins because you spent the summer together. You have already had a label placed on you, and it reduces your chance of meeting people on an equal basis. That goes for White people and Black people."

Parenting through the College Years

Although this section of the chapter has focused primarily on the influence of the college environment on students, we need to note that parents do not stop their close involvement with their daughters when they go to college. Although supportive college environments and programs may be viewed in many respects as part of surrogate parenting, this analogy is limited. Parents' continuing influence and support are clearly important in helping the daughters succeed in college.

During the interviews, the daughters emphasized that their relationships with their parents continue to be very important during the college years. Many daughters talk to their parents regularly—often with their mothers, and in some cases their fathers as well. In many cases, frank discussions of social and/or academic challenges take place. Several daughters described parents who were in regular contact with their academic advisors; furthermore, Meyerhoff Program staff ensure that parents are informed and engaged if academic or social difficulties arise.

The next excerpt, from a daughter who was a sophomore biology major at the time we interviewed her, describes the different kinds of support her mother continues to provide during the college years.

"My mom and I talk all of the time. She is supportive of me. In a lot of ways I would say she is like my best friend. I can tell my mother anything. She knows everything about me, basically. For instance, if I have a relationship problem with a guy, she can tell me everything about why a particular idea will or won't work. Concerning academics, this semester, oh my goodness, it is so hard. I am just doing the best I can do. I talk to my mom almost every day, and she says, 'Just do the best you can and try not to get stressed out.'"

Below, two more daughters share examples of support received during times of academic disappointment. The first daughter was a senior biochemistry major when she was interviewed, and in this case, her mother's support proved important when she "gave her all" to earn an A in a difficult biochemistry course, yet did not achieve her goal.

"I remember we studied so hard for the final, and in the end I thought I did well, but ended up getting a B—I missed an A by two points. I really have never been all that frustrated about a grade, but I felt like I'd put my all into it. It was like unheard of for me to do my absolute best, and fail to achieve my goal. I remember going home crying, and my mom came and hugged me. That's really one situation that sticks out in my mind. It was just that she was encouraging and let me know that it was okay. She said, 'It's okay, you know—it's not the end of the world. You did all that you could do. You did your best. You did all that God or anyone could ask of you.'"

The next daughter received several Cs the fall of her sophomore year.

"Last fall was the first time I really had struggles. I got a C in Organic Chemistry and a C in Physics. That was right before Christmas. And I

was just evil; I didn't buy any Christmas presents for anybody. I was like bah-humbug to everybody. My mother thought I was crazy [laughter]. She thought I was crazy to be crying over a C. She was just like, 'Get out of my face, because you're just ridiculous.' I guess she always knew that I was still going to do well, and that these little setbacks were not going to stop me."

Generally, it is knowing that their parents are there for them, continuing to care and support them, that appears most important to the daughters. The quote below illustrates this theme. It is from a daughter whose mother died when she was a teenager, and who hears from her father on a weekly basis.

"My father still calls me like once a week, to ask me how my grades are and how I am feeling, and how I am doing. So he really cares. He is always there."

Future Plans

The students we studied had, in most cases, well-developed and ambitious plans for their careers. Some were already enrolled in medical and graduate schools, while many others planned to pursue their M.D. and/or Ph.D. degrees upon graduation from college.[18] Over the course of their careers, these young women plan to conduct research, teach, practice medicine, and consult. They have high aspirations and seek to have an influence at the highest levels. Some expressed their dreams of one day becoming the Surgeon General of the United States, Dean of Harvard Medical School, and even Nobel Prize-winners. The desire to succeed at the highest levels reflects, in part, the young women's self-confidence, which has been fostered by their parents, the Meyerhoff Program, and the community. Early graduates of the Meyerhoff Program are well on their way to achieving their impressive goals—nearly 90 percent of the program's 225 graduates (through spring 2000) are pursuing graduate and professional degrees at institutions across the country in science, engineering, and medicine. The young women who have graduated from the program, however, do not wish solely to achieve personal success, for they also expressed the desire to "give back to their communities" and to work with "compassion and commitment." Sustaining these values speaks not only to their character as individuals, but also to the enduring influence of their parents, their communities, and the Meyerhoff Program.

Summary

In the first two sections of this chapter, we discussed the daughters' pursuit of math and science in their early years through high school. In this section we have described the components of the Meyerhoff Program, one program among a number in the country designed to help college-aged African Americans overcome the odds, earn undergraduate degrees in science and engineering, and go on to graduate and professional school.[19] We hope that from reading this chapter, parents will become more fully aware of the challenges that their daughters will face throughout their schooling. Parents should be prepared to help their daughters meet the challenges awaiting them at each level of their schooling, and support them in carefully selecting college and university environments that will empower them to succeed (see Appendix B).

In this chapter, as in the previous one, we focused primarily upon the academic challenges facing the daughters. Yet, clearly, the daughters also face a wide range of psychological and social challenges beyond the academic arena, all of which have a major influence on their development. It is to these challenges, and the ways that parents, the young women, and significant others have responded, that we now turn.

CHAPTER 6

Becoming a Black Woman
A Closer Look at Personal, Cultural, and Emotional Challenges

In the previous two chapters, we listened to the daughters, in their own voices, describe the myriad experiences that helped to promote their academic success, in general, and in math and science, in particular. As the daughters told their stories, and described their respective journeys to Black womanhood, they touched on several critical areas in their lives, beyond academics. In this chapter, we narrow our focus and take a closer look at their personal, cultural, and emotional challenges. (For the purposes of this discussion, "cultural" challenges refer to those pertaining to race, ethnicity, and gender.) As we listen to the daughters' voices, we learn that these young women share many experiences—some because they are women, some because they are Black, some because they are Black women, and some because they are human.

Specifically, we focus on the daughters' experiences in the following areas: (1) dating and sexual intimacy, (2) depression and substance abuse, (3) self-esteem and body-image, (4) racial and ethnic identity, and (5) race, gender, and their intersection. The challenges we discuss occurred both within and outside of school contexts, and from preschool through post-college years.

We often hear that every challenge presents an opportunity for growth. As we listen to the daughters describe their personal battles, we gain a better understanding of the nature of such challenges. In some instances, we also see how these obstacles became motivating forces in the young women's lives, and how they overcame the challenges. In addition, we learn about the many resources the daughters used to respond to personal, cultural, and emotional difficulties. For instance, parents often served as an important resource either by preparing their daughters for future challenges, having taught them values and given them advice, or by playing an active role at the time of the challenge. We also learn that religion and spirituality proved important to the majority of the daughters in terms of preparing them for and overcoming obstacles. We discuss the critical role of religion and spirituality at the end of this chapter.

Dating and Sexual Intimacy

Given the prevailing concerns in society about sexual behavior and teens (as noted in the first chapter), we asked the daughters what messages their parents conveyed to them regarding sex and dating. We learned that more than two thirds of them received a clear message from their parents regarding sexual behavior. The majority of those messages taught that premarital sex was wrong. Beliefs about premarital sex were communicated through discussions that focused, in some cases, on the mothers' own teen pregnancies and, in other cases, on teen pregnancies of family members, friends, neighbors, schoolmates, and even strangers in the news. For some daughters, the topic was not broached until they began dating in high school or college. There were some parents who focused primarily on prevention, teaching about the risks involved with premarital sex and the consequences of pregnancy and sexually transmitted diseases. This diversity of responses is consistent with what we learned from the parents, including those who dealt with these issues before they happened, those who dealt with the issues as they arose, and those who discussed the issues even though they were not immediately relevant.

The theme of parental discouragement of early sexual behavior was also reflected in the young women's survey responses. Specifically, 69 percent reported that parents stressed the importance of not having a child until their education was completed; 53 percent stated that parents emphasized sexual abstinence until adulthood or marriage; and 46 percent indicated that parents cautioned them to be responsible if they did engage in sexual activities (e.g., using contraception).

One way parents limited opportunities for premarital sex was by prohibiting or discussing dating. Nearly 60 percent of the daughters interviewed stated that their parents had stringent rules with regard to dating. Notwithstanding the various methods that most parents used to convey their beliefs about sex and dating, there were a few daughters who said that their parents never communicated with them about sex and dating. Below, we take a closer look at sex and dating from the daughters' perspectives, particularly regarding the decisions they made and the challenges they faced.

Decisions About Sexual Intimacy

Several of the daughters reported that they chose to abstain from sex as teenagers because of their personal values, or after seeing friends or family members become pregnant. In three instances, the daughters' decisions were made consciously in an attempt to break the family legacy of teen pregnancy. Other daughters were actively engaged in sex in high school or college, although their parents were not always aware of their activities. Some parents made discoveries about their teenage or college-age daughters' sexual behaviors and had to respond to sensitive situations. Two examples of these instances are illustrated below.

> *"[M]y mother knew because I told her I needed to go on the pill, and she was fine about it. She took me to the doctor and got me set up, asked me how I was doing. She was fine about it, but my dad probably didn't find out until years later. But it is pretty open with my mom, although she still said she didn't believe in premarital sex."*

> *"The day I told my father I was no longer a virgin, he cried, and that was one of the most touching experiences. That was like an affirmation that I was no longer a little girl, and he just didn't know what to do about that. Well he didn't fuss; he was just like, 'We have to do whatever we have to do to make sure that you are protected.' Neither one of my parents advocate premarital sex."*

Conflicts About Dating

Some of the young women indicated that, at times, they purposely hid the fact they were dating because they believed their parents would disapprove of their boyfriends. It also was a way to protect the young men from parental interrogation. Other young women described the conflicts that arose when one or both parents expressed disapproval of the dating relationship. Some of the reasons mentioned for parental disapproval included (1) the perception that the young man's values were different; (2) the fact that the young man was much older than the daughter; (3) that the young man was from a different ethnic and cultural background; and (4) the daughter was too young to date anyone. While some daughters were not able to reach any type of compromise with their parents, one solution formulated by Jamie's parents is presented below.

"It was like they realized that we were going to date behind their backs, so they might as well bring it out into the open. So he was invited over to dinner, and my dad would have one-on-one talks with him. And if he called, if my mom answered the phone, she would chat with him for a few minutes and ask him questions. The same kind of questions that she might ask me about—his interest in sex, his interest in me, what he does after school, etc. . . . Instead of putting the pressure on me not to have a boyfriend, they put themselves in my relationships."

Date Rape

In recent years, greater attention has been given to dating violence and date rape experienced by young women.[1] Several researchers have found that African American girls, in particular, tend to exhibit more emotional distress and behavioral problems as victims of, or witnesses to, dating violence compared with girls from other ethnic groups.[2] Thus, we also asked the daughters about the types of messages they received regarding rape. Only four of the daughters interviewed had been warned specifically about placing themselves in potentially harmful situations. The fathers appeared to play an important role in this area, given that three of the four young women received such messages from their fathers. This is consistent with what we learned from the fathers who said they instructed their daughters about "the world of men."

Depression and Substance Abuse

Female adolescents, in general, and academically gifted ones in particular, are thought to be at risk of depression due to increased academic pressures.[3] Furthermore, African American adolescents have been reported, in some instances, to have higher rates of depression than their White peers.[4] Interestingly, though, African American female adolescents have been reported to have lower rates of depression than their female counterparts from other ethnic groups.[5] Despite conflicting rates cited in the literature, the experience of depression is very real for Black girls and women. As the daughters told their stories, we learned how they struggled not only with depression, but also with related feelings of anger and guilt.

With regard to drug and alcohol use, African American female adolescents report lower levels of usage than their White counterparts.[6] However, because substance abuse is such a potentially devastating concern, we asked the daughters about their personal experiences with drugs and alcohol, including the parental messages they received. In the following sections, we take a closer look at the daughters' experiences with both depression and substance abuse.

Depression and Emotional Distress

A few of the daughters discussed depression, which varied in intensity from mild to severe, including suicide attempts. For each, the resulting emotional distress interfered temporarily with their ability to focus on their schoolwork. However, with strong parental support and sometimes with professional intervention, the daughters were able to resume their academic journeys, although for some the struggle continued. Monique's poignant story below is perhaps the best reminder that academic success does not protect against the devastation of depression.

> *"I think the challenge was when I was suffering from depression. I was hospitalized because I had tried to commit suicide and remember it being a very trying time. I had swallowed some medication, and I had taken the whole bottle . . . and on top of that, I had taken ibuprofen, too. Sometimes I take a look at myself, and I can tell I am suffering from depression. You think that you can cure yourself and that you don't need any help . . . but then I know that I do need help. [It] is not something that will really just go away."*

For several daughters, experiences with depression and related feelings of anger, guilt, and resentment followed devastating events, including parental separation or divorce, the death of a parent, and physical abuse. For those who experienced the breakup of their parents' marriage, feelings of sadness and anger led to difficulties in school. For others, indifference and numbness were more common. The quotes below represent the range of emotions the daughters experienced following their parents' separation or divorce.

> *"I always felt a little guilty for my parents divorcing, because I felt if I was a guy, my dad would have stayed, because he talked about how he wanted sons a lot."*

> *"For a long time, like all throughout high school, it just didn't bother me and I wasn't happy, I wasn't sad. It was just like, 'You two, if y'all can't get along then just split up. This is not going to affect me one way or the other.' It wasn't until I got older that it bothered me. . . . Before then, I just didn't allow myself to feel."*

In a few cases, a parent's remarriage led to additional feelings of despair. Although some stepparents were very involved in the young women's lives and were loved and accepted by the daughters, others had conflictual relationships with the daughters. Leanna, for example, felt that she constantly had to prove herself to her stepmother. In addition, she believed that she received differential treatment from her stepsiblings. As a result, she described feeling angry, resentful, and depressed to the point that she cried alone every night for years. Leanna learned to cope with her situation by immersing herself in her academics and striving for academic success.

> *"It was almost like I was in competition after awhile with my stepmother. When you are young, and you perceive that someone's not welcoming you, you figure it's something wrong with you when really it wasn't. I was kind of in a misery stage when I lived there. But it was something that made me think that I needed to do a little bit better academically."*

The death of a parent is typically traumatic. Several daughters described experiencing a range of emotions and reactions to the loss of a parent, including sadness, pain, and increased motivation to do well academically. In instances where the deceased parent's behavior, such as alcoholism, had contributed to familial distress or separation, feelings of despondency were often coupled with anger and resentment. Tanisha's description of her reaction to her parent's death provides us with a clear example of both the intensity and complexity of emotions related to such a trauma.

> *"I think I became a vegetable at that point, which probably helped me do well in school. I went through a lot of pain and a lot of emotional hangups, skeletons, whatever . . . when my father died, and my mother did too. And I think that was the beginning of the absolute focus, the shutting down of emotions, the blocking out of anything that can hurt you. . . . Since then, I've had a problem with emotions. And I know that has to at least have helped me focus. I was determined that nothing was going to bother me. I was going to do what I had to do, and maybe I'll make him proud one day. . . . Nobody helped me through it. I still, to this day, have not cried."*

Feelings of emotional despair were also prevalent for those daughters who experienced and/or witnessed physical abuse. In each case, the daughters described having distant and strained relationships with their fathers, which were marked by anger and resentment. Tracey, in her poignant account, explains how she overcame her feelings of hatred toward her abusive father, who was in and out of their household.

> *"I didn't [want] my father in the house. He hit us or abused us or her . . . he stressed her and stressed us with whippings or neglect. I was at the point in my life where I wasn't taking any mess, and I didn't think she deserved it either. . . . My mother felt that was not my place, but I loved my mother, and I didn't feel she should have to take that. He tried to raise us, with slapping us. He would come over for dinner, and if we didn't do it his way and treat him like a king, he didn't like that. So he would slap us, hit us, beat us, whatever it took. . . . He is certainly a different man now, and I guess that speaks to the power of God, in His ability to change people, and also in His ability to allow us to forgive. . . . Because right now, I have no animosity towards my father. I would do anything for him. I love him like I love any person, but I think a lot of people would hate their fathers, or hate their parents for what they have done. But I have no animosity because it is very easy for children or other people to hate, but we really learn about ourselves when we have to walk in that person's shoes. And who is to say that I wouldn't have acted the same way, if I had walked in his shoes."*

As the daughters struggled with such emotional challenges, they generally described their parents as being supportive. In dealing with such problems as depression or related emotional disturbances, parents also played an important role by identifying appropriate mental-health services for their daughters.

Drug and Alcohol Use

The daughters were asked specifically about messages from their parents regarding drug and alcohol use. More than half said that their parents warned them, through various means, of the potentially negative effects of drugs and alcohol. In survey responses, 45 percent reported that their parents placed "great emphasis" on not using alcohol, while 65 percent said that their parents placed "great emphasis" on not using drugs.

The content of the communications from their parents varied, but the common underlying message was that drugs and alcohol were wrong, and should not be touched. Some of the parents used their own experiences, or experiences of family members, to highlight the negative effects of using substances, as we heard in the parents' chapters. Examples of other methods used by parents to communicate messages to their daughters about drugs and alcohol included (1) involving them in church and Sunday school classes where teaching about drugs and alcohol occurred and (2) discussing related incidents as they arose in the news, in the community, or in the workplace. Other daughters said that their education about drugs and alcohol use came from watching the deleterious effects on friends and family members. Below, Celeste describes her observation of the use of drugs and alcohol by family members.

> *"I grew up in a household with people smoking weed. I knew how to roll a joint when I was nine years old. My sisters and I never wanted to touch it. . . . And it was just a regular thing, like smoking cigarettes. . . . My uncle had a problem with being addicted to cocaine, although he never did it in front of us, but that was like common family knowledge. . . . My grandfather was an alcoholic."*

For daughters with a parent who actively used alcohol, the lessons about the devastating impact of alcohol abuse were quite clear. In one case, drinking led to divorce, while in two other cases, drinking contributed to parental separation and the fathers' early deaths. In the poignant statement that follows, Rosalyn describes the painful manner in which she learned of the destructive potential of alcohol.

> *"As far as alcohol goes, my father is an alcoholic. So, I see how that has ripped between us. My parents are divorced because of it, and it affects me every year, everyday of my life. . . . My mom hasn't really talked to us about it because she knows we know what a problem it can be."*

Several of the daughters described instances where the messages their parents instilled helped them decide not to use drugs or alcohol, even when their friends were indulging. One daughter stated that she smoked cigarettes in the fifth grade, but stopped because she knew her mother would be angry. Two daughters of alcoholic fathers stated that even as adults, they do not drink often or heavily because of their experiences as children. In the following account, Carmen describes how she experimented with drugs and alcohol, stopped on her own, and was able to discuss it candidly with her mother.

> *"I told her that I had gotten drunk once or that I had smoked some stuff. Since she had done it, and since I told her I had stopped, she didn't really worry about it that much. She wasn't really mad. She knew it hadn't affected my grades or anything."*

Self-Esteem and Body Image

The literature suggests that Black girls report higher levels of self-esteem and more positive body images than White and Hispanic girls.[7] As discussed in Chapter 1, results from one study found that 40 percent of African American girls considered themselves attractive or very attractive, compared with only 9 percent of White girls. However, it is important not to overlook the other side of the coin—60 percent of the Black girls studied still considered themselves unattractive.[8] Among the daughters we interviewed, 60 percent discussed having low self-esteem due to concerns about their weight, clothing, and/or physical attractiveness. (Issues regarding self-esteem and appearance that are specific to race or ethnic-group membership are discussed in the next section on racial and ethnic identity.)

Given that these young women have enjoyed high levels of academic success, one might expect that positive feelings about their accomplishments would diminish the importance of threats to self-esteem in other areas of their lives. However, as we listened to their struggles, in some cases ongoing, we learned that academic success did not protect these daughters from the difficult experiences of self-doubt and insecurity.

Weight

Several daughters experienced problems because they were considered overweight. They described being teased by family members and/or friends. Some of the young women stated that they received little to no attention from the opposite sex until they lost weight in high school or college. In the following account, Carol explains how she was able to see her situation in a positive light despite the fact that she was regularly teased by her family for being overweight.

> *"I think the one thing with being overweight was that it probably gave me less opportunities for dating, but that may have been a good thing, because it gave me less opportunities to do things that I wasn't supposed to do."*

In some instances, they endured teasing from friends and/or family members. Below, Chanel recounts how implicit messages about thinness in her household, including jokes about weight, fostered her fears of becoming fat.

> *"The idea of being thin, that's always been the issue in our house. . . . I think it was more or less a subtle issue, not so much something that was talked about. . . . Not to put my dad down, but it was kind of perpetuated because of him, [the idea] of a thinner female."*

Mia describes her challenge of being teased by her brother because of her weight and because she wore braces.

> *"When I was younger, my brother used to always mess with me because I*

was a fat kid. His comments made me very self-conscious, just because it was like a constant thing. It wasn't like every once in a while. It wasn't like he ever apologized; he just said what he wanted to say, because that is what he felt. Yeah, I would definitely say he made me self-conscious. Always about how I looked and how I felt about myself. For a long time, I would say I felt bad about how I looked just because he was always talking about me. But after time passed and I got past that phase, I think now I am healed from it . . . after I finally lost weight and got the braces off and things like that. I guess then the attention I started getting for my appearance kind of healed me—just the fact that I must not be that bad since 'so and so' wanted to call me."

Clothing

Nearly one third of the young women described concerns related to their clothing or style of dress. Specifically, the daughters expressed that at some point they were self-conscious because they did not dress like the other students. For some, their parents could not afford to buy them fashionable or expensive clothing. For others, their parents insisted that they dress in a conservative manner. While the young women eventually learned not to let the teasing or comments bother them, some of the daughters tried to dress differently. This often led to conflicts of varying severity with their parents. Juanita describes a rather difficult experience, below.

"I think my freshman year of high school was the roughest time between my parents and me because I was discovering boys and makeup and cleavage. And I remember several times when I would come downstairs to go out to the mall and my mom would be like, 'I think there's a shirt that goes over that.' So I think that was the roughest time. That's when we butted heads the most. That's when I hated my mom, and I'm sure she didn't like me too much, and we had a lot of screaming matches about I can wear what I want or things like that. . . . I think that she didn't give up. She would try different tactics. Sometimes it just came down to screaming but she'd compliment me if I wore something that was modest, and she liked it. . . . I think eventually I grew out of it, and I became more interested in school and less interested in clothes. So it just kind of faded away slowly."

Physical Attractiveness

The daughters discussed a variety of concerns about their appearance (other than weight, and clothing). Some of the young women we interviewed described being teased by friends and family members because of a specific physical feature (e.g., large forehead, small breasts). Others, though not frequently teased, considered themselves to be "ugly" or unattractive, a perception often linked to a lack of interest from the opposite sex. Christine's account, below, is an example of the challenges, which continue for some, related to physical attractiveness.

> *"I think I always had low self-esteem about how I looked when I was younger. Like whenever my mom noticed that she would always say, 'But why, you're so pretty.' . . . And then around the age when boys start to matter, I guess I never really got any attention from boys. And one of my best friends was really pretty, and so guys were always talking to her, so I kind of felt left out in that. If I had any issues in my life, that's probably low self-esteem as far as physical appearance. . . . I can't think that I was ever teased or called ugly. Most of the time, I think I have resolved it. But to some extent, how I feel about myself is still strongly attached to . . . my boyfriend. If I have a boyfriend, then I think I must be okay, because somebody thinks I am pretty. But now I know that it doesn't really make sense to think that way. I can check myself when I start thinking stupid things like that, but it still happens. If I don't notice it right away, it can distract me from things."*

The Parental Role

With regard to issues concerning weight, clothing, and physical appearance, we learned from the above accounts that some parents played a role in providing reassurance for their daughters when they became aware of the girls' specific difficulties. Other parents conveyed general messages in an attempt to foster their daughters' overall feelings of confidence and self-worth. Such messages, however, did not prevent the young women from personally experiencing discomfort, nor did they help to resolve the situation quickly. Generally, the daughters had to bear some feelings of hurt, self-doubt, and/or self-consciousness before learning to cope with or resolve their particular issues. Yet it appears that the positive messages regarding self-esteem received from parents provided a foundation, which helped the daughters face, and eventually overcome, such challenges.

Racial and Ethnic Identity

The research literature discusses African American students having their "Blackness" questioned when they experience academic success. Successful students may be perceived as "acting White" or selling out. "Acting White" has been previously defined by African American students as displaying those values and behaviors perceived to be characteristic of White Americans, for example, speaking standard English, listening to White music, working hard and getting good grades in school, being on time, doing volunteer work, going to the opera, symphony, ballet, or rock concerts, and spending time in the library.[9] In other words, gifted African American students are sometimes perceived as having betrayed or abandoned their culture or community by achieving in school, which is sometimes viewed as a symbol of the dominant culture. It has been noted that African American girls and women who are academically successful must not only deal with the issue of "acting White," but also cope with the pressure of a subtle gender hierarchy, which is reflective of the larger society.[10]

African American individuals have also experienced challenges to their identity, a form of "within-group discrimination," for reasons unrelated to academic success. Although not well understood by some, differential treatment, based on skin color, hair texture, or physical features characteristic of African peoples, is an age-old phenomenon and continues to exist within the Black community.[11] Although many Blacks consider the issue to be "dead" or "taboo"[12] or too controversial to be discussed, the issue persists for African Americans. Historically, light-skinned women have often been preferred within the Black community, while negative associations were linked to having dark skin.[13] In one study, for example, African American college women expressed the belief that their male peers considered light skin to be more valued and attractive.[14] Similarly, among Black adolescents, those who reported themselves to be "lighter" or "darker" had lower levels of satisfaction with their skin color, and those who described themselves as "darker" had lower self-esteem.[15]

Relatedly, children of immigrant parents face unique challenges in trying to form an identity.[16] For example, foreign-born Blacks often distance themselves from American-born Blacks, whom they perceive as being lazy and undisciplined. American Blacks, in turn, form their own negative stereotypes about Blacks born in other countries.[17] Such "mutual negative stereotyping" can lead to conflicts between African Americans and the children of foreign-born Blacks.[18] There also is pressure on foreign-born children and adolescents as they develop their identities and must decide whether to identify as an American, as a member of their parents' ethnic group, or as one who shares both cultures.[19]

The research literature captures some of the challenges experienced by the daughters we interviewed. Their racial and ethnic identities have been questioned, primarily by Black peers, and in some cases by family members, for a number of reasons and within multiple settings. First, we listen carefully to the daughters' voices as they discuss instances where their racial identities have been challenged, because they were "nerds" or "too smart" or "acting White." Next, we explore threats to the daughters' ethnic identities that were based not on academic accomplishments, but on characteristics such as skin color, hair, physical features, and ethnic-group membership. Finally, we explore the role of parental messages in preparing these young women to deal with such challenges.

"Acting White"

Almost two thirds of the daughters interviewed recounted incidents in which they were teased or felt alienated for exhibiting behaviors that were considered to reflect White cultural norms. This is consistent with their survey responses, in which 82 percent of the daughters reported that they had been accused at least once of "being a nerd, acting White, or not being cool by their peers." The daughters were called such names as "Oreo," "nerd," and "White" because they were academically successful, or because they sounded or acted "White" according to their Black peers. Vanessa describes what was said about her in elementary school because of her limited interactions with African American peers.

"They had rumors going around that I was deaf and mute. I was quiet because I didn't know them. I also had a problem because I played field hockey. Field hockey is not a Black sport. . . . they called me an 'Oreo.'"

The responses to such attacks on identity varied. While the ridicule and isolation moved some to tears, others learned to have quick retaliatory responses, such as, *"Well, this nerd will be writing your paycheck one day."* Some daughters learned to ignore the teasing and reasoned that their peers were either jealous or would be less successful. Still others were eventually accepted by their peers, sometimes after those same classmates began to turn to them for help academically or had opportunities for interaction through sports or other extracurricular activities.

Several of the daughters coped with their situations by attempting to downplay their academic strengths, for instance, by not answering questions in class or minimizing their academic success. Such a strategy was often part of a larger repertoire of coping behaviors employed by the young women in order to live and function within two culturally distinct realms. Terms such as alternation[20] and code-switching[21] (e.g., switching between "standard English" and "Black English" depending on the context) have been used to characterize participation in, and negotiation of, two cultural realms, which is the reality for many African Americans. The two illustrative quotes which follow highlight the complexities involved with a "dual existence" (i.e., living separate lives) and learning how to bring those worlds together.

"My ethnicity was questioned, I was 'being White.' I didn't appreciate it. And when I was questioned, it was like, 'Well, maybe I should act more like how they would act.' I would still study and stuff, but I started to do certain things that were really out of the norm. And then that's when I started getting in trouble with my parents about certain things. Like my female friends would always hang around guys who were in high school, and I would start to do that. And my whole music changed. But I still always . . . focused on schoolwork. It's kind of like you had to live two separate lives. In school, I had to act like I didn't care what was happening in class . . . but when I got home, I worked extra hard so I could catch on to the stuff I wasn't paying attention to in class. Or to make sure that my presentation was really good to make up for the fact that I wasn't really paying attention. . . . But I would still have to have two separate lives— like how I was with my friends socially at a party, at the movies, and how I was when I turned my work in with my teachers."

" I got 'nerd,' I got 'White girl,' people still tell me I sound like a White girl. . . . I felt like I needed to keep those two worlds separate, those two

sets of friends, those two experiences, mostly because I felt like White people wouldn't understand. I think that Black people understand White culture, but White people don't understand Black culture. We have to live in White culture, whereas White people don't have to deal with Black culture unless they choose to. My way to deal with it—I had to put on two faces in a way. But as I got older, I was like to heck with that. . . . you know that comes with maturity."

Outward Appearance and Ethnic-Group Membership

Nearly 30 percent of the daughters described having their ethnic identity challenged at least once because of physical characteristics or cultural differences. Specifically, they described experiencing difficulties because of their skin color, hair texture, or prominent African features. Others' identities were questioned because their families had immigrated from Africa or the Caribbean.

Most described challenges related to skin color. They were teased by friends and/or family members because their complexions were considered either too light or too dark. For example, name-calling included "Old Yellow," " Sunshine," and "Big Bird" for the light-skinned daughters and "Tar Baby," " Brown Butterball," and "Blackie" for the dark-skinned daughters. Some of the lighter-skinned young women stated that they received preferential treatment because of their complexion, which they also perceived as offensive. Other daughters were not teased directly, but described their disapproval at seeing others ridiculed. Jana tells of a personal hurdle, which her grandfather was able to help her overcome.

"I remember when I was young, I had a severe color complex. I always say that it was because my brother and sister used to focus on, 'Oh, you're dark-skinned' and it was always kind of echoing in my mind. . . . I think I remembered the phrase 'tar baby' or something like that. I was very dark and ugly, but it was not only at home, it was also at school. When I was really down on myself, I used to go to my grandparents house—my grandfather noticed it. He was like my personal cheerleader, so that helped me a lot through that phase."

Within the Black community, issues pertaining to skin color often overlap with hair. Among the daughters interviewed, several commented on the preferential treatment they either experienced or witnessed involving girls and women with light skin and long hair. Conversely, those with "nappy" hair, particularly with dark complexions, were teased. For one daughter who had a perm, however, her peers accused her of trying to "be White." As the daughters became older and more self-confident, some chose to return to natural hairstyles. Despite their comfort with their hair, they stated that they continued to receive strange looks or negative comments from others, including family members. Some of the daughters mentioned the media's role in perpetuating skewed definitions of beauty within the Black community. Below, Janine captures both the complexity and gravity of this issue.

"I guess I think I have very strong feelings on the way the media portrays women and the way the media portrays Black women. For the longest time growing up, I guess I didn't think I was ugly, but I didn't really think I was attractive. And I guess I didn't [have] an appreciation for beauty the way I see it now because of the influences. . . . Even today, you open up an Ebony or Jet magazine and you look at the ads, the women in the ads are invariably either light skinned or have long hair. We have a very skewed perception of what beauty is, and I guess I just ran into this head on. Even though my parents fostered a strong sense of self-pride and self-esteem in me, I still have problems. . . . I would look at people and say, 'Oh gosh, she is so pretty, I wish I could look like her.' And I don't think any child should have to do that. I think there are a lot of issues mostly among the Black race, at least growing up where I was, where self-hate is fostered in children."

In addition to skin color and hair texture and/or length, a few of the daughters also encountered problems because of their facial features. In these cases, having a broad nose or big lips, features associated with African descendants, brought ridicule from friends and/or family members. Jana took a rather drastic measure in an attempt to bring the negative comments in elementary school to an end. She stated, *"I went through this phase of putting this swimming thing that pinches your nose, that synchronized swimmers use, to kind of pinch my nose a little bit so it wouldn't look as wide."*

For the daughters whose families were from Caribbean or African countries, threats to their identities were not based solely on complexion, hair, or physical features, but also on any differences that reflected their ethnic group membership. In these cases, their parents instilled traditional cultural values and traditions. They were expected, for instance, to follow certain customs and were to identify themselves as a member of their respective ethnic group. Araba stated, *"It's like you live in two different worlds,"* when comparing her ethnically based household to the other settings (i.e., school and work) in which she lives and functions.

Such cultural differences, rather than being cause for celebration and appreciation, have often been the basis for discrimination from other Blacks. Cynthia, for example, is very proud of her West Indian heritage and, as her parents taught, describes herself as "Black" rather than as "African American." She is annoyed with American Blacks who, because of their difficulties accepting and appreciating within-group cultural differences, choose to ignore such differences and expect all Blacks to conform and adopt "American" attitudes and behaviors. For Cynthia, this act of ignoring cultural differences is also a form of discrimination.

"I think there are very big differences between the groups culturally, and I think Caucasians tend to separate themselves, but Blacks always tend to put themselves in this huge group. So, it's just interesting to me that we feel that we should do that, and we impose that on others. I find that stupid and disturbing, and I always have throughout my college career. And some of the things I find that African Americans tend to say, I find very disturbing. . . . It's hurtful, and they don't even realize it, so I guess that's the way they're brought up."

The Parental Role

Parents' messages varied regarding challenges to their daughters' identities based on academic success (e.g., "acting White"), skin color, hair, physical features, or ethnic-group membership. In many cases, the daughters did not receive any relevant parental messages, while in other cases, the communications received continued to perpetuate the very beliefs with which the young women were struggling. For example, when daughters were teased by family members because of their complexions, there was no explicit mention of parental concern or intervention, perhaps because such teasing was accepted as a benign family tradition. Janine was shocked and disappointed at her mother's vehement disapproval of her boyfriend because he was dark-skinned and from a different culture.

In contrast, however, some of the young women described receiving messages from their parents that were positive and affirming. In one of the stories above, we learned of the grandfather who helped remove the stigma associated with dark skin. We also learned of parents, born in other countries, who consciously instilled a sense of ethnic pride in their daughters. Other positive messages included, *"You're pretty, and it's what's inside that counts,"* and, in reference to the accusation of acting White, *"You cannot act a color."* Finally, in another case, it was an older sister who conveyed the very powerful message, *"Do not fall victim to stereotypes."*

In the following account, Eva discusses her parents' foreign-born influence as she struggled to forge an identity from childhood through adulthood.

"When I was little, my best friend was this Caucasian girl. That was when I was confronted with the whole issue of beauty. Being young and not really understanding what was going on, I wanted to have her eyes, I wanted to have her hair, I wanted to talk like her, I wanted to walk like her, and I wanted her skin, and on and on. I just wanted them to clone her. . . . I don't think until I was in college did I really begin to appreciate me for who I am and the good things or the positive things about the way Black women are typically shaped or the way we look. . . . [My parents] kind of gave me the impression that I wasn't Black like someone who was born and bred from parents who were born here. And I understand that; that was just their whole approach to it. As I began to read more when I came to college . . . I have kind of gotten away from that. I identify myself both with my West Indian heritage, as well as my African American roots."

Race, Gender, and Their Intersection

Within the larger society, Black women are members of two historically oppressed groups. A number of concepts have been offered to describe the potential ramifications of such shared-group membership, such as "double disadvantage"[22] and "double whammy."[23] A similar view is that Black women are "twice victimized" since "the double jeopardy of race and gender complicates the problems of identity" because they "must respond to the desires and expectations of Black men and to White cultural values and norms."[24] African American women, regardless of race, have historically sought to overcome their imposed secondary status. African Americans, regardless of gender, have battled against the ravages of oppression and discrimination. A contrasting view, however, is that because of affirmative action, Black women have a "double advantage" because they have a preferred status over Black men in the labor market.[25]

It is not surprising that when asked about experiences of discrimination related to race and gender, more than three fourths of the daughters reported having at least one such encounter. As we listen to the daughters describe such experiences in their own voices, we also hear them speak of incidents related to their success in areas traditionally occupied by White men—math and science. At the end of this section, the critical role of parental messages specific to race and gender is explored.

Race

Nearly two thirds of the daughters interviewed reported experiences where they believed they were discriminated against because of their race. Within academic settings, several daughters described feeling as if they had to prove themselves constantly. Some stated that peers, who in some cases assumed that awards or scholarships were received only because of their race, questioned their intelligence. For example, one daughter commented that even if she stated, "The sky is blue," her Asian lab partner would not believe her unless the teaching assistant told him "that the sky was really blue." In other instances, the young women recalled that teachers graded them more harshly than their peers or expected them to perform poorly. The stories below are representative examples of the daughters' experiences, which were not only complex but also often hurtful. First, we hear Tyra describe the challenges faced after she fought, along with her parents, to move up to a gifted-and-talented math class.

"And I got moved up, and I got As. There were other people in class who got Cs and they didn't get moved down, but I was threatened with, 'If you get a C, then you will definitely have to go down.'... I was really hurt. I just couldn't believe that they would sit there and tell me these things. It finally dawned on me that they were telling me this because I was like the only Black person in the class. The other White kids asked me for help

on things but [would] get lower grades and nobody would ever say any-thing to them. . . . It just made me more determined to work harder and prove to them that I belonged in these classes. It made me realize that you can encounter racism anywhere. It may not be overt, but [they] will do undercover things to make it known that they don't think you belong."

Next, Eva tells of an experience with a professor at the college level.

"He questioned my ethnicity and said, 'Your hair is not Black. . . . where are your parents from?' So, we had a little discussion on that, and that let me know that . . . his expectations were higher because he thought I wasn't Black. I guess had he known, he wouldn't really have expected much from me. When he found out it was me who had the highest score on his exam, then all of a sudden his expectations changed because now he thought . . . we need something to explain this. . . . She must not be Black or [her] hair doesn't exactly look Black, so then his expectations took a reverse. . . . I think initially I didn't stand out to him."

Finally, Cynthia talks about her parents' influence on how she handled discrimination by teachers at different levels of schooling.

"I had some problems with two teachers when I was in high school, and my parents took care of it. . . . In college, I've had some issues, and it's a different story because it's one of those things where you have to deal with it on your own. You can't deal with it the way you would like to because this is your professor, and he determines your grade. But I think I'm able to deal with it because that's how my parents deal with it, and I know I don't have to yell and scream. That's ignorant because that doesn't make you any better. In general, the biggest weapon is just obtaining your education."

The daughters also described experiences of discrimination that occurred outside of the classroom. Some of the young women were treated fairly in school by peers, but were never invited to the parties or sleepovers held by those same peers. Others described feeling alienated by neighbors. For instance, one daughter stated that her family was told there was a three-year waiting list to join the swim club in their neighborhood, while the White family which moved in after them was accepted immediately. Still, others encountered racism from total strangers, such as being followed around in stores or stared at in elevators. Two daughters tell us of their challenges with peers, neighbors, and strangers, respectively.

"I remember one specific incident when I was on the bus and [a boy] was talking about me to his friend, and he said that my skin color was the same as doo doo or poop. That hurt. It didn't make me angry, and it didn't make me sad, but it hurt my feelings. And when I was in junior high, I went ice-skating with some friends of mine, and some kid called me a nigger and that was the second of two incidences in my life where somebody has called me a nigger. That made me angry, and I wanted to fight with him about it, but he was bigger than I was, so we didn't fight, but I yelled at him."

"We moved when I was fourteen to an all-White neighborhood . . . very hostile environment. They did not want us there. They made it clear they did not want us there. At the signing of the house, they offered my mom the money that we were paying for the house to not move in. . . . The owner of the house wanted to throw us a party to introduce us to the neighbors, but we didn't have the party because no one was going to come. I remember one time when my two younger sisters and I got locked out of the house, we went around my neighborhood . . . trying to ask them if we could use their phones. It was raining and we were little girls, and no one would let us [use the phone]. So, we ended up having to walk a lot of miles to the nearest pay phone It was just very hostile. They didn't want us there, so we kept to ourselves."

In this third account, Allison tells us what happened after a White, male stranger followed her and told her she was beautiful.

"I was just so scared. He [was] getting closer to me, and I was like what is he trying to do? And he stuck out his hand and said, 'I'm so and so,' and I shook his hand, and he kissed my hand . . . and then as he walked by, I noticed a swastika on the left side of his lower back, a green swastika, and then I noticed that he was bald, he was a skinhead. I took my food, I ran to the nearest bathroom. I must have washed my hand fifteen million times. What was he doing? Was he trying to stick me with something? The whole week after that I just kept looking at my hand,

waiting for it to fall off. I was like, why would he have said those things? I felt like he was being patronizing, because if you don't believe in that stuff then why are you going around with a Nazi symbol on your back and a shaved head. To me, that wasn't even like racism, that was just blatant hate. . . . It really, really shook me up."

Gender

Although incidents of gender-based discrimination were less common for the daughters interviewed than race-based discrimination, more than one quarter encountered problems specific to their gender, which seemed to become more prevalent as they grew older. Some of the daughters mentioned that when they were in a group of boys or men, they often were not taken seriously. Within classroom settings, from elementary school through college, especially in math and science classes, several young women stated that they had encountered teachers who preferred to call on male students, expected male students to perform better than female students, and made subtle discriminatory remarks against female students. Some of the young women commented that among their male professors, those from other cultures tended to have less favorable attitudes toward women than their White professors. Camille, Juanita, and Tanisha, respectively, comment on their experiences with gender-based discrimination in the "real world."

"You do tend to get picked over, that happens a lot. Like if I go to a career fair, many times I've been standing next to a man, or you know, just . . . a guy, someone my age. I could've been there first . . . and especially if it's a man presenter, he will tend to talk to the man. You know, I'll just stand there . . . it happens a lot. I'm just trying to practice being a little more verbal in those situations."

"I think it is hard because as a female, you are expected to have this professional, pretty, but not too pretty appearance. Like you cannot walk into this science corporation looking like a glamour girl. But then at the same time, if you're downright ugly, then you still won't have a chance. And you can't be fat. But it is important, and you know that if you are attractive, or if you are well built . . . you are more likely to get a job. And it's terrible, but that's just the way it is, especially if you are a woman.

Because a lot of times it is men doing the hiring and men don't necessarily care how chubby another man is. . . . There is so much pressure put on women anyway to look good and to be the perfect size, and to be Barbie. . . . No matter how smart you get, it is still going to come into play."

"I work with men everyday, and the gender thing is very real. . . . There are still a whole lot of men who feel like women are not their equivalent, that women are good for wives and should speak when they're spoken to and shouldn't be in positions of power . . . in their conversations with each other, in the way that men have their exclusive clubs, like golf. A lot of business deals go on along with golf games, smoking cigars at the bar, drinking brandy. It's a guy-thing, and we're not going to be part of it."

The Intersection of Race and Gender

Above, we learned that the daughters in this sample faced an array of challenges, some specific to their race, others specific to gender. In addition, there were many instances when obstacles were related to both identifying characteristics. More than one third of the daughters interviewed described facing challenges because of their "double minority" status. Most of these daughters also described encountering specific obstacles because of either their race or gender. Still, they acknowledged that in some instances, the duality of their existence was central to their experiences. Specifically, most stated that because they were both Black and female, they were expected to do poorly and had to work extra hard to prove themselves, particularly in the areas of math and science. Some commented that even when both factors play a role, depending on the situation, the relative weight of each would change. Only one daughter stated that a positive consequence of being Black and female is preferential treatment (i.e., a "double advantage"). The complexity of the issues is best revealed in the voices of the daughters.

"I know in middle school, especially, I would try to do well just because I knew that being a woman, or being a girl and being Black, I wasn't supposed to do as well. . . . I was treated differently and not necessarily in a negative manner. Sometimes being a woman, you get preferential treatment, or sometimes even being Black you get preferential treatment [but] not all the time. One time on a summer job, I was told 'you are

going to do X, Y, and Z,' but when it came down to it, I only had the opportunity to do half [of] what was initially said. And I think it was because I was a woman and I was Black and because I was young. All three of those things."

"Sometimes you can't tell if [people] are treating you a certain way because you are Black or you are a woman or what. . . . People will ask a question, and I will give them the answer . . . always being second-guessed, then the teacher would come back and say the same thing. But that happens all the time, and now I'm a teaching assistant for the bio-chemistry lab, and I don't know how people think I actually got that position, but I actually do know what I'm talking about. I don't look stu-pid . . . that's the way I am treated a lot of times, like I am really stupid. I think it is more like a race issue because I don't think that so many peo-ple think that women are intellectually inferior. Obviously I am a woman, it's more obvious that people call me a Black woman. I'm Black first, and then I am a woman. That's what people see. They don't see me as being a woman who is Black."

"I definitely think I was more memorable or stood out more [in classes] because I was a Black female. . . . I mean it is expected that math and science are men-dominated fields, however, a lot more women are start-ing to come through. Personally, I think it's more a gender issue than a race issue."

"It's still a little bit surprising to me that I am still having to prove that I am worthy to get these assignments, or I am worthy to be pro-moted . . . and not feel like I have to explain that just because I am a woman, or just because I am Black, doesn't mean that I can't do the same thing you are, or do it better. I think there is still a little bit of resentment sometimes, being young, successful, smart, Black, being a woman."

The Parental Role

More than 80 percent of the daughters stated that they received messages from their parents specific to race and/or gender. The nature and context of the communications varied across families. For instance, some parents provided general commentary on the state of American society. They gave their daughters such messages as they would have to work "twice" or "three times" or "ten times" as hard to succeed because they were Black (or Black and female). Other parents offered their perspectives on such issues after they, their daughters, or others experienced injustices. Messages involving socialization were often transmitted when parents and other family members discussed their experiences as African Americans and/or women in society. There were also parents who took special efforts to instill cultural knowledge and pride by exposing their daughters to Black history through stories, museums, and other cultural events.

Overall, messages specific only to gender were less common, while race-specific messages were predominant. In some cases, parents discussed potential challenges to being Black and female. Given the obstacles described by the daughters, above, it is likely that the transmission of such messages provided them with an internal resource they could draw upon in times of challenge. Below, two daughters describe the messages from their parents, which are specific to race and refer to the complexities of race relations and the subtleties of racism, respectively.

"On one hand, my mom had White acquaintances, so I had an interaction with people from different races on a regular level. But she also always just made me aware. Like I remember one time we were watching TV, and it was about a Ku Klux Klan [in] the area. I remember I was scared . . . but she would tell me . . . 'It's because they are afraid of Black people.' I didn't understand how the Ku Klux Klan was afraid of Black people. It didn't make sense to me. But I see what she's saying now. She just always, with comments and different educational programs and different things said, 'This is real, this is the reality of it.'"

"You don't distrust White people, but you do have to kind of look out for yourself and make sure that you are watching your back . . . that it was out there and that you had to deal with it. . . . You can't use it as an excuse, you have to keep going."

Regarding potential gender-based challenges, some of the daughters received inspiring messages to persevere regardless of their gender. Several young women described receiving conflicting messages, often subtle and indirect, of a double standard when their brothers were allowed to have more freedom or received less discipline. Still, their parents encouraged them by conveying that they could be self-sufficient or achieve anything when dealing with the larger society. Below are three examples of such communications.

"Well, as far as being female, my father just tells me every once in a while that, 'You are going to have to stand out, something about you is going to have to catch people's attention, you know, for you being female.'"

"My mother would talk about how women were encouraged when she was growing up to do a lot of things, I mean besides maybe being a teacher. She would tell us stuff like that so we could appreciate things now, like the doors that have opened up for women, for instance."

"My mom and my grandmother were like, 'You don't need a man to make you feel like you have some worth. You have things to offer to other people.' When I do have pride, I attribute that to my mom just because she's strong, and she knows what she wants, and she can do all this stuff without necessarily my father having to do it. . . . I've looked at my mom and grandma, and that's how I get some of the attributes I have."

Finally, more than one quarter of the daughters interviewed described receiving messages that addressed both race and gender. The theme of having to work extremely hard in order to succeed was common in these messages. In the following quotes, we hear the daughters repeat the words which served not only to instruct, but also to inspire.

"[My parents said] that nobody's going to give you anything; don't think that you are going to get anything for free. You are going to have to work extra hard, not only to do well, but to fight against people's prejudices or preconceived notions about you based on your race or gender. What can I say, the statistics were stacked against me being Black and female, and so I was going to have to work hard."

"She told me that because I was Black it was going to be difficult compared to somebody else. 'You are going to be judged harder.' Being female

is going to add on to that, cause men are supposedly better. 'It's going to be harder so you have to watch how you behave. Watch what you do and how you act. You have to work harder for it.'"

"They have helped me to understand what it means to be a Black woman in this world and to be competent and proud of that, but also to keep perspective, and let me know that that is not my only defining feature."

Religion and Spirituality as a Resource

Throughout this and previous chapters, we have heard the young women mention several sources from which they drew strength. Parents played a major role in providing support and messages to warn, encourage, and advise. Both verbal and nonverbal communications from peers and extended family served to encourage or discourage certain behaviors at different stages of the young women's lives. They also relied upon internal resources, including personal motivation, determination, intelligence, and pride to help them in the face of challenge. In the above accounts, several daughters spoke of God's role in helping them to overcome a particular challenge. Additionally, the church often served as a vehicle through which messages about drugs, alcohol, dating, and premarital sex were conveyed. Most of the daughters described how their religious or spiritual experiences provided them with critical resources such as values, character, strength, and support. As we heard throughout the chapter, it was these resources which often helped them confront and overcome specific challenges.

Specifically, nearly 80 percent of the sample described either religion or spirituality as having played a significant role in their lives. Only a small percentage definitively stated that neither religion nor spirituality was a factor at any point in their development. The daughters' experiences in this area were diverse. Some daughters were raised in the church, have always been active in church, and developed close, personal relationships with God at an early age. Others were also exposed to church as children, but did not become personally interested and involved until high school or college. For some young women, organized religion and church attendance were not central, but faith in God and sound morals were the basis of their spirituality. Several daughters were introduced to religion not by their parents but by other family members. Still others are presently struggling to decide what role, if any, religion and/or spirituality will play in their lives. Thus, the paths to religion and spirituality were quite diverse. The illustrative quotes that follow highlight both the diversity and complexity of the daughters' experiences with religion and spirituality.

"I went through stages in high school where I wanted to be a Muslim, or I wanted to be a Buddhist, or I was an atheist or agnostic. . . . I have been on a journey. Right now, it is a very important part, like I definitely believe [in] God, and I think I have a close relationship with Him, and that plays a big role in as far as . . . what I want to do. I think I am here for a purpose . . . to help other people."

"I think religion is one of those things, when just implied, it is not as effective. So like my parents have grown up in a Catholic environment, and there wasn't any question about that, it was just like 'that's what you are, that's what you do, you know the rules.' But it wasn't like any further . . . teaching in the house about it . . . it was kind of like Sundays and that was it. So, that made it even more individualized for me. The major role that it has played is presenting a lot of contradictions in my life for me to deal with [and] having to decide when and where religion was going to be the deciding factor. And for that reason, I think I have developed a lot more along the lines of spirituality versus religion. It's something that I am still struggling with now."

"I've been going to church since I was born. All the people at church know me, they know my whole family. I think that my parents have always stressed that God gives you special gifts. . . . He doesn't give them to everybody, so you should cherish the gifts that He gives. God made me smart, so I am going to do whatever I need to do to make sure it stays that way."

"I've spent I guess most of my life, if not my whole life, going to church. Towards the end of my high-school years, I had a greater desire to have a closer relationship with God. . . . I guess I've pretty much grown up knowing there was a God and that He played some role in my life, and more so in college . . . it's like He's played a bigger role, or I've recognized His role more."

Summary

In this chapter, we continued to weave the daughters' accounts of personal, cultural, and emotional challenges into a multifaceted tapestry. We learned that academic success did not protect them from experiencing problems ranging from dating conflicts and perceptions about their physical appearance to depression and discrimination. There are obstacles with which some of the daughters continue to struggle (e.g., low self-esteem, death of a parent, differential treatment based on race and/or gender). However, in many instances, we heard that their challenges motivated them not only to persevere and overcome specific obstacles, but also, in several cases, to work harder to achieve academic success. Religion, spirituality, self-motivation, pride, and even anger and frustration served as resources which the daughters often relied upon to negotiate difficult obstacles. Parents were valuable resources and helped the daughters to face both expected and unexpected challenges in a variety of ways. We close with a summary of the parental actions and messages which the daughters described as helpful to them as they faced personal, cultural, and emotional challenges along their developmental journeys to Black womanhood.

Parental Messages and Behaviors Helpful to Daughters

1. Maintain a policy of either no dating or dating with strict conditions, including meeting the young man before the date, allowing dating only in groups, enforcing curfews, and personally supervising the dates in the home.
2. Emphasize abstinence from sexual behavior until either adulthood or marriage.
3. Encourage daughters not to have children until after obtaining an education.
4. Caution daughters to be responsible about engaging in sexual activity, including using contraception to prevent pregnancy and sexually transmitted diseases.
5. Warn them not to place themselves in potentially harmful situations, in order to avoid date rape or sexual assault.
6. Convey the message that drugs and alcohol are harmful and wrong.
7. Offer caring and support, and seek out professional resources if necessary, regarding depression and emotional distress.

8. Involve daughters in church or teach Biblical principles in the home, which provide teachings that sex, drugs, and alcohol are unacceptable.
9. Instill positive and affirming messages to promote self-confidence, self-respect, and self-pride.
10. Provide reassurance and support upon learning about daughters' struggles with self-esteem or with teasing by peers.
11. Expose them to history and cultural activities in order to promote cultural pride and awareness.
12. Impart the message that daughters must work two, three, or ten times as hard as others in order to be successful because of their race and/or gender.
13. Teach by example and by recounting stories of the parents' own challenges regarding drugs, alcohol, premarital sex, and prejudice and discrimination from both Blacks and Whites.

CHAPTER 7

Raising Successful
African American Young Women
What We Have Learned

A Parent's Pledge

*I pledge to: Listen to my children. . . . Communicate with my children. . . .
Teach my children right from wrong and be a good role model for them. . . .
Spend time with and pay attention to my children. . . . Educate my children
in mind, body, and soul. . . . Work to provide a stable family life for my children. . . . Vote for my children to ensure them fair treatment and opportunity. . . . Speak out and stand up for my children's needs and support effective groups that help children.*

MARIAN WRIGHT EDELMAN, LANTERNS: A MEMOIR OF MENTORS[1]

It is important to remember that the young women in our study
are successful not simply in general, but they have excelled in
high school and college math and science courses and performed well on
standardized tests. Their success is especially significant in the light of
recent legal decisions regarding affirmative action. These decisions make it
more difficult for minority children to gain admission to some of the nation's
colleges and universities. The critical challenge minority children face is that
if their grades and test scores—the traditional measures of success—are not
as competitive as those of their White or Asian counterparts, these underrepresented minority groups may not be able to take advantage of all the
educational and career opportunities available in our society. Therefore, we
must do all we can to strengthen and elevate the academic performance of
these students well before they enter college.

We know that schools and teachers are critical in the educational process,
and understandably they receive a great deal of attention when we look at
student-achievement levels. However, we need to focus much more attention on the role of families in this process, particularly in preparing daughters for success in school. Both parents and daughters agreed that parental
or family support, in addition to natural ability, was a major reason for the

daughters' success. We have learned that raising African American girls to become high-achieving women in science is a complex and exciting challenge. The past six chapters have focused on what we have learned from slightly more than one hundred families of successful African American college women in science. The book uses and analyzes the voices of the parents and daughters to illuminate the journeys of these families over three generations. What emerges from their diverse perspectives and backgrounds is a rich and colorful tapestry that helps us understand the values, practices, and strategies that have led to the daughters' success.

The daughters in our study come from a variety of familial, geographic, educational, and economic backgrounds. They come from two-parent and single-parent homes where some of the parents have a college education and others do not; they come from urban environments as well as suburban and rural settings; they have attended private and parochial schools and larger public schools; and their economic backgrounds range from lower- to middle-income. In organizing this book, we have taken the time to distinguish among the different types of home environments so that parents who read the book may learn more about families whose circumstances may be similar to their own. Most important, regardless of the differences among the families, all of them are fortunate to have daughters who have excelled in school. Also, regardless of the families' circumstances, we find that the mothers, in most instances, have played the most pivotal role in the girls' upbringing. This observation is not meant to undervalue the very important role that fathers have played, or can play, in the lives of their daughters. Nor, based on examples we encountered, is it intended to suggest that other individuals—whether a grandparent or aunt, for example—cannot be effective in playing critical parenting roles.

Education Across Generations

We first looked at the backgrounds of the parents in our study in order to understand how the parents' view of their own upbringing influenced the way they raised their daughters. Sometimes these parents had not thought about how significant their own childhood experiences and relationships with their parents had been in shaping their own parental styles. We found that understanding these connections can shed valuable light on how parents can work effectively with their children.

Most of the parents grew up in two-parent homes, which were typical of life in the 1940s and 1950s and even the early 1960s. Many of the families during that period emphasized the belief that education "makes the difference," and the primary lifetime focus for many of these parents has been on working hard and succeeding in spite of the odds. Just as many of them were reared in religious homes where strong discipline was exercised, many of these parents have worked hard to provide a similar environment for their children. One of the major differences, however, between the homes of the students we studied and the childhood homes of their parents is that a substantial number of the students' families, reflecting current trends, have gone through divorce. We found that two fifths of the daughters we interviewed lived without a second parent for many years due to divorce or separation, or because their single parent never married.

The Mothers' Voices

When we asked the mothers what factors were most important in their daughters' academic success, about half suggested that the daughters were highly self-motivated, while the other half believed strongly that the family's involvement with the daughter, especially in highlighting the importance of education, was the primary reason. Other frequently cited factors included the support of teachers and involvement in the church.

From listening to the mothers in this book, it is clear that most, if not all, have understood the importance of being vigilant in order to ensure that their daughters stayed on track and received the level of attention and support they deserved from the family and the schools. Many of these mothers have been constantly concerned that someone, or some circumstance, might become an obstacle to their daughters' success primarily because of the daughters' race or gender. To address this concern, these mothers have sent an important message to their daughters: that obstacles and challenges are inevitable, but that individuals have the power to overcome the odds and succeed through hard work, self-discipline, and perseverance.

These mothers tended to be very knowledgeable about their daughters' strengths, the challenges the daughters faced, and the approaches they had taken as parents to address those challenges effectively. These mothers have proven to be experts on their daughters, and they have been constantly aware of the need to help their daughters understand not only the growing opportunities available to African American women, but also serious challenges such as drug abuse, crime, and teenage pregnancy. The mothers pushed their daughters to have high expectations for themselves so that they could respond to the increasing opportunities available to young people who are well prepared academically.

Many of the mothers we studied encountered teachers who were impressed by their daughters' abilities and expected a great deal from them. Some of these teachers were helpful in providing opportunities in laboratories, special programs, and advanced classes. At the same time, over one third of the mothers reported that their daughters had been misplaced in low-level courses, and that they, the mothers, had to advocate on behalf of their children and to insist that they be placed in higher level courses, particularly in math and science.

Even though high-achieving, some of the girls we studied did get into trouble in earlier years, from missing school to being suspended to running away. But the mothers never gave up hope, sometimes seeking help from others and continuing to work hard not to lose their children to negative, at times even dangerous, influences. Many focused on providing their daughters with appropriate information and teaching them how to use problem-solving skills to think through potentially dangerous situations, to recognize choices, and to understand the consequences of those choices. The mothers were willing to go to any length necessary to protect their children. In dealing, for example, with issues and challenges such as self-esteem and physical appearance, premarital sex and pregnancy, and drug and alcohol abuse, mothers stressed the importance of open and honest communication, trust, and healthy relationships with the daughters. In a number of cases, the mothers (and fathers) taught lessons to their daughters by using personal stories involving either themselves or relatives who had problems, for example, with drug or alcohol abuse.

Most of the mothers also point to people outside of the immediate family, including extended family members, teachers, counselors, church members, and friends, who were able to reinforce with their daughters important messages and values. In fact, a number of mothers talked about the significance of the African proverb, "It takes a village to raise a child."

While we were not surprised to find that there were some issues the daughters chose not to tell their mothers about until much later, if at all, we found that, on the whole, the mothers knew their daughters extremely well, especially their strengths and weaknesses and the challenges they faced.

Most important, the mothers worked to counter negative influences coming from outside the home, and they were determined to take a proactive approach in building their daughters' self-esteem and confidence. Mothers of girls who were in predominantly White settings spent a great deal of time helping their daughters to avoid listening to racial stereotyping, to feel good about their appearance while looking different from classmates, and to be confident in their ability to succeed academically.

To varying degrees, the mothers (and fathers) showed pride in their daughters but were concerned about how people, in general, would treat them. These families were (1) constantly working to keep lines of communication open, especially by avoiding quick judgments, (2) using personal experiences and stories to teach lessons about right and wrong, with an emphasis on avoiding the wrong crowds, (3) helping the girls appreciate the significance of being both Black and female in America, (4) constantly working to sensitize the daughters to racism and sexism, and empowering them to avoid being paralyzed when they encountered these negative influences, (5) emphasizing the importance of support from family, church, and community, (6) teaching them to believe in themselves, and (7) setting high expectations.

The Fathers' Voices

We were interested in hearing the fathers' voices in part because so little has been written about the relationship between African American men and their daughters. While the fathers we interviewed come from a variety of educational and economic backgrounds, we found several themes that ran fairly consistently through the interviews with this group. First, and in most cases, the fathers' role was very important, but rarely as critical to the girls' upbringing as the role of the mothers. Second, in interacting with their daughters, some of the fathers focused as much on preparing them for life as on their doing well in school. Third, fathers expressed grave concerns about the potential danger to their daughters of associating with the wrong crowd or being pressured by boys to become sexually active. Fourth, even though many of the fathers in our study had every confidence that their daughters could succeed in math and science and become scientists, physicians, and engineers, they frequently expressed concerns about how their daughters would be treated in the larger world as the girls became adults. It was this last theme that motivated fathers to emphasize to their daughters that they would have to work much harder than others to succeed because the playing field was not always level.

When asked why their daughters had succeeded, most of the fathers attributed success to family support and strong communication. Some of the messages that they communicated to their daughters included (1) avoiding being in the wrong crowd or trusting boys too quickly, which can easily lead to undesirable behavior and related consequences, (2) spending time on academics and constructive work rather than focusing on romantic or dating-related issues too soon, (3) being involved in athletics, band, or other extracurricular activities, which can help the daughters avoid negative situations, (4) realizing the importance of hard work, especially in the light of prejudice and discrimination, and for a few fathers (5) becoming highly educated as a vehicle for helping the entire family move out of difficult situations (e.g., unsafe neighborhoods).

In a number of cases, the fathers spoke of their daughters' mothers as excellent role models who had helped their daughters develop healthy habits and values. Some of the fathers also mentioned the importance of the church community. Many felt too that they were more involved with their daughters than their neighbors were with their respective daughters. The fathers in our study were very impressive in that the overwhelming majority not only knew how their daughters were performing academically in school, but also regularly attended athletic events and other school programs.

Those fathers who were actively involved, like the mothers, reported having to work with the schools on a number of occasions in order to have their daughters placed in advanced placement courses. Also, in those cases where the fathers had a college education, they tended to play the largest role in their daughters' lives, e.g., not only supporting their daughters in athletics but working with them on homework, going with the daughters to physical therapy, or helping them find productive summer employment.

In general, the fathers spent a great deal of time teaching their daughters about men, trying to make them as knowledgeable as possible about relationships with the opposite sex, and preparing them for the world of work. The fathers tended to be very protective of their daughters, frequently talking with them about choices and the consequences involved in dating. In fact, some of the fathers we interviewed were very careful to get to know the boys their daughters dated, in order to help protect them. Also, it was encouraging to encounter a few cases in which the fathers discussed sexuality with their daughters from a male perspective. In some cases, fathers began discussing issues involving sex, drugs, and crime with their daughters at a young age for purposes of prevention. In other cases, they talked with their daughters about these issues as they were reported on in newspapers and on television, thus using the news as an opportunity to teach important lessons.

While we saw many positive examples of the influence and involvement of men in the home, we also learned of the devastating impact of drugs, alcohol, and abusive behavior by some fathers. Clearly, men with substance abuse problems or who are unemployed will be much less likely to be effective parents, and, thus, the question of effective parenting is especially tied to these kinds of important societal issues. Subsequent research on successful relationships between fathers and daughters needs to look at these issues as well as relationships between young African American women and other important male figures, including uncles, ministers, siblings, and teachers.

Many, though not all of the parents we studied—both fathers and mothers—used opportunities to talk with their daughters about what it means to be Black and female, not only in school but in life generally. These parents pointed to other young Black girls who made unwise choices and were forced to assume the responsibilities of parenting at an early age. They also recognized that often their daughters were under more pressure than other high-achieving girls because they were African American. Because of the daughters' rare status as high-achievers, on the one hand they were sometimes given additional onerous responsibilities by the school; on the other hand, at times, the girls were considered unpopular by other Black children. Nevertheless, these parents constantly told their daughters to avoid perceiving themselves as victims, but rather to focus on what they could do to overcome the odds.

The Daughters' Voices

We cannot overemphasize the importance of knowing that the young women in our study represent rarely publicized examples of high achieving young African American women, that they come from diverse socioeconomic backgrounds and family situations, and that their success can clearly be traced in part to effective parenting and specific, sometimes special, actions taken by their families. Such actions range from moving the entire family from one neighborhood to another in order to remove the daughter from a gang to initiating counseling for a daughter when she was experiencing serious emotional problems. All of the young women point to at least one or more adults who have provided special support and nurturing. Significantly, the young women in our study and their parents believe that it is largely because of this kind of support that the girls have developed the self-esteem, good habits, and strong reading and problem-solving skills needed to do well in school.

In our interviews, we asked the daughters questions similar to those we posed to the parents, focusing primarily on why they thought they had succeeded. What is significant is that their responses are generally similar despite the demographic differences among them, and their messages are consistent with what we heard from the parents. The first message is that the daughters placed a great deal of importance on education. They also understood that their parents had very high expectations and were willing to provide the necessary support to ensure that they had every chance to meet those expectations. Many of the daughters expressed appreciation for the hard work of their parents in ensuring the financial stability of the family.

Regarding their maternal and paternal relationships, the daughters consistently responded positively about their relationships with their mothers, though they often reported having experienced some "bumpy" periods. They consistently saw their mothers as being more involved than their fathers in the personal aspects of their development. In the cases of the fathers, the messages were varied. The daughters saw their fathers as being more task-oriented than their mothers, for example, providing transportation, helping with homework, and offering support at their athletic events. While some of the daughters viewed their fathers as being very supportive and actively involved in their lives, others reported that their fathers either were not present or had a negative influence on the family because of drugs, alcohol, or abusive behavior.

From the daughters' perspective, there were a number of specific factors that contributed substantially to their success and reflected their overall feeling that their parents had been a major resource for them in their upbringing. The following themes were identified consistently throughout our interviews.

1. **The Importance of Reading**. A parental focus on reading, including reading to the children at an early age, and the value of everyone's read-

ing in the home were identified. In fact, reading was a much more frequently cited pastime in the home than television-watching.

2. **High Expectations Accompanied by Encouragement.** Almost every daughter in our study reported that her parents expected and encouraged her to do well academically because of their expressed view that education was extremely important. Also, the parents placed much emphasis on praising academic achievement.

3. **Demonstrating Parental Interest.** The parents consistently showed interest in their daughters' homework, often monitoring the time they spent working on it. Even when the daughters were in high school, almost half of the parents continued to place a great deal of emphasis on the importance of homework, and the majority of these young students regularly talked with their parents about their school work.

4. **Parents' Interaction with Teachers.** Three quarters of the mothers and two fifths of the fathers reported making a conscious effort to get to know their daughters' teachers. The parents spent a great deal of time ensuring the placement of their daughters in appropriate programs and courses.

5. **Extracurricular Activities.** From the daughters' perspective, one of the most important roles parents played was encouraging and supporting them in activities outside the classroom, from athletics, band, and multicultural clubs to science clubs and community service. The daughters understood the value of these activities in helping them to develop positive habits and to keep them focused constructively during nonschool hours.

The daughters also identified a variety of other factors that contributed to their academic success. Most mentioned individual teachers, principals, counselors, church members, or coaches who played a major role in their success. Most important, the majority of students were able to point to at least one teacher or counselor, if not more, who believed in them and expected the most from them in terms of their academic performance. In many cases, for example, teachers (both Black and White) insisted that students enroll in gifted and talented programs. (Several of the daughters, however, cited instances of racism or sexism in the classroom, and some seemed to feel that teachers had higher expectations of Asian and White students.) Many students alluded to advice from some of these influential adults regarding placement in special math and science programs and to connections with African American role models in science, engineering, and medicine. In addition, these influential adults emphasized the need for making sure that girls have early positive experiences in math and science and opportunities for hands-on science experiences, for example, in science museums and with educational toys such as chemistry sets. They also suggested that parents seek information about math/science enrichment opportunities for their children. Finally, they stressed the importance of parents (1) having their children see them reading, (2) playing educational games with their daughters, (3) setting clear expectations with consequences, (4) learning to listen in a nonjudgmental way, and (5) exposing the girls to a variety of career options in science.

The daughters pointed to the importance of support from student peers who shared similar academic values and aspirations, and it was this support which often helped to counter the teasing and cruelty from students who were not as academically interested or capable. They pointed also to the close monitoring of their behavior by parents, especially mothers, who emphasized strong limits and discipline. As the girls grew up, they knew that their mothers were especially watchful and would consistently administer appropriate punishment when their behavior exceeded established boundaries. The daughters' appreciation for the sacrifices their parents made also was an important factor. Particularly moving were the stories of those young women who were motivated to succeed academically because of the dire circumstances of their families' poverty and the hard work of their parents, particularly single mothers. In fact, some of these young women understood that the only way out of such circumstances was to succeed in school. In addition, a number of the young women focused on the importance of spirituality and religion in helping them to cope with a variety of difficult situations, from having feelings of low self-esteem to resisting the temptations of getting caught up in the drug culture. Many were especially appreciative of the role of the church in applauding their high academic achievement. Finally, for some of the young women in our study, "having a dream" was an important reason cited for their success.

Dating, Discipline, Church Attendance, Intellectual Development

From our conversations with daughters and parents, we found especially interesting some of the perspectives shared by parents and daughters regarding the experiences the families had in common outside the classroom. It might be surprising to some readers, for example, that some of the families did not allow their daughters to do any dating through high school, and that others were very careful to get to know the boys chosen by their daughters and to monitor their activities as closely as possible. These parents were clearly strict and demanding on the one hand, yet communicative and loving on the other. The daughters indicated that when they looked back on their teenage years from their perspective as young women, they could understand why their parents acted as they did. Interestingly, the daughters' and parents' stories and their interpretations of the past were very similar, leading us to have even more confidence in the accuracy of their reports.

With regard to discipline, in the early years, parents used a variety of methods, including physical punishment in some cases, particularly before the children were old enough to reason. But as the daughters became older, most parents tended to focus on helping them understand the consequences of their actions, usually by grounding them or by taking away for a period of time something that was valuable to the girls. The parents noted, however, that in carrying out the discipline, being consistent and following through with the consequences required considerable time, attention, and energy on their part. Although it is much easier to forget to follow through or to make light of inappropriate behavior, it is important that children see that parents mean what they say, and that the children understand that there are undesirable consequences to inappropriate behavior. What seems most important is for parents not to act simply out of anger, but rather to take time to think through the disciplinary actions that will teach children appropriate lessons. The challenge parents face is to balance discipline, on the one hand, with efforts to instill self-esteem and an earnest desire to be smart, on the other. Many of the daughters in our study came to appreciate the efforts of their parents in this regard.

Regarding the daughters' intellectual development and interest in science, the parents agreed that the first years of the girls' lives were critical, and these parents spent a great deal of time reading to them and focusing on basic skills involving numbers, letters, shapes, and colors. These parents also purchased such educational aids as junior chemistry sets, doctors' kits, tinker toys, and computer games in mathematics, science, and reading. Most important, these parents spent time playing educational games with their children.

Finally, the vast majority of the families and daughters were churchgoers and/or spiritual, and both the parents and daughters viewed their experiences in this regard as an important part of the daughters' upbringing. For example, in some churches, the youth were given opportunities to be active in the service, including speaking, reading scripture, reading announcements, participating in the choir, and helping with younger children. At other churches, the students received special recognition for high academic achievement, including having their names read and receiving applause for making the honor roll. Most important, the young people received a variety of positive messages that reinforced the importance of doing well in school, contributing constructively through church activities, and serving as positive role models for other young people. Both parents and daughters agreed that the church provided excellent examples of educated African Americans who could also talk with the daughters about some of life's important lessons. They also agreed that participating in Sunday school and church helped to instill those values that helped create the foundation for making the best choices later in life.

The Meyerhoff Scholars Program: The College Years

Throughout the book, we refer to the Meyerhoff Scholars Program, one of the leading programs in the nation designed to increase the number of minorities, especially African Americans, who succeed academically in science and engineering in preparation for research careers in these fields. One of the challenges that some of the young women in the program faced was that even when they had done well in math and science at the elementary and secondary levels, they encountered difficulty in these disciplines in college. Sometimes, the problems stemmed from inadequate academic preparation, weak study habits, not being accustomed to stiff competition, and experiencing difficulty adjusting to being away from home. We found that the Meyerhoff Program was instrumental in strengthening the skills and building the confidence of these young women.

Early on, the Meyerhoff students begin working in research laboratories with faculty on campus and with other scientists in laboratories throughout the nation and even internationally. Some start working in labs on campus year-round beginning in their sophomore year while taking classes. These early research experiences give them superb opportunities to understand the demands, frustrations, and exhilaration of research, including, most important, learning the value of curiosity, asking good questions, and perseverance in seeking answers. These experiences also help the student become comfortable in the laboratory, which is significant because she often is the only woman or Black, or one of only a few, in these settings. They learn how to work in teams with people different from themselves, and they develop confidence in their ability to contribute substantively. In fact, many become published authors in refereed science journals while they are undergraduates.[2] These experiences also help them make decisions about their post-graduate education and subsequent careers. Indeed, the overwhelming majority have chosen to pursue graduate and professional education in the sciences, medicine, and engineering.[3]

In addition, the young women have received valuable insights from graduates of the program, many of whom are now in doctoral and medical programs throughout the nation. This is consistent with one of the distinguishing characteristics of the program—that each cohort, or group of Meyerhoff Scholars, is expected to serve as big sisters (and big brothers) to younger Meyerhoff Scholars. These relationships have been invaluable, especially during times of trouble and crisis for the students. Part of the ethos of the program is based on the adage that "much is required of those to whom much is given." These young women are taught to feel responsible for one another, for younger Meyerhoff students, and for young schoolgirls whom they tutor and mentor throughout the year. This sense of responsibility to serve and set an example for others often serves as an additional motivation to excel.

It is very important that the Meyerhoff Program also values the ongoing emotional support and advice that parents give their daughters, even during their college years. In fact, parents provide useful information about the daughters to program staff (who frequently serve as surrogate parents), and these parents help each other in addressing problems as the need arises. We have found that even after their daughters graduate, these parents continue to be closely involved in their daughters' lives and decisions. Perhaps one of the critical factors leading to the success of these young women is their willingness to accept advice, a quality that families encouraged throughout the daughters' upbringing.

These young women know that they will be among the small number of African American female research scientists, physicians, and engineers in the nation. Their parents and the Meyerhoff Program are preparing them to accept these roles with both confidence and humility, with a special commitment to high achievement, solving problems, and service to others.

Implications

We have learned a great deal from the voices of these successful young women, their parents, and other adults who have been influential in the students' lives about effective strategies for working with African American children. Based on these voices, we are able to offer a number of suggestions to parents, policy-makers, educators, and communities.

When standardized test scores show that children cannot read or compute at grade level, most people immediately point fingers at the teachers, schools, or families. Few people look carefully enough at the situation to understand that in many integrated settings, minority children in a class may not be achieving while other children are scoring at grade level and above in the same class with the same teacher. It would be simplistic to attribute this discrepancy to racism or discrimination. The fact is that in many urban settings, most of the teachers and children are minorities, and large numbers, if not the majority of these children, are reading below grade level. It is certainly appropriate for school systems to focus increasing attention on providing teachers with additional support and training in working with children from diverse racial and economic backgrounds. Nonetheless, it is equally important to focus increased attention on ways of connecting parents to the school for the purpose of emphasizing the significant role families play in preparing children to learn and, in this case, to achieve in math and science. We agree with Willie Pearson that, "if Black participation and performance in science is to improve significantly, Black parents . . . will have to play a more active role in any such efforts. These parents must be made more aware of the economic opportunities available in scientific and technical fields."[4] In the healthiest of communities, schools have been effective largely because of their ability to sustain ongoing communication between parents and teachers. Parents of girls and young women need opportunities to interact with teachers in order to provide them with additional knowledge about their daughters and to receive feedback from teachers about their daughters' performance and behavior in the school.

To be effective, schools also must work on being as welcoming as possible, understanding that some parents can feel intimidated in those settings by teachers and educators. This is especially the case for parents who, themselves, had bad experiences in the past, either as students or as adults. Sometimes, parents who are already active in the school can be asked to serve as liaisons to other parents who have been reluctant to become involved. In many cases, while parents care deeply about their children, they do not understand the benefits of actively participating in the schools. Unfortunately, many parents become involved only when a crisis occurs. Parents who have been involved with the schools and have had positive experiences tend to be more trusting of teachers and administrators. Both teachers and parents can be more effective with the child when she receives consistent messages from these two sets of important adults in her life. Many school officials and teachers become frustrated after attempting to engage parents who do not respond. Our advice to school systems is to continue focusing on the practices that have proven most effective in reaching out to families, including serving meals, providing babysitting services, and offering prizes or other incentives for active participation by parents. Some of these strategies may seem somewhat controversial; however, many of today's parents simply do not recognize or fully appreciate how important their involvement in the schools is to their children's academic success.

What the schools can do is to ensure that teachers, counselors, and others work together to understand the special challenges that African American girls and young women face in school—from sometimes having onerous responsibilities at home (e.g., helping other siblings and doing chores) to being pressured by peers and influenced by popular culture to act in ways that make academic achievement especially difficult. We strongly suggest that schools develop programs for these young women and others that promote academic success by providing special support services similar to those in the Meyerhoff Program, and that provide special incentives, possibly similar to those given student athletes (special apparel, opportunities to be in the spotlight, special recognition, opportunities to travel). Elements of the Meyerhoff Program that might be used include (1) creating an environment that provides rewards for academic achievement, (2) supporting young women in forming groups to discuss in general the significance of being a girl or woman of color, and to talk specifically about their academic performance, (3) providing young girls with role models who are successful African American women, including college students, and other mentors who are women with an interest in helping, (4) encouraging these students to create and use study groups in those classes that are most challenging, and (5) encouraging parents of these students to engage in ongoing discussions about common challenges and effective strategies. This last point is important because parents also need opportunities to talk with other parents. Our interviews with parents lasted much longer than we might have expected because they were hungry for opportunities to reflect on their experiences and to learn from others because many had younger children whom they were still rearing. Schools, churches, and community associations should be considered as possible settings for discussions among parents and others interested in helping the girls and young women. It is especially helpful for parents of older students, both those who have been successful and those who have not, to talk to parents of younger students about their experiences, and even to form mentoring relationships.

While all of the young women we studied were academically successful, many of them experienced difficulty in school at some point relating to teachers' expectations. Many of the parents talked about having to serve as advocates for their daughters when, for example, they were placed in low-level classes. We strongly suggest that schools form focus groups to learn about the perceptions of African American parents regarding teachers' treatment of their daughters. Only through these discussions can schools and parents build the kind of trust that will lead to a better understanding of the decisions that teachers and schools make about children. It is interesting, however, that many of the students who took advanced placement and gifted-and-talented courses referred to one or more teachers or counselors who believed in them and insisted that they take the most rigorous courses in order to fulfill their potential. Schools should look carefully at the role of teachers and counselors in advising students about middle-school programs because it is these courses that will determine the level of rigor of the students' high-school programs.

We have already touched on the important role that is attributed to the church and spirituality by the parents and the daughters. The challenge is to encourage more African American families to consider participating in faith-based or other activities that can reinforce appropriate values and provide children with opportunities to interact with other successful adults. This strategy is especially important in the light of the general decline, for example, in church attendance.[5]

We also agree with Pearson that, "within the Black community, more can be done to utilize retired persons with training in mathematics and science. . . . Retirees could supplement the school system and develop intervention

programs based on churches, recreation centers, and housing projects. . . .
[Also,] predominantly Black fraternities, societies, and professional organizations can contribute substantially to scholarships and to intervention programs as volunteers."[6]

Finally, we strongly support the major initiatives of agencies such as the
National Science Foundation, the National Institutes of Health, and NASA,
as well as those of higher education institutions across the country focusing
on K-16 projects that connect universities and schools in working with
teachers and children to improve performance in math and science. To
increase the number of African American children who are excited about
math and science and succeed in these areas, we will need to continue placing increased emphasis on math-and-science education at the K-8 level.
Girls need to engage in a variety of hands-on science and math activities that
show connections to real life and that teach them to think critically and reinforce the joys of solving problems.

Advice for Fathers and Mothers

From our discussions with daughters and parents, we have identified several
key themes to guide parents in raising their daughters, including six components, or effective strategies, of parenting that the mothers and fathers in our
study used to support their daughters' intellectual development and to help
them move successfully, and relatively smoothly, into womanhood.

1. **Child-focused love** involves self-sacrifice and active parental involvement in the daughter's life and is reflected by loving, encouraging,
   instilling self-confidence and self-respect, challenging, and supporting
   the daughter. It also involves accepting the fact that the child may fail at
   times, yet resiliently recover and learn from occasional failure. It means
   paying particularly close attention to the daughter's academic and personal development, including interacting with teachers, attending parents' nights, serving as an advocate when necessary, attending children's
   performances or sports activities, and being willing to be constructively
   critical when appropriate. It also means constantly monitoring the
   daughter's general state of being.
2. **Continually setting high expectations** for a child is essential, particularly regarding academic achievement, and when a daughter falls short,
   parents should follow up by seeking explanations from her and commu-

nicating with the schools. It is important, too, to emphasize to daughters that they may have to work much harder than others in order to excel simply because the world is not always fair.

3. **Open and honest communication** is perhaps the most important parenting strategy. It is essential for parents to communicate with their children in every way possible and to listen carefully to each daughter and always to believe she can succeed. Through their words and actions, parents should convey to their daughters a "can do" attitude about excelling in education and in the daughter's future careers. Parents should work also to keep lines of communication open in sensitive areas. Regarding sexuality, for example, parents are encouraged to talk openly with their daughters about such issues as pregnancy and disease prevention, and they should stress the importance of exercising appropriate responsibility.

4. **Strict limit-setting** involves establishing rules and holding the child accountable for focusing on her school work, being respectful, and acting honestly. When the child deviates, it is important that consequences be imposed swiftly and reasonably. As the daughter moves into young womanhood, it is wise to be very careful in developing a dating policy with relatively strict conditions, for example, insisting on meeting the young man before the date, enforcing curfews, personally supervising dates in the home, and cautioning daughters to avoid possibly harmful situations that could lead to date-rape or sexual assault.

5. **Drawing upon community resources** is important because parenting cannot effectively be done in isolation. Parents should avail themselves and their daughters of the influence of libraries, museums, and other community institutions and organizations that enrich a child's life. Based on our observations, parents also would be well advised to take responsibility for involving the entire family in church or faith-based activities, and when problems arise, soliciting advice and help from other churchgoers in the parenting process. Parents should pursue other community resources when they face serious challenges involving their daughters. When, for example, a daughter's behavior becomes particularly difficult to handle, or when a daughter is experiencing depression, excessive anxiety, or other psychological problems, parents should consider seeking appropriate mental health services, recognizing that many young people benefit from this type of intervention.

6. Parents should take time regularly to *expose their daughters to African*

American history and culture, including activities that promote cultural awareness and pride, and *engage in conversations about the importance and challenges of being a woman and African American in American society*. Parents should consider talking with their daughters about the state of American society, in general, and about issues involving race and gender, in particular. Also, it is helpful when parents provide personal perspectives on the role and importance of working hard and of having high self-esteem. Most important, parents should strive to be sure that their daughters feel comfortable in coming to them for support when challenges arise in their lives.

In addition to the six parenting components discussed above, we also encourage parents to be very mindful of the need to *balance career and parenting responsibilities*. This has become especially important given our increasingly fast-paced culture. We recommend spending as much time together as a family as possible. Also, effective parenting of girls or young women when they are physically sick sometimes involves making adjustments in work schedules or jobs in order to be able to provide the daughters with the appropriate level of support. At times, when it may be impossible to adjust the work schedule, parents may need to seek support from relatives or friends.

Advice for Young Women

From observing the lives of the successful young African American women in our study, we learned a great deal about what Black girls must do as they develop and grow in order to become high-achieving young women. Above all, they must develop as strong individuals, both intellectually and in terms of having a healthy sense of self. Equally important, they must recognize the value of, and become skillful at, interacting with a variety of others who can be supportive, even instrumental in their success.

Regarding individual growth, an African American girl or young woman must come to appreciate her strengths and her potential to succeed. She must have, or be encouraged to have, a dream or vision of what she wants to become, seeing herself, for example, in the role of scientist, physician, or engineer. She also needs to be passionate about pursuing her vision, and to have a sense of control over her destiny. She must recognize the importance of hard work and persistence in developing the intellectual and academic skills needed to achieve her vision, and she must not be willing to settle for being less than the best. She must learn, too, to feel comfortable being the only African American and/or the only woman in her classroom or laboratory.

Regarding interactions with others, the young women in our book demonstrated the importance of being willing to ask for advice and seek help, of having a genuine interest in associating with others, of wanting to seek out role models and mentors, and of learning how to work in teams or study groups to solve problems. They also demonstrated the value of having strong relations with family members, often gaining support by talking with parents and staying in contact with other family members. Similarly, they showed that strong relations with others in the community are important. Most of the young women discovered and developed important personal qualities by working with children or others who were less fortunate than they were. Finally, they taught us about the importance of young women determining the nature of their relationships with other people, whether those relationships involve friendship, dating or socializing, or studying. Young women should be mindful about the consequences of their interactions with others, including their physical and emotional protection.

The Task Ahead

Clearly, the amount of research on African American girls has been very limited. It is encouraging to see that the research agenda of the American Psychological Association includes important proposed work on adolescent girls of color. It also is important to remember that this group is very diverse. When focusing on African Americans, in particular, the fact is that these girls and young women come from a variety of socioeconomic backgrounds and are raised in many different settings in terms of geographic location and the number of adults in the home. Regardless of background, however, they share the status of being in a world that for a variety of reasons would set low expectations for them and provide them with limited opportunities. They are caught between their geographic and ethnic communities, which may suggest one set of behaviors for survival, and the school community, which sometimes requires a different set of behaviors to ensure success.

The young women in this book, with the help of families, have managed to survive successfully in their communities and to excel in their schools. Their parents have taught them that regardless of the odds, they can achieve their goals through hard work, confidence, and belief in self. In fact, these parents are constantly telling their daughters how smart they are and that education makes the difference between success and failure. Just as was the case in the past, families of African American girls and young women in this new century will need to be strong advocates for their children, standing up for them and holding them accountable. They must be proactive, and in the words of one community member interviewed, *"remain as fanatical a parent as possible until they are twenty-one."* Parents of successful children also can be very helpful as role models for other parents by encouraging them to become more involved in the schools and to spend more time with their children, and by telling their stories of what it means to raise a talented young African American woman. These parents have praised, pushed, and cajoled their daughters to be the best, and they have prepared them to be successful professionals in science and engineering. Even more important, however, these young women will serve as role models for thousands of other young girls, thereby increasing the chances that they, too, can overcome the odds.

Overview of the Study Procedure

Interview Samples

Letters were sent to the parents of current African American female Meyer-hoff students in good standing, along with parents of program graduates, inviting them to group interviews on the UMBC campus. Parents were then contacted by telephone by the African American male associate director of the program and an African American female graduate student to schedule the group interviews. Parents who were unable to attend any of the group sessions were scheduled for individual sessions either in person or by telephone. The parents were informed that the interviews would form the basis of a book on parenting African American young women, and would be videotaped and audiotaped, but that individuals would not be identified in publications. After the initial mailing, additional single, non-college-educated parents were further recruited via telephone, so as to have a large enough sample to gain insight into this important subgroup.

In 1998 and 1999 a total of forty-six mothers were interviewed by the African American female director of the Meyerhoff Scholars Program (eight groups) and the African American female coauthor (seventeen individual interviews). The African American male associate director of the program interviewed twenty-seven fathers (eight groups and five individual interviews). Prior to the start of each group and in-person individual interview, parents completed a brief questionnaire. Parents who were interviewed by phone returned their questionnaires by mail.

Daughters who were currently enrolled in the Meyerhoff Program, as well as program graduates from one-parent and non-college-educated house-holds, were invited to take part in the research by the associate director of the Meyerhoff Program and an African American female graduate student. In 1998 and 1999, sixty-six individual interviews were conducted, by phone and in person, by the African American female coauthor and the aforemen-tioned graduate student. Prior to the start of each in-person individual interview, daughters completed a brief questionnaire. The currently enrolled students completed a longer questionnaire at a Meyerhoff meeting in winter 1999. Program graduates who were unable to personally attend individual sessions were interviewed by phone and returned both questionnaires by mail.

In addition, questionnaires focused on factors leading to success in school were administered to Meyerhoff students attending the required six-week, pre-college summer bridge programs on the UMBC campus in the summers of 1991–99.

Trustworthiness of Data

Several steps were taken to enhance the credibility and trustworthiness of the qualitative data. The four interviewers participated in a training session facilitated by a faculty member with expertise in qualitative research. The selection of Meyerhoff Program staff to conduct the group parenting interviews ensured, in most cases, that the fathers and mothers interviewed had a positive, trusting relationship with the interviewer. The program has been extremely effective in empowering Black women to succeed in college and to go on to graduate or professional school, and many parents in particular seemed to welcome the opportunity to "give back" to the program leaders.

The decisions to interview multiple family members whenever possible and to use both qualitative and quantitative methods ensured multiple data sources and formats. This approach helped us to establish and support the veracity of our findings. Finally, a multiracial research team worked on the development of the interview and questionnaire measures, and the quantitative and qualitative data analysis.

Interview Analysis

All parenting and school experience interviews were transcribed, resulting in over 1000 single-spaced pages. Analysis proceeded on two related fronts. A trained, multiracial coding team of graduate and undergraduate students developed a coding system under the direction of two of the coauthors and a consulting faculty member. The coding system developed focused on the presence or absence of various factors which emerged from the thematic analysis as contributing to academic achievement (see Hrabowski, Maton, and Greif, 1998). The transcripts were reviewed and coded for major themes, until agreement was reached by teams of two coders. (Initially, all five members of the coding team reached consensus in the coding categories for ten transcripts, prior to breaking up into groups of two). Summary sheets with descriptive background information were also completed.

APPENDIX B

Minority Student Development Programs

The National Science Foundation (NSF)

The NSF is a major funding agency for science and mathematics education in the United States. The NSF also coordinates programs promoting science, math, engineering, and technology (SMET) with other federal and state agencies. These programs focus on all levels of education, from preschool to graduate school and beyond. Many of the science and math programs the daughters in this book participated in are, at least partially, funded by the NSF. The National Science Foundation annually documents the number of science and mathematics degrees awarded to minority students as part of their goal of increasing the number of minorities in science and mathematics.

NSF student development programs are grouped into three areas of focus: pre-college, undergraduate, and graduate.

Pre-college opportunities, aimed at elementary-and secondary school students are grouped under the Urban Systemic Program (USP). The two programs supported under this initiative are the Comprehensive Regional Centers for Minorities (CRCM) and the Partnerships for Minority Student Achievement (PMSA). These programs aim to forge alliances between schools, institutions of higher education, community organizations, and private industry both to foster minority student interest in science, math, and technology and to increase minority performance in these fields.

Undergraduate programs provide outreach assistance and scholarships to increase the number of degrees awarded to minorities in science, math, and technology. The two programs supported under this initiative are the Louis Stokes Alliances for Minority Participation Program (LSAMP) and the Historically Black Colleges and Universities (HBCU) Initiative. The LSAMP program is designed to develop the comprehensive strategies necessary to strengthen the preparation and increase the number of minority students whom successfully complete baccalaureates in SMET fields. The

HBCU Initiative seeks to address historical under-representation of minorities in baccalaureate and doctoral degree ranks in science, engineering, and mathematics.

At the graduate-school level, the National Science Foundation focuses on supporting minority researchers through the Centers of Research Excellence in Science and Technology (CREST) and the Alliances for Graduate Education and the Professoriate (AGEP). These programs aim to expand a diverse student presence in SMET disciplines by upgrading the capabilities of the most research-productive minority-servings institutions, implementing innovative models for recruiting, mentoring, and retaining minority students, and developing strategies for identifying and supporting under-represented minorities who want to pursue academic careers.

To locate the programs in your area contact:

The Division for Human Resource Development
National Science Foundation
Room 815
4201 Wilson Boulevard
Arlington, VA 22230
(703) 292-8640

The National Science foundation also awards fellowships in math, science, and engineering at both the graduate and undergraduate levels. In addition, they provide a listing of research opportunities for minority students. A list of publications and information about NSF programs can be found at www.nsf.gov and/or www.nsf.gov/cgi-bin/getpub?nsf0065.

The National Institutes of Health (NIH)

NIH is the principal biomedical research agency of the U.S. Department of Health and Human Services. The National Institute of General Medical Sciences (NIGMS) is the component of NIH that primarily supports basic biomedical research that is not targeted to specific diseases or disorders. NIGMS has four divisions that support research and research training in basic biomedical science fields. The Division of Minority Opportunities in Research (MORE) is particularly designed to increase the number of minority biomedical scientists. Support is available at the undergraduate, graduate, postdoctoral, and faculty levels, as well as for education and research infrastructure improvements.

The MORE Division has three components: Minority Access to Research Careers (MARC), Minority Biomedical Research Support (MBRS) Branch, and Special Initiatives.

The MARC Branch offers special research training support to four-year colleges, universities, and health professional schools with substantial enrollments of minority students. The branch's goals are to increase the number and competitiveness of underrepresented minorities engaged in biomedical research by strengthening the science curricula at minority-serving institutions and increasing the research training opportunities for students and faculty at these institutions. There are several student-based components of the MARC programs including the Undergraduate Student Training in Academic Research (U*STAR) experience, the Post-Baccalaureate Research Education Program (PREP), predoctoral fellowships, and ancillary training activities grants that provide support for meetings, conferences, technical workshops, and any other training activities that are harmonious with the overall objective of the MARC Branch.

The objective of the MBRS Branch is to increase the number of researchers who are members of minority groups that are underrepresented in the biomedical sciences. The MBRS Branch awards grants to two or four year colleges, universities, and health professional schools with substantial enrollments of minorities. These grants support research by faculty members, strengthen the institutions' biomedical research capabilities, and provide opportunities for students to work as part of a research team. MBRS program components include the Support of Continuous Research Excellence (SCORE) Program, the Research Initiative for Scientific Enhancement (RISE) Program, and the Initiative for Minority Student Development (IMSD) Program.

The Special Initiatives division develops and launches new research, research training programs and other initiatives for minority scientists. These include the Bridges to the Future Programs (Bridges to the Baccalaureate Degree and Bridges to the Doctoral Degree), which are co-sponsored by the Office of Research on Minority Health (another component of the NIH). The division is also responsible for organizing meetings and other activities that build networks among individual and educational institutions to promote minority participation in sponsored research.

A list of publications and information about NIH programs can be found at www.nih.gov and/or www.nigms.nih.gov.

The National Aeronautics and Space Administration (NASA)

NASA is committed to spreading knowledge of aeronautics and space research. NASA has two programs committed to providing minority students with research and educational opportunities. NASA's Office of Equal Opportunity Programs established the Minority University Research and Education Division (MURED) in 1990 to increase the Agency's responsiveness to Federal mandates related to Historically Black Colleges and Universities (HBCUs) and Other Minority Universities (OMUs). The MURED is responsible for formulating and executing the agency's Minority University Research and Education Program (MUREP) budget and developing agency wide policies, procedures and guidelines that enhance the involvement of HBCUs and OMUs in the agency's mission. Secondly, the National Council for Minorities in Engineers (NACME) has led the national effort to increase the representation of successful African American, Latinos, and American Indians in engineering. NACME advances its mission through partnership with industry, government, and the education community. Additional information about NASA's programs can be found at www.nasa.gov.

NOTES

Preface

1 Hrabowski, Maton, and Greif 1998.
2 American Psychological Association 1999.
3 Bok and Bowen 1998.

Chapter 1: Successful African American Young Women and Their Families

1 The National Center for Health Statistics reported in October 1999 that teenage birth and pregnancy rates for girls ages 15–19 declined approximately 18 percent nationwide from 1991 to 1998.
2 Ventura, Mathews, and Curtin 1998. National Vital Statistics Reports, 47, p. 12. In 1997, there were 342,029 births to White women, 15–19 years old, and 130,401 births to Black women, 15–19 years old. The birth rates that year for White and Black women in this age group were 46.8 per 1000 girls and 89.5 per 1000 girls, respectively. For Black teenagers, 15–19 years old, the birth rates have dropped sharply from 115.5 per 1,000 in 1991 to 89.5 in 1997.
3 Pipher 1994, p. 44.
4 Kusimo 1997, pp. 7–15.
5 Among the several books Brumberg discusses, the following are especially pertinent to this study: Niobe Way, *Everyday Courage: The Lives and Stories of Urban Teenagers* (New York, 1998); *Souls Looking Back: Life Stories of Growing Up Black*, ed. by Andrew Garrod, Janie Victoria Ward, Tracy Robinson, and Robert Kilkenny (New York, 1999); and Pamela Haag, *Voices of a Generation: Teenage Girls Report About Their Lives Today* (New York, 2000).
6 American Psychological Association 1999, pp. 2–3.
7 Ibid., p. 10.
8 Majors, Billson, and Mancini 1992.
9 Steinberg, Dornbusch, and Brown 1992.
10 Carroll 1997, p. 94.
11 Chenoweth 1998, p. 24.
12 College Board 1999.
13 Statistical Abstract of the U.S. 1999, table no. 304: Enrollment status, by race, Hispanic origin, and sex: 1975 and 1997.
14 U.S. Department of Education, National Center for Education Statistics, [1999]. Also see U.S. Department of Education, National Center for Education Statistics, [2000], Table 2a, and U.S. Department of Education, National Center for Education Statistics, 2000.
15 National Science Foundation 2000.
16 U.S. Department of Education, National Center for Education Statistics, [2000], Selected degree conferred by Title IV eligible, degree granting institutions, by race/ethnicity, field of study, and gender: 50 states and District of Columbia, 1996–97.

17 Maton, Hrabowski, and Schmitt 2000.
18 Miller 1995, p. 159.
19 College Board 1999, p. 9.
20 Ibid. Reaching the top: A report of the national task force on minority high achieve-
    ment, p. 9.
21 McWhorter 2000.
22 Ibid., p. 2.
23 Hrabowski, Maton, and Greif 1998.
24 Taylor, Gilligan, Sullivan 1995, pp. 78–79.
25 Ibid., pp. 43–44.
26 Ibid., p. 74.
27 Fordham 1996, p. 115.
28 Ibid., p. 330.
29 American Association of University Women (hereafter AAUW) 1999, p. 6.
30 Haag 1999, p. 69.
31 Cited in Phillips 1998, p. 21.
32 Ibid., p. 20.
33 Gibbs 1996, in Leadbeater and Way 1996, p. 321. These data reflect some of the find-
    ings or a study of a multiethnic sample of urban adolescent and early teenage females,
    ages 12–16.
34 Ibid., p. 316.
35 Cited in Phillips 1998, p. 26. Smoking rates for African American teenage girls (12.2
    percent) are substantially lower than those for White and Hispanic teenage girls—40
    percent and 33 percent respectively.
36 Ibid., p. 24.
37 Ibid., p. 8.
38 Grantham and Ford 1998, par. 35–36.
39 Ibid., par. 37.
40 Phillips 1998, p. 33.
41 AAUW 1992, p. 66.
42 Phillips 1998, p. 36.
43 Weiler 1999, par. 3.
44 Ibid., par. 15.
45 Ibid., par. 19.
46 Ibid., par. 22.
47 Ibid., par. 25.
48 U. S. Department of Education, Office for Civil Rights 1997, p. 1.
49 Ibid.
50 Ibid.
51 AAUW 1992, p. 81.
52 Ibid.
53 Phillips 1998, p. 68.
54 Ibid.
55 AAUW 1992, p. 82.
56 Phillips 1998, p. 68.
57 Weinstein et al. 1991.
58 Lips 1989, p. 204.
59 AAUW 1992, pp. 118–19.

60 Callahan and Reis 1996, p. 179.
61 Ibid., p. 183.
62 Grantham and Ford 1998, par. 5.
63 AAUW 1992, p. 122.
64 Ibid., p. 123.
65 Callahan and Reis 1996, p. 184.
66 Malcom et al. 1998.
67 Betz 1997, pp. 108–9.
68 AAUW 1992, p. 59.
69 Phillips 1998, p. 68.
70 Educational Testing Service 1995.
71 National Research Council 1995.
72 U.S. Department of Labor 1997, par. 2.
73 Billingsley 1992, p.17.
74 Phillips 1998, p. 11.
75 Lips 1989, p. 199.
76 Taylor, Gilligan, Sullivan 1995, pp. 43–44, 79.
77 Phillips 1998, p. 11.
78 Reid 1985, pp. 204, 206–7.
79 Ibid., pp. 207–8.
80 Lips 1989, p. 207.
81 Ibid.
82 Reid 1985, p. 208.
83 Additional information regarding methodology and data analysis is contained in Appendix A.
84 U.S. Bureau of the Census 1998.
85 Kusimo 1997, p. 8.
86 Ibid., p. 14.

Chapter 2: Mothers of Academically Successful Daughters

1 Boyd-Franklin 1989 and Peters 1997 are among a number of authorities on African American families who make this point.
2 Bennett 1988.
3 Ibid., p. 222.
4 Bennett 1988.
5 Sterling 1997, p. xvii.
6 Lerner 1992, p. xxii; Reid-Merritt 1996 makes a similar point.
7 Lerner 1992, p. xxiii.
8 Collins 1991, p. 118.
9 U.S. Bureau of the Census 2000.
10 U.S. Bureau of the Census 1995.
11 Also potentially affecting African American male employability is the "invisibility syndrome" (see Franklin and Boyd-Franklin 2000).
12 U.S. Bureau of the Census 1999, Table 2: Selected economic characteristics of people and families, by sex and race: March 1998.
13 U.S. Bureau of the Census 1998.

14 U.S. Bureau of the Census 1999, Table 1: Selected social characteristics of the population, by sex, region, and race.

15 The issue of a young Black woman coming to respect the domestic work of her mother as part of her own growth process is discussed by Moore 2000.

16 See Jencks and Philips 1998.

17 Mothers were asked to indicate on a five-point scale to what degree various statements were accurate, with "not at all accurate," (score of 1) at one extreme, "completely accurate," (score of 5) on the other extreme and "somewhat accurate" (score of 3) in the middle. Scores of 4 and 5 were grouped together indicating the statement was accurate to a high degree.

18 The mothers were offered a scale with "great emphasis," "some emphasis," and "little emphasis" as possible responses.

19 The mothers were given a series of statements on the questionnaire and were asked to respond using a five-point scale with "no worry at all" on one extreme, "a great deal of worry" on the other, and "some worry" as the mid-point.

20 Peters 1997, p. 177.

21 Ibid., p. 179. Davis et al. (2001) found successful African American high school females were positively influenced by contextual factors, including family structure, religion, and the neighborhood. See also Furstenburg (2001) for another view of the impact of the neighborhood on child well-being and Marshall et al. (2001) for the impact of neighbors, friends, and family on parental effectiveness.

Chapter 3: Fathers of Academically Successful Daughters

1 Collison 1999.

2 U.S. Bureau of the Census 1998.

3 Hill 1997.

4 Allen and Connor 1997, p. 55.

5 Ibid., 56.

6 Ibid.

7 Medical schools have also opened up. Minority enrollment increased in medical schools by 43 percent between 1986 and 1994 before declining slightly in the next two years, particularly at public institutions (Carlisle, Gardner, and Liu 1998).

8 Billingsley 1992, p. 180.

9 Williams 1998, p. 79.

10 Rasheed and Rasheed 1999, in writing about therapy with African American fathers, encourage them to co-create with their children a narrative that is positive in nature and protects the relationship from the intrusion of destructive outside influences. These influences often have depicted the father negatively. Communication with children can help to combat this (p. 94).

11 Fathers were asked to indicate on a five-point scale to what extent various statements were true, with "not at all accurate" (score of 1) at one extreme, "completely accurate" (score of 5) on the other extreme, and "somewhat accurate" (score of 3) in the middle. Scores of 4 and 5 were combined, indicating a high degree of accuracy, for various items.

12 A five-point scale was used where responses ranged from "no worry at all" at one extreme to "a great deal of worry" on the other extreme, with "some worry" as a midpoint.

13 Pleck 1997, p. 90.

Chapter 4: A Diversity of Family Contexts

1   See, for example, Leadbeater and Way 1996. Furthermore, most of the research has focused on lower-income Black youths, with very little research focused on working-class or middle-class Black youth.

2   See, e.g., Johnson, Roberts, and Worell 1999. More generally, many researchers in recent years have argued for a strengths-based rather than a deficits-based approach to research on Black families and youth (e.g., Arnold 1995; Hill 1999; Hurd, Moore and Rogers 1995; Logan 1996; McAdoo 1997; Taylor, Jackson, and Chatters, 1997; Yoshikawa and Seidman 2000).

3   See, e.g., McLaughlin, Irby, and Langman 1994.

4   See, e.g., Floyd 1996; Ford 1994; Gordon 1997; McCubbin, Thompson, Thompson & Futrell 1998.

5   See, e.g., Werner and Smith 1992.

6   Maton and Salem 1995. More generally, Luster and McAdoo 1994 argue for the importance of "understanding the processes (e.g., activities, roles, relationships) in the family, school, and community that contribute to success" among African American children (p. 1093). Many other writers in recent years have stressed the importance of adopting a broad, ecological model to understand African American youths' positive development (e.g., Hill, 1999; Taylor, Jacobson, and Roberts, 2000). Maton 2000 asserts that capacity-building, group empowerment, relational community-building and culture challenge together are necessary to make a difference in our social problems, including the transformation of the educational opportunities available for many African American youth.

7   This finding is consistent with many previous studies on Black families, which have found that positive maternal or family process variables, not family structure (or indicators of family socioeconomic status per se) are linked to a range of educational and psychosocial positive outcomes for Black youth (e.g., Apfel and Seitz 1996; Battle 1997; Boyd-Franklin 1989; Bradley et al. 1987; Burchinal, Follmer, and Bryant 1996; College Board 1999; Dornbusch, Ritter and Steinberg 1991; Ford et al. 1998; Prom-Jackson, Johnson, and Wallace 1987; Ricciuti 1999; Salem, Zimmerman, and Notaro 1998; Slaughter-Defoe et al. 1990; Steinberg, Elmen, and Mounts 1989).

8   See, e.g., Staples and Johnson 1993, ch. 8. In addition to different challenges and stresses, the research literature suggests differences in variables ranging from communication style to family climate in single-parent vs. two-parent Black homes (e.g., Jayakody, Chatters, and Taylor 1993; Prom-Jackson, Johnson, and Wallace 1987; Thornton et al. 1990; Tolson and Wilson 1990).

9   The importance of maternal education for educational attainment among Black young adults was found, for instance, in a widely cited study by Wilson and Allen 1987. McLoyd and Jozefowicz 1996 found a link between maternal education and life course expectations for African American middle-school students. Luster and McAdoo 1996 found that the link between maternal education and longer-term education attainment involved intervening impacts on both academic motivation and personal behavior of the young child. Thornton et al. 1990 found that mothers with higher levels of education were more likely to impart messages and socialize their children concerning racial matters than those with lower levels of education; this was especially the case with older, highly educated mothers. Harris, Terrel, and Allen 1999 found a relationship between maternal education and maternal teaching behavior in a sample of African American mothers.

10 As general support for this point, Cohen 1987 found that "white collar" parents tend to influence the academic achievement of their children through expectations and modeling, while "blue collar" parents did so through expectations only.

11 The general importance of economic resources or socioeconomic status for educational attainment was discussed in Chapter 1. Many more specific links to academic preparedness or to parenting practices exist as well (cf. Taylor 1997). For instance, in terms of academic preparedness, Entwisle and Alexander 1990 found that among Baltimore City children, math reasoning skills at the start of grade one was related to economic resources in the home. Concerning child-rearing, Spencer 1990 found, in a sample of black parents, that middle-income parents enlisted more community resources for help in child-rearing (e.g., literature, medical sources), were more likely to rate the role of the father as equally important in child-rearing, and were more likely to rate church attendance as "extremely important."

12 Steinberg, Dornbusch, and Brown 1992 in a large sample of high-school students found that the absence of peer support for achievement was especially undermining of academic achievement for black youth. Researchers have found a link between neighborhood socioeconomic status and other characteristics and various youth academic and social outcomes (e.g., Connell 1999; Elliot et al. 1996; Hope 1995; Sampson 1999) and have explored the specific educational and social challenges of life in poor urban neighborhoods in particular (e.g., Figiueira-McDonough 1998; Luster and McAdoo 1996). The link between school (and school system) resources and educational quality and outcomes has long been established (e.g., Coleman et al. 1966; College Board 1999; Roscigno 2000).

13 See, e.g., Banks 1989; Hudson 1991; Slaughter and Johnson 1988; and Tatum 1997 for discussions of the challenges of developing a positive racial identity for students growing up in varied neighborhood environments.

14 See Seidman, Aber, and French (forthcoming) for a concise summary of the influence of the transition to middle and high school on youth academic and social adjustment. Recent students focused on African American youth include Gutman and Midgley 2000 and Newman et al. 2000.

15 Thornton et al. 1990 examined the sociodemographic correlates of racial socialization and found high levels in families from higher socioeconomic status subgroups. Thornton 1997 further reports a differentiation of type of racial socialization linked to family sociodemographic characteristics.

16 There has been surprisingly little empirical research specifically examining the nature of the mother-adolescent daughter relationship focused solely on African Americans. One exception is Cauce et al. 1996, who describe various aspects of this relationship, including closeness, conflict, and control.

17 Research has shown a direct link between regular patterns of reading to children when they are young and subsequent school performance (e.g., Romotowski and Trepaneir 1977). In terms of TV-watching, Christenson, Rounds, and Gorney 1992, based on their review of available research, emphasize the importance of parents limiting TV viewing to enable the child to participate in other, educationally related activities (for a recent study comparing the influence of TV-watching vs. homework on educational outcomes, see Aksoy and Link 2000).

18 Research has consistently shown that parents of successful African American students place a high value on education and the pursuit of high status careers (e.g., Clark 1983; Ford 1993; Johnson 1992; Wilson, Cooke, and Arrington 1997).

19 Not surprisingly, research has indicated that reinforcement and feedback on homework produce higher student achievement (e.g., Keith 1987), and parental enforcement of consequences for completion or noncompletion may improve effectiveness (e.g., Harris, 1983). Research on lower-income Black families has found that use of firm and consistent monitoring of home activities and study time (Clark 1983) and of specific strategies to aid students in their homework (Gutman and McLoyd 2000) have been linked to higher achievement.

20 The high-school questionnaire item was, "In high school my parent(s) monitored the amount of time I spent studying." Students indicated the accuracy of the statement on a five-point scale ranging from "not at all accurate (1) to "somewhat accurate" (3) to "very accurate" (5). Responses of 3, 4, or 5 were considered indications of at least some parent monitoring.

21 The importance of parental involvement in education has been demonstrated in numerous studies (e.g., Clark 1983; Farber and Iversen, 1998; Garibaldi 1992; Sanders 1998; Smith and Hausafus 1998; Snodgrass 1991; Wilson, Cook, and Arrington 1997; Yan 1999). As summarized by Christenson, Rounds, and Gorney 1992, "Parents participate in education both at school and at home. There is a substantial body of literature that documents the positive effects of parent involvement on student achievement. There is some evidence to show that the effects are most comprehensive when parents are involved both at home and at school. Parent involvement in home learning activities that support school instruction is a strong, significant correlate of academic outcomes for students" (p. 192).

22 Parent school involvement has been found in many studies to be an important predictor of student academic success (e.g., Christenson and Hurley 1997, Christenson, Rounds, and Gorney 1992; Cole-Henderson 2000; Desimone 1999; Gutman and Eccles 1999; Haynes and Comer 1996; Smith-Maddox 1999; Yan 1999; Yonezawa 2000). Mutual respect and cooperation between schools and Black families in particular contributes greatly to Black children's academic success and school adjustment (e.g., Slaughter-Defoe et al. 1990; Smith, Bouette, Zigler, and Finn-Stevenson, forthcoming 2000). In one longitudinal study, Luster and McAdoo 1996 found that maternal involvement in kindergarten was an important predictor of academic motivation and long-term educational achievement, through age 27.

23 Based on their review of the research literature, Christenson, Rounds, and Gorney 1992 concluded that "a positive parent-child relationship is related to academic success. Parents who accept, nurture, encourage, and are emotionally responsive to their child's developmental needs tend to have children who are successful in school. This affective relationship is not associated with IQ, SES, or gender of the child" (p. 188). Floyd 1996 found that a supportive, nurturing family environment was linked to success among academically successful, resilient, African American high school seniors. Mason et al. 1994 found that high-quality parenting, and specifically maternal control, can play an important role protecting African American adolescents from the negative influence of problem peers.

24 Christenson, Rounds, and Gorney 1992, in their review of this literature, conclude, "Parental discipline characterized by setting clear standards, enforcing rules, and encouraging discussion, negotiation, and independence is associated with positive academic outcomes. Over- and under-control are correlated negatively with student achievement" (p. 190). They also indicate that the evidence of a link between parenting style and academic outcome is stronger for White than African American families.

McLoyd 1998 reports that in poor, inner-city neighborhoods very strict and highly directive parenting, combined with warmth, helps children resist environmental forces that might lead to low academic achievement.

25 Many researchers have found a strong relationship between realistic, high parent expectations for children's school performance and positive academic performance for children in general (for a review, see Christenson, Rounds, and Gorney 1992) and in studies of African American children in particular (e.g., Entwisle and Alexander 1990; Ford et al. 1998; Gill and Reynolds 1999; Halle, Kurtz-Costes, and Mahoney 1997; Reynolds 1998; Reynolds and Gill 1994).

26 Researchers have emphasized the importance for children's academic achievement of a positive link between the family and community cultural and social resources, both for youth in general (e.g., Bronfenbrenner 1986), and for African American youth in particular (e.g., Bowman and Howard 1985; Ogbu 1988; Sanders 1998; Slaughter-Defoe et al. 1990). The importance of nonparental sources of positive influence was a major finding in the interviews with academically successful minority students carried out by Bowser and Perkins 1991.

Hillary Clinton's 1996 best-selling book emphasizes the importance of community connectedness for families and youth. As aptly stated by Andrew Billingsley 1992, "One of the most powerful truths about families is that they cannot be strong unless they are surrounded by a strong community" (p. 70).

27 Consistent with findings in the current study, the Black church has repeatedly been found to be a strong support for Black families, and for Black youth (e.g., Ellison 1997; Kim and McKenry 1998; Mattis and Jaegers, forthcoming; McAdoo 1995; Sanders 1998; Sanders and Herting 2000; Walsh 1998).

28 For a discussion of importance of teacher support as a protective factor, see, e.g., Floyd 1996, Sanders 1998, and Smith, Boutte, Zigler, and Finn-Stevenson (forthcoming). For a discussion of the importance of teacher expectations, see Ferguson 1998; Kolb and Jussim 1994; and Weinstein 1998. The samples of academically successful working-class youth interviewed by Bowser and Perkins and of African American low-income youth interviewed by Floyd 1996 both emphasized the critical influence of positive, personal, mentoring relationships developed with concerned, committed educators in the school.

29 The importance (and challenges) of peer support for academic success among African American youth has been affirmed in various school and peer contexts (e.g., Cauce 1986; Clark 1991; Cooper and Datnow 2000; Datnow and Cooper 1997; Fordham 1996; Ogbu 1988; Patchen 1982; Steinberg 1996; Steinberg, Dornbusch, and Brown 1992; Wilson, Cooke, and Arrington 1997; Wilson-Sadberry, Winfield, and Royster 1991). Teacher encouragement of parental involvement is another important facet of teacher influence (e.g., Gavin and Greenfield 1998).

30 The importance of extracurricular involvements has been documented in various studies and builds upon the view that meaningful engagement in activity is a key facet of positive youth development (e.g., Maton 1990; McLaughlin, Irby, and Langman 1994).

31 Within each subgroup discussed in this chapter, extended family members were cited by some of the daughters as important influences and sources of support. As noted by one daughter, "All of my extended family have impacted me and encouraged me." The importance of extended family support for Black parents and youth was discussed by the mothers and fathers interviewed (Chapters 2 and 3, respectively), and has been emphasized by a number of researchers (cf. Hrabowski, Maton, and Greif 1998; Hunter

1997; McCabe, Clark, and Barnett 1999; Scales and Gibbons 1996; Taylor, Casten, and Flickinger 1992; Taylor 1996; Taylor, Chatters, and Jackson 1997; Wilson 1995).

32 The nature, frequency, and some of the correlates of racial socialization by African American parents has increasingly been a topic of academic research, and suggests the importance of racial socialization and ethnic identity as protective resources for African American youth (e.g., Bowman and Howard 1985; Clark 1991; Loomis 2000; Marshall 1995; Miller 1999; Richards 1997; Sellers, Chavous, and Cooke 1998; Shorter-Gooden and Washington 1996; Thornton et al. 1990; Ward 1996).

33 Interestingly, Paulson 1994 found that what best predicts achievement is an adolescent's perceptions of the parenting they received, not the actual behavior of the parents.

Chapter 5: Parenting and Educating for Success in Math and Science

1 Clewell, Anderson, and Thorpe 1992 reported that positive attitudes toward math and science declined for both female and minority students as they reached the junior high school years.

2 See, e.g., Clewell, Anderson, and Thorpe 1992; Hill, Petus and Hedin 1990; Leder 1990; McClendon and Wigfield 1998; Smith and Hausafus 1998; Yong 1992 for a discussion of factors which interfere with the development and maintenance of interest in the sciences for female and ethnic minority students.

3 Catsambis 1995.

4 Studies highlighting the importance of one or more of these factors, many focused explicitly on minority students, include Dick and Rallis 1991; Ellis 1993; Garcia 1988; Gibbons 1992; Hill, Pettus, and Hedin 1990; McClendon and Wigfield 1998; Naizer 1993; Oakes 1990; O'Brien, Martinez-Pons, and Kopala 1999; Parsons 1997; Reynolds 1991; Seymour and Hewitt 1997; Singer, Smith, and Hausafus 1998; Vetter 1994.

5 See Clewell, Anderson, and Thorne 1992, and Martin 2000, for a more comprehensive list of recommendations.

6 The material in this section is drawn to a large extent from Maton, Hrabowski, and Schmitt 2000; a number of the interview excerpts are from the daughters interviewed for the current book.

7 See, e.g., Bowen and Bok 1998; Breland 1979; Fleming and Garcia 1998; Ramist, Lewis, and McCamley-Jenkins 1994; Willingham et al. 1990.

8 For prior research on these and related factors, see Allen 1992; Betz 1997; Brown and Clewell 1998; Campbell, Denes, and Morrison 2000; Frierson 1998; Gandara and Maxwell-Jolly 1999; Garrison 1987; Leslie and Oaxaca 1998; Malcolm et al. 1998; Mervis 1998; Miller 1999; Nettles 1988; Seymour and Hewitt 1997; Steele 1997; Thurmond and Cregler 1999.

9 See, e.g., Nettles 1988; Seymour and Hewitt 1997.

10 See, e.g., Allen 1992; Hilton et al. 1989; McHenry 1997; Nettles 1988; Redmond 1990; Seymour and Hewitt 1997.

11 See, e.g., Fries-Britt 1994; Gandara and Maxwell-Jolly 1999; Garrison 1987; Nettles 1988.

12 Bonsangue and Drew 1995; Gandara and Maxwell-Jolly 1999; Kosciuk 1997; Seymour and Hewitt 1997; Springer, Stanne, and Donovan 1999; Treisman 1992.

13 See, e.g., Atwater and Alick 1990; Gandara and Maxwell-Jolly 1999; Hilton et al. 1989.

14 See, e.g., Gandara and Maxwell-Jolly 1999; Hilton et al. 1989.

15 See, e.g., Gandara & Maxwell-Jolly 1999; Hilton et al. 1989; Seymour and Hewitt 1997.
16 See, e.g., Gandara and Maxwell-Jolly 1999; Glennan, Baxley, and Farren 1985; Grandy 1998; Hilton et al. 1989; Seymour and Hewitt, 1997.
17 The administration of surveys and interviews have been funded, over the years, from grants from NSF, and earlier from the Sloan Foundation, to evaluate the effectiveness of the Meyerhoff Program.
18 Research (funded from NSF) is currently under way on the academic success and psychosocial adjustment of the Meyerhoff students (and comparison samples) to their graduate- and professional-school environments.
19 For a description of other programs, see Gandara and Maxwell-Jolly 1999.

Chapter 6: Becoming a Black Woman

1 O'Keefe and Treister 1998 found that 46 percent of adolescent girls from a multiethnic sample had experienced some form of physical violence from dating partners. Phillips 1998, in reviewing studies of sexual abuse and rape, reported that sexual abuse is usually underreported by adolescent girls and that rape perpetrators are often familiar to the victims. Haag and the American Association of University Women Educational Foundation 2000 found that adolescent girls from diverse ethnic backgrounds were concerned about the absence of school policies against sexual harassment and violence.
2 Harway and Liss 1999 abstract from several studies that African Americans may be at higher risk for dating violence and rape, and associated complications, because they are less likely to disclose that it occurred.
3 Roberts, Roberts, and Chen 1997 report that female adolescents, regardless of race, had significantly higher reports of depressive symptoms and also related impairments in functioning at home, in school, and with peers. Sands and Howard-Hamilton 1995 describe gifted female adolescents as prone to depression when issues such as self-concept, gender role expectations, and peer relationships can become overwhelming.
4 Roberts, Roberts, and Chen 1997 found that African American adolescent males and females report significantly more symptoms of depression than their White peers, although less than Mexican American adolescents.
5 Cited in Phillips 1998. A lower percentage of symptoms was reported among Black adolescent girls compared with White, Hispanic, and Asian girls.
6 Brannock and Schandler 1990 found lower levels of drinking among Black female adolescents than among White counterparts. Gottfredson and Koeper 1996 found lower levels of drug use among Black female adolescents compared with White counterparts. However, Curtis-Boles and Jenkins-Monroe 2000 report that the prevalence of drug and alcohol use among African-American women has risen in recent years.
7 In Parker et al. 1995 African American female adolescents were found to have more flexible perceptions of beauty and more acceptance of physical selves than White peers. Tashakkori 1993 found that African American adolescent males and females reported higher self-esteem than White counterparts.
8 Cited in Phillips 1998.
9 Fordham and Ogbu 1986, in their study of high-achieving African Americans, found

pressure among Blacks to "act Black" and were seen as having adopted conflicting cultural values (i.e., acting White).

10 Fordham 1993.

11 Bond and Cash 1992; Okazawa-Rey, Robinson, and Ward 1987; and Russell, Wilson, and Hall 1993 note that color consciousness in the Black community is rooted in slavery. For example, lighter-skinned Blacks (i.e., those who were presumed to have White blood) were historically considered more attractive and received preferential treatment. These phenomena have been perpetuated through the years due to a variety of societal factors.

12 Russell, Wilson, and Hall, 1993, p. 2.

13 Okazawa-Rey, Robinson, and Ward 1987 provide a historical overview of the preference for African American women who were of lighter complexions within the Black community and within the larger society.

14 Bond and Cash 1992.

15 Robinson and Ward 1995. Woody and Neville 2000 similarly found that female African American college students who were less satisfied with their skin color were also less satisfied with their overall appearance.

16 De Las Fuentes and Vasquez 1999.

17 Waters 1996 reports results based on a study of adolescent children of Black immigrants from Haiti and English-speaking Caribbean islands. In her study, 42 percent adopted "American" identities, 30 percent adopted "strong ethnic" identities, and 28 percent adopted "immigrant" identities.

18 Ibid. p. 68.

19 Ibid.

20 Greene 1996 defines "alternation" as a pattern among African Americans whereby they "move between" two distinct cultural realms or use strategies to adapt to, and negotiate within, both Black and White cultural realms or settings.

21 E.g., Chimezie 1985 describes linguistic "code-switching" as switching between Black dialect and standard English depending on the context or setting.

22 Blake 1999, p. 84.

23 Nkomo and Cox 1989, p. 826.

24 Okazawa-Rey, Robinson, and Ward 1987, p. 99.

25 Nkomo and Cox 1989, p. 826.

Chapter 7: Raising Successful African American Young Women

1 Edelman 1999, pp. 155–58.

2 The Meyerhoff Scholars regularly contribute as coauthors on articles appearing in scholarly scientific journals such as *Science*, *Nature: Structural Biology*, and the *Journal of Molecular Biology*.

3 Including the first group of graduates in 1993, some 225 Meyerhoff students have earned degrees in science and engineering through the spring of 2000, with 88 percent (199) either currently engaged in or having completed post-graduate study at institutions nationwide. (The remaining twenty-six graduates are either employed (24) or undecided (two). The 199 graduates matriculated into the following post-graduate programs: Ph.D. (91); M.D./Ph.D. (23); M.D. (44); master's (32); D.D.S. (one); J.D. (one); post-baccalaureate (seven).

4 Pearson and Bechtel 1989, p.140.
5 Although precise data are not readily obtainable, one source indicates that the number of 12th grade students who report weekly religious attendance has declined from 2 out of every 5 students (41%) in 1976 to 1 out of every 3 students (31–33%) since 1987. (Department of Health % Human Services, 1999).
6 Pearson and Bechtel 1989, p. 151.

REFERENCES

Aksoy, T., and C. R. Link. 2000. A panel analysis of students' mathematics achievement in the US in the 1990s: Does increasing the amount of time in learning activities affect math achievement? *Economic Educational Review 19*: 261-77.

Allen, W. D., and M. Connor. 1997. An African-American perspective on generative fathers. In A. J. Hawkins and D. C. Dollahite, eds., *Generative fathering: Beyond deficit perspectives*, pp. 52-70. Thousand Oaks, Calif.: Sage.

Allen, W. R. 1992. The color of success: African-American college student outcomes at predominately white and historically black public colleges and universities. *Harvard Educational Review 62*: 45-65.

American Association of University Women. 1992. *How schools shortchange girls—The AAUW report: A study of major findings on girls and education*. New York: Marlowe and Company.

American Association of University Women. 1999. *Gender gaps: Where schools still fail our children*. New York: Marlow and Company.

American Psychological Association; Task Force on Adolescent Girls. 1999. *A new look at adolescent girls: Strengths and stresses*. Washington, D.C.: American Psychological Association.

Apfel, N., and V. Seitz. 1996. African American adolescent mothers, their families, and their daughters: A longitudinal perspective over twelve years. In B.J. Leadbeater and N. Way, eds., *Urban girls: Resisting stereotypes, creating identities*, 1996, pp. 149-70.

Arnold, M. S. 1995. Exploding the myths: African-American families at promise. In B. B. Swaderner and S. Lubeck, et al., eds., *Children and families "at promise": Deconstructing the discourse of risk*. SUNY Series, the social context of education, pp. 143-62. Albany: State University of New York Press.

Astin, A. W. 1982. *Minorities in American higher education: Recent trends, current perspectives, and recommendations*. San Francisco, Calif.: Jossey-Bass.

Astin, A. W. 1990. *The black undergraduate: Current status and trends in the characteristics of freshmen*. Los Angeles: University of California, Higher Education Research Council.

Astin, A. W. 1993. *What matters most in college? Four critical years revisited*. San Francisco, Calif.: Jossey-Bass.

Atwater, M. M, and B. Alick. 1990. Cognitive development and problem-solving of Afro-American students in chemistry. *Journal of Research in Science Teaching 27*: 157-72.

Baldwin, A. Y. 1991. Gifted Black adolescents: Beyond racism to pride. In M. Bireley and J. Genshaft, eds., *Understanding the gifted adolescent: Education, developmental, and multicultural issues*, pp. 231-39. New York: Teachers College Press.

Banks, J. A. 1989. Black youth in predominantly white suburbs. In R. L. Jones, ed., *Black Adolescents*, pp. 65-77. Berkeley, Calif: Cobb and Henry.

Battle, J. 1997. The relative effects of married versus divorced family configuration and socioeconomic status on the educational achievement of African American middle school students. *Journal of Negro Education 66*: 29-42.

Bennett, L., Jr. 1988. *Before the Mayflower: A history of Black America*, 6th ed. New York: Penguin Books.

Betz, N. 1997. What stops women and minorities from choosing and completing majors in science and engineering? In D. Johnson et. al., Eds., *Minorities and girls in school: Effects on achieve-*

ment and performance. Leaders in psychology, vol. 1.; pp. 105–40. Thousand Oaks, Calif.: Sage.

Billingsley, A. 1992. *Climbing Jacob's Ladder*. New York: Simon & Schuster.

Blake, S. 1990. At the crossroads of race and gender: Lessons from the mentoring experiences of professional Black women. In A. J. Murrell, F. J. Crosby, and R. J. Ely, Eds., *Mentoring dilemmas*, pp. 83–104. Mahwah, N. J.: Lawrence Elrbaum Associates.

Blankenhorn, D. 1995. *Fatherless America: Confronting our most urgent social problem*. New York: Basic Books.

Bok, D., and W. G. Bowen. 1998. *The shape of the river: Long-term consequences of considering race in college and university admissions*. Princeton, N.J.: Princeton University Press.

Bond, S., and T. F. Cash. 1992. Black beauty: Skin color and body images among African-American college women. *Journal of Applied Social Psychology* 22 (11): 874–88.

Bonsangue, M. V., and D. E. Drew. 1995. Increasing minority students' success in calculus. *New Directions for Teaching and Learning*, no. 51: 23–33.

Bowen, W. G., and D. Bok. 1998. *The shape of the river: Long-term consequences of considering race in college and university admissions*. Princeton, N.J.: Princeton University Press.

Bowman, P., and C. Howard. 1985. Race-related socialization, motivation, and academic achievement: A study of black youth in three-generation families. *Journal of the American Academy of Child Psychiatry* 24: 134–41.

Bowser, B. P., and H. Perkins. 1991. Success against the odds: Young black men tell what it takes. In B. P. Bowser, ed., *Black male adolescents: Parenting and education in community context*, pp. 183–200. Lanham, Md.: University Press of America.

Boyd-Franklin, N. 1989. *Black families in therapy: A multi-systems approach*. New York: Guilford Press.

Bradley, R.H., S. L. Rock, B. M. Caldwell, P. T. Harris, and H. M. Hamrick. 1987. Home environment and school performance among black elementary school children. *Journal of Negro Education* 56: 499–509.

Brannock, J. C., and S. L. Schandler et al. 1990. Cross-cultural and cognitive factors examined in groups of adolescent drinkers. *Journal of Drug Issue* 20 (3): 427–42.

Brazziel, W. F., and M. E. Brazziel. 1997. Distinctives of high producers of science and engineering doctoral starts. *Journal of Science Education and Technology* 6: 145–53.

Breland, H. M. 1979. *Population validity and college entrance measures*. New York: College Entrance Examination Board.

Bronfenbrenner, U. 1986. Ecology of the family as a context for human development: Research perspectives. *Developmental Psychology* 22: 723–42.

Brown, S. V., and B. C. Clewell. 1998. *Project Talent Flow: The Non-SEM Field Choices of Black and Latino Undergraduates with the Aptitude for Science, Engineering and Mathematics Careers*. January. Final Report to the Alfred P. Sloan Foundation.

Brumberg, J. J. November 2000. When girls talk: What it reveals about them and us. *Chronicle of Higher Education*, B7–10.

Burchinal, M. R., A. Follmer, and D. M. Bryant. 1996. The relations of maternal social support and family structure with maternal responsiveness and child outcomes among African American families. *Developmental Psychology* 32: 1073–83.

Callahan, C., and S. Reis. 1996. Gifted girls, remarkable women. In K. Arnold, K. Noble, and R. Subotnik, eds., *Remarkable women: Perspectives on female talent development*, pp. 171–92. Cresskill, N.J.: Hampton Press.

Callan, P. 1994. Equity in higher education: The state role. In M. Justiz, R. Wilson, and L. Bjork, eds., *Minorities in higher education*. Phoenix, Ariz.: American Council on Education and Oryx Press.

Campbell, G., Jr., R. Denes, and C. Morrison. eds. 2000. *Access denied: Race, ethnicity, and the scientific enterprise.* New York: Oxford University Press

Carlisle, D. M., J. E. Gardner, and H. Liu. 1998. The entry of underrepresented minority students into US Medical schools: An evaluation of recent trends, *American Journal of Public Health* 88: 1314–18.

Carroll, R. 1997. *Sugar in the raw: Voices of young Black girls in America.* New York: Crown Trade Paperbacks.

Catsambis, S. 1995. Gender, race, ethnicity, and science education in the middle grades. *Journal of Research in Science Teaching* 32: 243–57.

Cauce, A. 1986. Social networks and social competence: Exploring the effects of early adolescent friendships. *American Journal of Community Psychology* 14: 607–28.

Cauce, A.M., Y. Hiraga, D. Graves, N. Gonzales, K. Ryan-Finn, and K. Grove. 1996. African American mothers and their adolescent daughters: Closeness, conflict, and control. In B.J. Leadbeater and N. Way, eds., *Urban girls: Resisting stereotypes, creating identities,* pp. 100–116.

Chenoweth, K. 1998. The College Board decries preparation gap. *Black Issues in Higher Education* 15, no. 15.

Chimezie, A. 1985. Black biculturality. *Western Journal of Black Studies* 9: 224–35.

Christenson, S. L., and C. M. Hurley. 1997. Parents' and school psychologists' perspectives on parent involvement activities. *School Psychology Review* 26: 111–30.

Christenson, S. L., T. Rounds, and D. Gorney. 1992. Family factors and student achievement. *School Psychology Quarterly* 7: 178–206.

Clark, M. L. 1991. Social identity, peer relations, and academic competence of African-American adolescents. *Education and Urban Society* 24: 41–52.

Clark, R. 1983. *Family life and school achievement: Why poor black children succeed or fail.* Chicago: University of Chicago Press.

Clewell, B. C., B. T. Anderson, and M. E. Thorpe. 1992. *Breaking the barriers: Helping female and minority students succeed in mathematics and science.* San Francisco, Calif.: Jossey-Bass.

Clinton, H. 1996. *It takes a village: And other lessons children teach us.* New York: Simon and Schuster.

Cohen, J. 1987. Parents as educational models and definers. *Journal of Marriage and the Family* 49: 339–49.

Cole-Henderson, B. 2000. Organizational characteristics of schools that successfully serve low-income urban African-American students. *Journal of Education for Students Placed at Risk* 5: 79–91.

Coleman, J. E., E. Q. Campbell, C. J. Hobson, J. McPartland, A. M. Mood, F. D. Weinfield, and R. L. York. 1966. *Equality of educational opportunity.* Washington, D.C.: Government Printing Office.

College Board 1999. 1999 profile of college-bound seniors. New York.

Collins, P. H. 1991. *Black feminist thought.* New York: Routledge, Chapman, and Hall.

Collison, M. N.-K. 1999. Researching fatherhood, *Black Issues in Higher Education* 16 (5): 23–26.

Connell, P. 1999. Comment on "What Community Supplies." In R. F. Ferguson and W. T. Dickens, eds., *Urban problems and community development,* pp. 279–92. Washington, D.C.: Brookings Institution Press.

Cook, P. J., and J. Ludwig. 1997. Weighing the "burden of 'acting white'": Are there race differences in attitudes towards education? *Journal of Policy Analysis Management* 16: 256–78.

Cooper, R. and A. Datnow. 2000. African-American student success in independent schools: A model of family, school, and peer influences. In M. G. Sanders et al., eds., *Schooling students*

placed at risk: Research, policy, and practice in the education of poor and minority adolescents,
pp. 187–205. Mahwah, N.J.: Lawrence Erlbaum Associates.

Curtis-Boles, H., and V. Jenkins-Monroe. 2000. Substance abuse in African American women. *Journal of Black Psychology* 26: 450–69.

Datnow, A., and R. Cooper. 1997. Peer networks of African American students in independent schools: Affirming academic success and racial identity. *Journal of Negro Education* 66: 56–72

Davis, L., J. H. Williams, and M. Johnson-Reid, et al. 2001. Choices for life for adolescent success. Paper presented at the Annual Program Meeting of the Council on Social Work Education, Dallas, February.

De Las Fuentes, C., and M. Vasquez. 1999. Immigrant adolescent girls of color: Facing American challenges. In N. G. Johnson, M. C. Roberts, and J. Worrell, eds., *Beyond appearance: A new look at adolescent girls,* pp. 131–50. Washington, D.C.: American Psychological Association.

Department of Health and Human Services, Trends in the Well Being of America's Children and Youth. 1999. Section 4: Social Development, Behavioral Health, and Teen Fertility. SD 1.3. Religious Attendance & Religiosity.

Desimone, L. 1999. Linking parent involvement with student achievement: Do race and income matter? *Journal of Educational Research* 93: 11–30.

Dick, T. P., and S. F. Rallis. 1991. Factors and influences on high school students' career choices. *Journal for Research in Mathematics Education* 22: 281–92.

Dornbusch, S. M., P. L. Ritter, and L. Steinberg. 1991. Community influences on the relation of family statuses to adolescent school performance: Differences between African Americans and non-Hispanic Whites. *American Journal of Education* 99: 543–67.

Duderstadt, J. J. 1990. America at the crossroads: The challenge of science education. In W. R. Wineke and P. Certain, eds., *The freshman year in science and engineering: Old problems, new perspectives for research universities,* pp. 21–27. University Park, Pa.: Alliance for Undergraduate Education.

Edelman, M. Wright. 1999. *Lanterns: A memoir of mentors.* Boston: Beacon Press.

Educational Testing Service. 1995. College bound seniors: 1995 profile of SAT program test takers. Princeton, N.J.: Educational Testing Service.

Elliot, D. S., W. J. Wilson, D. Huizing, R. J. Sampson, A. Elliott, and B. Rankin. 1996. The effects of neighborhood disadvantage on adolescent development. *Journal of Research in Crime and Delinquency* 33: 389–426.

Elliott, R., A. C. Strenta, R. Adair, M. Matier, and J. Scott. 1995. *Non-Asian minority students in the science pipeline at highly selective institutions. Report to the NSF.* Washington, D.C.: National Science Foundation.

Ellis, R. S. 1993. Impacting the science attitudes of minority high school youth. *School Science and Mathematics* 93: 400–07.

Ellison, C. G. 1997. Religious involvement and the subjective quality of family life among African Americans. In R.J. Taylor, S.J. Jackson, and L.M. Chatters, eds., *Family life in Black America,* pp. 117–31.

Entwisle, D. R. and K. L. Alexander. 1990. Beginning school math competence: Minority and majority comparisons. *Child Development* 61: 454–71.

Falconer, J. W. and H. A. Neville. 2000. African American college women's body image: An examination of body mass, African self-consciousness, and skin color satisfaction. *Psychology of Women Quarterly* 24: 236–43.

Farber, N. B. and R. R. Iverson. 1998. Family values about education and their transmission among black inner-city young women. In A. Colby, J. Boone, et al., eds., *Competence and character through life,* pp. 141–67. Chicago: University of Chicago Press.

Ferguson, R. F. 1998. Teachers' perceptions and expectations and the Black-White test score gap. In C. Jencks and M. Phillips, eds., *The Black-White test score gap* (pp. 273-317). Washington, D.C.: Brookings Institution Press.

Figiueira-McDonough, J. 1998. Environment and interpretation: Voices of young people in poor inner-city neighborhoods. *Youth and Society* 30: 123-63.

Fleming, J. and N. Garcia. 1998. Are standardized tests fair to African American Americans?: Predictive validity of the SAT in black and white institutions. *Journal of Higher Education* 69: 471-96.

Floyd, C. 1996. Achieving despite the odds: A study of resilience among a group of African American high school seniors. *Journal of Negro Education* 65: 181-89.

Ford, D. Y. 1993. Black students' achievement orientation as a function of perceived family achievement orientation and demographic variables. *Journal of Negro Education,* 62: 47-66.

Ford, D. Y. 1994. Nurturing resilience in gifted black youth. *Roeper Review* 17: 80-85.

Ford, D. Y., and J. J. Harris III. 1995. Underachievement among gifted African American students: Implications for school counselors. *School Counselor* 42 (3): 196-204.

Ford, D.Y., L. B. Wright, T. C. Grantham, and J. J. Harris. 1998. Achievement levels, outcomes, and orientations of Black students in single- and two-parent families. *Urban Education* 33: 360-84.

Fordham, S. 1993. "Those loud Black girls": (Black) women, silence, and gender "passing" in the Academy. *Anthropology and Education Quarterly 24: 3-22.*

Fordham, S. 1996. *Blacked out: Dilemmas of race, identification, and success at Capitol High.* New York: Dryden Press.

Fordham, S. and J. U. Ogbu. 1986. Black students' school success: Coping with the "burden of 'acting white.'" *Urban Review* 18: 176-206.

Franklin, A. J. and N. Boyd-Franklin. 2000. "Invisibility syndrome: A clinical model of the effects of racism on African-American males, *American Journal of Orthopsychiatry* 70: 33-41.

Frierson, H. T. 1998. *Diversity in Higher Education,* Volume 2. Stanford, CT: JAI Press.

Fries-Britt, S. L. 1994. A test of Tinto's retention theory on the Meyerhoff Scholars: A case study analysis. Ph.D. dissertation, University of Maryland, College Park.

Furstenburg, F. F. 2001. Managing to make it: Afterthoughts. *Journal of Family Issues* 22: 150-62.

Gainen, J. 1995. Barriers to success in quantitative gateway courses. In J. Gainen and E. Willemsen, eds., *Fostering success in quantitative gateway courses.* San Francisco: Jossey-Bass.

Gandara, P., and J. Maxwell-Jolly. 1999. *Priming the pump: A review of programs that aim to increase the achievement of underrepresented minority undergraduates. A Report to the Task Force on Minority High Achievement of the College Board.* New York: College Board.

Garcia, J. 1988. Minority participation in elementary science and mathematics. *Education and Society* 1: 21-23.

Garibaldi, A. M. 1992. Educating and motivating African American males to succeed. *Journal of Negro Education:* 61: 4-11.

Garrison, H. H. 1987. Undergraduate science and engineering education for Blacks and Native Americans. In L. S. Dix, ed., *Minorities: Their underrepresentation and career differentials in science and engineering. Proceedings of a workshop.* Washington, D.C.: National Academy Press.

Garrod, A., J. V. Ward, T. L. Robinson, R. Kilkenny. 1999. *Souls looking back: Life stories of growing up black.* Routledge.

Gavin, K. M., and D. B. Greenfield. 1998. A comparison of levels of involvement for parents with at-risk African American kindergarten children in classrooms with high versus low teacher encouragement. *Journal of Black Psychology* 24: 403-17.

Gibbons, A. 1992. Minority programs that get high marks. *Science* 258: 1190–96.

Gibbs, J. T. 1996. Health-compromising behaviors in urban early adolescent females: Ethnic and socioeconomic variations. In B.J. Leadbeater and N. Way, eds., *Urban girls: Resisting stereotypes, creating identities*, pp. 309–327.

Gill, S. & A. J. Reynolds. 1999. Educational expectations and school achievement of urban African American children. *Journal of School Psychology* 37: 403–24.

Glennan, R.E., D. M. Baxley, and P. J. Farren. 1985. Impact of intrusive advising on minority student retention. *College Student Journal* 19: 335–38.

Gordon, E. W.. 1997. Introduction: The resilience phenomenon in ethnic minority adolescent development. In R. D. Taylor and M. C. Wang, eds., *Social and emotional adjustment and family relations in ethnic minority families,* pp. 1–4. Mahwah, N.J.: Lawrence Erlbaum Associates.

Gottfredson, D.C., & C. S. Koper. 1996. Race and sex differences in the prediction of drug use. *Journal of Consulting and Clinical Psychology* 64 (2): 301–13.

Grandy, J. 1998. Persistence in science of high-ability minority students: Results of a longitudinal study. *Journal of Higher Education* 69: 589–620.

Grantham, T. C., and D. Y. Ford. 1998. A case study of the social needs of Danisha: An underachieving gifted African-American female. *Roeper Review* 21 (2): 96–102.

Greene, B. 1994. African American women. In L. Comas-Diaz and B. Greene, eds., *Women of color: Integrating ethnic and gender identities in psychotherapy*, pp. 10–29. New York: Guilford Press.

Greene, M. L. 1996. Sociocultural orientation among talented African-American college students in a race-specific program: Patterns, predictors, and correlates. Ph.D. dissertation, University of Maryland, Baltimore County.

Gutman, L. M. and J. S. Eccles. 1999. Financial strain, parenting behaviors, and adolescents' achievement: Testing model equivalence between African American and European American single- and two-parent families. *Child Development* 70: 1464–76.

Gutman, L. M., and C. Midgley. 2000. The role of protective factors in supporting the academic achievement of poor African American students during the middle school transition. *Journal of Youth and Adolescence* 29: 223–48.

Gutman, L. M., and V. C. McLoyd. 2000. Parents' management of their children's education within the home, at school, and in the community: An examination of African-American families living in poverty. *Urban Review* 32: 1–24.

Haag, P. 1999. *Voices of a generation: Teenage girls report on sex, schools, and self: A report o nteenage girls from the American Association of University Women's Sister to Sister Summit.* Washington, D.C.: AAUW.

Haag, P. and the American Association of University Women Educational Foundation. 2000. *Voices of a generation: Teenage girls report about their lives today.* New York: Marlowe and Company.

Halle, T. G., B. Kurtz-Costes, and J. L. Mahoney. 1997. Family influences on school achievement in low-income, African American children. *Journal of Educational Psychology* 89: 527–37.

Harris, J. R. 1983. Parent-aided homework: A working model for school personnel. *School Counselor* 31: 171–76.

Harris, Y.R., D. Terrel, and G. Allen. 1999. The influence of education context and beliefs on the teaching behavior of African American mothers. *Journal of Black Psychology* 25: 490–503.

Harway, M., and M. Liss. 1999. Dating violence and teen prostitution: Adolescent girls in the justice system. In N. G. Johnson, M. C. Roberts, and J. Worrell, eds., *Beyond appearance: A new look at adolescent girls*, pp. 277–300. Washington, D.C.: American Psychological Association.

Haynes, N. M, and J. P. Comer. 1996. Integrating schools, families and communities through successful school reform: The school development program. *School Psychology Review* 25: 501–06.

Hill, O. W., W. C. Pettus, and B. A. Hedin. 1990. Three studies of factors affecting the attitudes of blacks and females toward the pursuit of science and science-related careers. *Journal of Research in Science Teaching* 27: 289–314.

Hill, R. 1997. *The strengths of African American families: Twenty-five years later*. Washington, D.C.: R and B Publishers.

Hill, S. A. 1999. *African American children: Socialization and development in families*. Thousand Oaks, Calif.: Sage.

Hilton, T. L., J. Hsia, D. G. Solorzano, and N. L. Benton. 1989. *Persistence in science of high-ability minority students*. Princeton, N.J.: Educational Testing Service.

Hope, J. 1995. The price they pay for the places they live: A case study of the association of educational achievement and aspirations with residential incongruence among middle-class black adolescents. In C. K. Jacobson et. al., eds., *American families: Issues in race and ethnicity*, pp. 407–27. New York: Garland.

Hrabowski, F. A. III, K. I. Maton, and G. L. Greif. 1998. *Beating the odds: Raising academically successful African American males*. New York: Oxford University Press.

Hrabowski, F. A. III., and K. I. Maton. 1995. Enhancing the success of African-American students in the sciences: Freshmen year outcomes. *School Science and Mathematics* 95: 18–27.

Hudson, R. J. 1991. Black male adolescent development deviating from the past: Challenges for the future. In B. P. Bowser, ed., *Black male adolescents: Parenting and education in community context*, pp. 271–81. Lanham, Md.: University Press of America.

Hunter, A. G. 1997. Counting on grandmothers: Black mothers' and fathers' reliance on grandmothers for parenting support. *Journal of Family Issues* 18: 251–69.

Hurd, E. P., C. Moore, and R. Rogers. 1995. Quiet success: Parenting strengths among African Americans. *Families in Society* 76: 434–443.

Jayakody, R., L. M. Chatters, and R. J. Taylor. 1993. Family support to single and married African American mothers: The provision of financial, emotional, and child care assistance. *Journal of Marriage and the Family* 55: 261–76.

Jencks, C., and M. Philips et al., eds. 1998. *The Black-White test score gap*. Washington, D.C.: Brookings Institute.

Johnson, N. G., M. C. Roberts, and J. Worrell. 1999. *Beyond appearance: A new look at adolescent girls*. Washington, D.C.: American Psychological Association.

Johnson, S. T. 1992. Extra-school factors in achievement, attainment and aspiration among junior and senior high-age African American youth. *Journal of Negro Education* 61: 99–119.

Keith, T. T. 1987. Homework. In A. Thomas and J. Grimes, eds., *Children's needs: Psychological perspectives*, pp. 275–82. Washington, D.C.: National Association of School Psychologists.

Kim, H. K., and P. C. McKenry. 1998. Social networks and support: A comparison of African Americans, Asian Americans, Caucasians, and Hispanics. *Journal of Comparative Family Studies* 29: 313–25.

Kolb, K. J., and L. Jussim. 1994. Teacher expectations and underachieving gifted children. *Roeper Review* 17: 26–30.

Kosciuk, S. 1997. *Impact of the Wisconsin Emerging Scholars first-semester calculus program on grades and retention from fall '93–'96*. Madison: University of Wisconsin, LEAD Center.

Kusimo, P. S. 1997. *Sleeping Beauty redefined: African American girls in transition*. U. S. Dept. of Education, Office of Educational Research & Improvement (OERI), ERIC Report ED 407 207, Washington, D.C.

Leadbeater, B. J. R. and N. Way, eds. 1996. *Urban girls: Resisting stereotypes, creating identities*, introduction, pp. 1–14. New York: New York University Press.

Leder, G. C. 1990. Gender differences in mathematics: An overview. In E. Fennema and G. C. Leder, eds., *Mathematics and Gender*, pp. 10–26. New York: Teachers College Press.

Lerner, G. 1992. *Black women in white America: A documentary history*. New York: Vintage.

Leslie, L. L. and R. L. Oaxaca. 1998. *Women and minorities in higher education*. Volume 14, Higher Education Handbook of theory and research. New York: Agathon Press.

Lips, H. M. 1989. Gender-role socialization: Lessons in femininity. In J. Freeman, eds. *Women: A feminist perspective*, pp. 197–216. Mountain View, Calif.: Mayfield.

Logan, S. L., ed., 1996. *The Black family: Strengths, self-help, and positive change*. Lawrence: University of Kansas.

Loomis, D. M. C. 2000. Relations among ethnic identity, self-esteem, and contextual factors among academically successful African American college students. M.A. thesis, University of Maryland, Baltimore County.

Luster, T., and H. McAdoo. 1994. Factors related to the achievement and adjustment of young African American children. *Child Development* 65: 1080–94.

Luster, T., and H. McAdoo. 1996. Family and child influences on educational attainment: A secondary analysis of the High/Scope Perry preschool data. *Child Development* 67: 26–39.

Majors, R., C. Billson, and J. Mancini. 1992. *Cool pose: The dilemmas of black manhood in America*. New York: Lexington Books.

Malcom, S.M., V. V. Van Horne, C.D. Gaddy, and Y. S. George. 1998. *Losing ground: Science and engineering graduate education of black and hispanic Americans*. Washington, D. C.: American Association for the Advancement of Science.

Malcom, S.M., Y. S. George, and V. V. Van Horne, eds. 1996. *The effect of changing policy climate on science, mathematics, and engineering diversity*. Washington, D.C.: American Association for the Advancement of Science.

Marshall, N. L., A. E. Noonin, K. McCartney, F. Marx, and N. Keefe. 2001. It takes an Urban village: Parenting networks of urban families. *Journal of Family Issues* 22: 163–82.

Marshall, S. 1995. Ethnic socialization of African American children: Implications for parenting, identity development, and academic achievement. *Journal of Youth and Adolescence* 24: 377–96.

Martin, D. B. 2000. *Mathematics success and failure among African-American youth: The roles of sociohistorical context, community forces, school influence, and individual agency*. Mahwah, N. J.: Lawrence Erlbaum Associates.

Mason, C.A., A. M. Cauce, N. Gonzales, and Y. Hiraga. 1994. Adolescent problem-behavior: The effect of peers and the moderating role of father absence and the mother/child relationship. *American Journal of Community Psychology* 22: 723–43.

Massey, W. E. (1992). A success story amid decades of disappointment. *Science* 258: 1177–79.

Maton, K. I. 1990. Meaningful involvement in instrumental activity and well-being: Studies of older adolescents and at-risk inner city teenagers. *American Journal of Community Psychology* 18: 297–320.

Maton, K. I. 2000. Making a difference: The social ecology of social transformation. *American Journal of Community Psychology* 28: 25–57.

Maton, K. I., and D. A. Salem. 1995. Organizational characteristics of empowering community settings: A multiple case study approach. *American Journal of Community Psychology* 23: 631–56.

Maton, K. I., F. A. Hrabowski, and C.L. Schmitt 2000. African American college students excelling in the sciences: College and post-college outcomes in the Meyerhoff Scholars Program. *Journal of Research in Science Teaching* 37: 629–54.

Mattis, J.S., and R. J. Jagers. Forthcoming. Toward a relational framework for the study or religiosity and spirituality in the lives of African Americans. *Journal of Community Psychology*.

McAdoo, H. P. 1995. Stress levels, family help patterns, and religiosity in middle- and working-class African American single mothers. *Journal of Black Psychology* 21: 424–39.

McAdoo, H. P., ed.. 1997. *Black families*, 3rd ed.. Thousand Oaks, Calif.: Sage.

McCabe, K.M., R. Clark, and D. Barnett. 1999. Family protective factors among African American youth. *Journal of Clinical Child Psychology* 28: 137–50.

McClendon, C., and A. Wigfield. 1998. Group differences in African American adolescents' achievement-related beliefs about math and science: An initial study. *Journal of Black Psychology* 24: 28–43.

McCubbin, H. I., E. A. Thompson, A. I. Thompson, and J. A. Futrell, eds. 1998. *Resiliency in African-American families*. Thousand Oaks, Calif.: Sage.

McHenry, W. 1997. Mentoring as a tool for increasing minority student participation in science, mathematics, engineering, and technology undergraduate and graduate programs. *Diversity in Higher Education* 1: 115–40.

McLaughlin, M. W., M. A. Irby, and J. Langman. 1994. *Urban sanctuaries: Neighborhood organizations in the lives and futures of inner-city youth*. San Francisco: Jossey-Bass.

McLoyd, V. C. 1998. Socioeconomic disadvantage and child development. *American Psychologist* 53: 185–204.

McLoyd, V. C., and D. M. H. Jozefowicaz. 1996. Sizing up the future: Predictors of African American females' expectancies about their economic fortunes and family life courses. In B.J. Leadbeater and N. Way, eds., *Urban girls: Resisting stereotypes, creating identities*, pp. 355–79.

McWhorter, J. H. 2000. *Losing the race: Self-sabotage in black America*. New York: Free Press.

Mervis, J. 1998. Wanted: A better way to boost numbers of minority Ph.D.s. *Science* 281: 1268.

Miller, D. B. 1999. Racial socialization and racial identity: Can they promote resilience for African American adolescents? *Adolescence* 34: 493–501.

Miller, L. S. 1995. *An American imperative: Accelerating minority educational advancement*. New Haven: Yale University Press.

Moore, B. S. 2000. The Black woman professional. From mammy to mentor: A tribute to the work of my mother. *Social Work Perspectives* 11: 8–14.

Naizer, G. L. Science and engineering professors: Why did they choose science as a career? *School Science and Mathematics* 93: 321–24.

National Campaign to Prevent Teen Pregnancy. 2000. Teen pregnancy facts and stats: General facts and stats. Washington, D.C.: Published by the author. National Research Council. 1995. *The National Scholars Program: Excellence with diversity for the future*. Washington, D.C.: National Science Foundation.

National Science Foundation. 1996a. *Science and engineering degrees: 1966–94* (NSF 96–321). Arlington, Va.: National Science Foundation.

National Science Foundation. 1996b. *Selected data on science and engineering doctorate awards, 1995* (NSF 96–3030). Arlington, Va.: National Science Foundation.

National Science Foundation. 1999. Women, minorities, and persons with disabilities in science and engineering: 1998 (NSF 99–338). Arlington, Va.

National Science Foundation. 2000. Women, minorities, and persons with disabilities in science and engineering: 1999.

National Task Force on Minority High Achievement. 1999. *Reaching the top: A report of the national task force on minority high achievement*. New York: College Board Publications.

Nettles, M. T., ed., 1988. *Toward black undergraduate student equality in American higher education*. New York: Greenwood Press.

Newman, B. M., M. C. Meyers, and P. R. Newman, et al. 2000. The transition to high school for academically promising, urban, low-income African American youth. *Adolescence* 35: 45–66.

Nkomo, S. M., and T. Cox, Jr. 1989. Gender differences in the upward mobility of Black managers: Double whammy or double advantage? *Sex Roles* 21 (11/12): 825–39.

O'Brien, V., M. Martinez-Pons, and M. Kopala. 1999. Mathematics self-efficacy, ethnic identity, gender, and career interests related to mathematics and science. *Journal of Educational Research* 92: 231–36.

O'Keefe, M., and L. Treister. 1998. Victims of dating violence among high school students: Are the predictors different for males and females? *Violence Against Women* 4 (2): 195–223.

Oakes, J. 1990. Opportunities, achievement, and choice: Women and minority students in science and mathematics. In *Review of Research in Education*, ed. D. B. Cazden, pp. 153–222. Washington, D.C.: American Educational Research Associations.

Ogbu, J. 1988. Cultural diversity and human development. In D. Slaughter, ed., *Black children and poverty: A developmental perspective*, pp. 11–28. San Francisco: Jossey Bass.

Okazawa-Rey, M., T. Robinson, and J. V. Ward. 1987. Black women and the politics of skin color and hair. *Women and Therapy* 6 (1–2): 89–114.

Okwu, J. 1999. *As I am: Young African American women in a critical age*. San Francisco: Chronicle Books.

Parker, S., M. Nichter, N. Vuckovic, C. Sims, and C. Ritenbaugh. 1995. Body image and weight concerns among African American and White adolescent females: Differences that make a difference. *Human Organization* 54 (2): 103–14.

Patchen, M. 1982. *Black-White contact in schools: Its social and academic effects*. West Lafayette, Ind.: Purdue University Press.

Paulson, S. E. 1994. Relations of parenting style and parental involvement with ninth-grade students' achievement. *Journal of Early Adolescence* 14: 250–67.

Pearson, W., Jr., and H. K. Bechtel, eds. 1989. *Blacks, science, and American education*. New Brunswick: Rutgers University Press.

Peters, M. F. 1997. Parenting of young children in black families. In H. P. McAdoo, ed., *Black families*, 3rd ed., pp. 167–82. Thousand Oaks, Calif.: Sage.

Phillips. L. 1998. *The girls report: What we know and need to know about growing up female*. Washington, D.C.: National Council for Research on Women.

Pipher, M. 1994. *Reviving Ophelia: Saving the selves of adolescent girls*. New York: Ballantine Books.

Pleck, J. H. 1997. Paternal involvement: Levels, sources, and consequences. In M. E. Lamb, ed., *The role of the father in child development*, pp. 66–103. New York: John Wiley and Sons.

Prom-Jackson, S., S. T. Johnson, and M. B. Wallace. 1987. Home environment, talented minority youth, and school achievement. *Journal of Negro Education* 56: 111–121.

Ramist, L., C. Lewis, and L. McCamley-Jenkins. 1994. *Student group differences in predicting college grades: Sex, language, and ethnic groups*. New York: College Entrance Examination Board.

Rasheed, J. M., and M. N. Rasheed. 1999. *Social work practice with African American men: The invisible presence*. Thousand Oaks, Calif.: Sage.

Redmond, S. 1990. Mentoring and cultural diversity in academic settings. *American Behavioral Scientist* 34: 188–200.

Reid, P. T. 1985. Sex-role socialization of black children: A review of theory, family, and media influences. *Academic Psychology Bulletin* 7: 201–12.

Reid-Merritt, P. 1996. *Sister power: How phenomenal black women are rising to the top*. New York: John Wiley and Sons.

Reynolds, A. J. 1991. The middle schooling process: Influences on science and mathematics achievement from the longitudinal study of American youth. *Adolescence* 26: 133–58.

Reynolds, A. J. 1998. Resilience among Black urban youth: Prevalence, intervention effects, and mechanisms of influence. *American Journal of Orthopsychiatry* 68: 84–100.

Reynolds, A. J., and S. Gill. 1994. The role of parent perspectives in the school adjustment of inner-city Black children. *Journal of Youth and Adolescence* 23: 671–94.

Ricciuti, H. N. 1999. Single parenthood and school readiness in White, Black, and Hispanic 6- and 7-year olds. *Journal of Family Psychology* 13: 450–65.

Richards, H. 1997. The teaching of afrocentric values by African American parents. *The Western Journal of Black Studies* 21: 42–50.

Roberts, R. E., C.R. Roberts, and Y. R. Chen. 1997. Ethnocultural differences in prevalence of adolescent depression. *American Journal of Community Psychology* 25 (1): 95–110.

Robinson, T.L, and J. V. Ward. 1995. African American adolescents and skin color. *Journal of Black Psychology* 21 (3): 256–74.

Romotowski, J. and M. Trepaneir. 1977. *Examining and influencing the home reading behaviors of young children.* (ERIC Document Reproduction Service No. ED 195-938.

Roscigno, V. J. 2000. Family/school inequality and African-American/Hispanic achievement. *Social Problems* 47: 266–90.

Rosenthal, R. 1994. Interpersonal expectancy effects: A 30-year perspective. *Current Directions in Psychological Science* 3: 176–79.

Russell, K., M. Wilson, and R. Hall. 1993. *The color complex: The politics of skin color Among African-Americans.* New York: Doubleday.

Sabot, R., and J. Wakeman-Linn. 1991. Grade inflation and course choice. *Journal of Economic Perspectives* 5: 159–70.

Salem, D.A., M. A. Zimmerman, and P. C. Notaro. 1998. Effects of family structure, family process, and father involvement on psychosocial outcomes among African American adolescents. *Family Relations* 47: 331–41.

Sampson, R. J. 1999. What "communtiy" supplies. In R. F. Ferguson and W.T. Dickens, eds., *Urban problems and community development,* pp. 241–292. Washington, D.C.: Brookings Institution Press.

Sanders, M. G. 1998. The effects of school, family, and community support on the academic achievement of African American adolescents. *Urban Education* 33: 385–409.

Sanders, M. G. and J. R. Herting. 2000. Gender and the effects of school, family, and church support on the academic achievement of African-American urban adolescents. In M. G. Sanders et al., ed., *Schooling students placed at risk: Research, policy, and practice in the education of poor and minority adolescents,* pp. 141–61. Mahwah, N.J.: Lawrence Erlbaum Associates.

Sands, T., and M. Howard-Hamilton. 1995. Understanding depression among gifted adolescent females: Feminist therapy strategies. *Roeper Review* 17 (3): 192–95.

Scales, P. C., and J. L. Gibbons. 1996. Extended family members and unrelated adults in the lives of young adolescents: A research agenda. *Journal of Early Adolescence* 16: 365–89.

Seidman, E., J. L. Aber, and S. E. French. In press. Restructuring the transition to middle/junior high school: A strengths-based approach to the organization of schooling. In K. I. Maton, C. Schellenbach, B. Leadbeater, and A. Solarz, eds., *Investing in children, youth, families and communities: Strengths-based research and policy.* Washington, D.C.: American Psychological Association.

Sellers, R. M., T. M. Chavous, and D. Y. Cooke. 1998. Racial ideology and racial centrality as predictors of African American college students' academic performance. *Journal of Black Psychology* 24: 8–27.

Seymour, E., and N. M. Hewitt. 1997. *Talking about leaving: Why undergraduates leave the sciences*. Boulder, Colo.: Westview Press.

Shorter-Gooden, K., and N. C. Washington. 1996. Young, Black, and female: The challenge of weaving an identity. *Journal of Adolescence* 19: 465–75.

Slaughter, D. T., and D. T. Johnson, eds. 1988. *Visible now: Blacks in private schools*. Westport, Conn.: Greewood.

Slaughter-Defoe, D.T., K. Nakagawa, R. Takanishi, and D. J. Johnson. 1990. Toward cultural/ecological perspectives on schooling and achievement in African- and Asian-American children. *Child Development* 61: 363–83.

Smith, E. P., S. Boutee, E. Zigler, and M. Finn-Stevenson. Forthcoming. The role of schools in promoting resilience in children and youth. In K. I. Maton, C. Schellenbach, B. Leadbeater, and A. Solarz, eds., *Investing in children, youth, families, and communities: Strengths-based research and policy*. Washington, D.C.: American Psychological Association.

Smith, F. M., and C. O. Hausafas. 1998. Relationship of family support and ethnic minority students' achievement in science and mathematics. *Science Education* 82: 111–25.

Smith-Maddox, R. 1999. The social networks and resources of African American eighth graders: Evidence from the National Educational Longitudinal Study of 1988. *Adolescence* 34: 169–83.

Snodgrass, D. M. 1991. The parent connection. *Adolescence* 26: 83–87.

Spencer, M. B. 1990. Parental values transmission: Implications for the development of African American children. In H. E. Cheatham and J.B. Stewart, eds. *Black Families: Interdisciplinary perspectives*, pp. 111–30. New Brunswick, N.J.: Transaction Publishers.

Staples, R., and L. B. Johnson. 1993. *Black families at the crossroads: Challenges and prospects*. San Francisco: Jossey-Bass.

Steele, C. 1997. A threat in the air: How stereotypes shape intellectual identity and performance. *American Psychologist* 52: 613–29.

Steele, C. M., and J. Aronson. 1995. Stereotype threat and the intellectual test performance of African Americans. *Journal of Personality and Social Psychology* 69: 797–811.

Steinberg, L. 1996. *Beyond the classroom: Why school reform has failed and what parents need to do*. New York: Simon and Schuster.

Steinberg, L., J. D. Elmen, and N. S. Mounts. 1989. Authoritative parenting, psychosocial maturity, and academic success among adolescents. *Child Development* 60: 1424–36.

Steinberg, L., S. M. Dornbusch, and B. B. Brown. 1992. Ethnic differences in academic achievement: An ecological perspective. *American Psychologist* 47: 923–29.

Sterling, D., ed. 1997. *We are your sisters: Black women in the nineteenth century*. New York: Norton.

Tashakkori, A. 1993. Race, gender, and pre-adolescent self-structure: A test of constuct-specificity hypothesis. *Personality and Individual Differences* 14 (4): 591–98.

Tatum, B. D. 1997. Out there stranded? Black families in White communities. In H. P. McAdoo, ed., *Black families*, 3rd ed., pp. 215–32. Thousand Oaks, Calif.: Sage.

Taylor, J. M., C. Gilligan, and A. M. Sullivan. 1995. *Between voice and silence: Women and girls, race and relationship*. Cambridge, Mass.: Harvard University Press.

Taylor, R. D. 1996. Adolescents' perceptions of kinship support and family management practices: Association with adolescent adjustment in African American families. *Developmental Psycholog*, 32: 687–95.

Taylor, R. D. 1997. The effects of economic and social stressors on parenting and adolescent adjustment in African-American families. In R. D. Taylor and M. C. Wang, eds., *Social and emotional adjustment and family relations in ethnic minority families*, pp. 35–52. Mahwah, N.J.: Lawrence Erlbaum Associates.

Taylor, R. L. 1991. Childrearing in African-American families. In J. E. Everett, S. S. Chipungu, S. Leashore, and R. Bagart, eds., *Child welfare: An Africentric perspective*, pp. 119–55. Princeton, N.J.: Rutgers University Press.

Taylor, R.D., L. Jacobson, and D. Roberts. 2000. Ecological correlates of the social and emotional adjustment of African American adolescents. In R. Montemayor, G. R. Adams, and T.P. Guyllotta, eds., *Adolescent diversity in ethnic, economic, and cultural contexts.* Advances in Adolescent Development Book Series, volume 10, pp. 208–234. Thousand Oaks, Calif.: Sage.

Taylor, R.D., R. Casten, and S. M. Flickinger. 1992. Influence of kinship social support on the parenting experiences and psychosocial adjustment of African-American adolescents. *Developmental Psychology* 29: 382–88.

Taylor, R.J., L. M. Chatters, and J. S. Jackson. 1997. Changes over time in support network involvement among Black Americans. In R.J. Taylor, S.J. Jackson, and L.M. Chatters, eds., *Family life in Black America*, pp. 293–316.

Taylor, R.J., S.J. Jackson, and L. M. Chatters, eds. 1997. *Family life in Black America.* Thousand Oaks, Calif.: Sage.

Thornton, M. C., L. M. Chatters, R. J. Taylor, and W . R. Allen. 1990. Sociodemographic and environmental correlates of racial socialization by black parents. *Child Development* 61: 401–409.

Thornton, M. D. 1997. Strategies of racial socialization among Black parents: Mainstream, minority, and cultural messages. In R. J. Taylor, J. Sidney, et al., eds., *Family life in Black America*, pp. 201–15. Thousand Oaks, Calif.: Sage.

Thurmond, V. B., and L. L. Cregler. 1999. Why students drop out of the pipeline to health professions careers: A follow-up of gifted minority high school students. *Academic Medicine* 74: 448–51.

Tinto, V. 1987. *Leaving college: Rethinking the causes and cures of student attrition.* Chicago: University of Chicago Press.

Tolson, T.F.J., and M. N. Wilson. 1990. The impact of two- and three-generational black family structure on perceived family climate. *Child Development* 61: 416–28.

Treisman, U. 1992. Studying students studying calculus: A look at the lives of minority mathematics students in college. *College Mathematics Journal* 23: 362–72.

U. S. Bureau of the Census 1999. Statistical Abstract of the U. S. Table No 304. Enrollment Status by Race, Hispanic Origin, and Sex: 1975 and 1997. Washington, D. C.

U. S. Bureau of the Census. 1998. Current Population Reports: Household and Family Characteristics: March 1998, P20–515. Washington, D.C.: Government Printing Office.

U. S. Bureau of the Census. 2000. Current Population Reports: Money Income in the United States, 1999, p. 60–209. Washington, D.C.: Government Printing Office.

U.S. Bureau of the Census. 1995. Women in the United States: A profile - Statistical brief. Washington, D.C.; Two-thirds of African American families have children, Census Bureau reports.

U.S. Bureau of the Census. 1999. Internet release date: 2/24/99. http://www.census.gov/ population/socdem/race/black/tabs 98.

U.S. Department of Education, National Center for Education Statistics. [1999]. The condition of Education, 1999 Section II. Quality of education environments (elementary/secondary). Retrieved May 1, 2000, from http://nces.ed.gov/pubs99/condition99sec-2.html.

U.S. Department of Education, National Center for Education Statistics. 2000. Educational Equity for Girls and Women NCES 2000–030, by Yupin Bae, Susan Choy, Claire Geddes, Jennifer Sale, and Thomas Snyder. Washington, D.C.: U.S. Government Printing Office.

U.S. Department of Education, National Center for Education Statistics. 2000. Integrated Postsecondary Education Data System. Retrieved May 1, 2000, from http://nces.ed.gov/ipeds/data.html#data.

U.S. Department of Education, Office for Civil Rights. 1997. Elementary and secondary school civil rights compliance report. Projected values for the nation. Washington, D.C.

U.S. Department of Labor, Women's Bureau. 1997. Facts on working women: Black women in the labor force, March 1997, No. 97-1. Washington, D.C.

Ventura, S. J., T. J. Mathews, and S. C. Curtin. 1999. Declines in teenage birthrate. 1991–98: Update of national and state trends. *National Vital Statistics Reports*, 47 (26).

Ventura, S.J., T. J. Mathews, and S. C. Curtin. 1998. Declines in teenage birth rates, 1991–97: National and state patterns. *National Vital Statistics Reports* 47 (12).

Vette, B. M. 1994. The next generation of science and engineers: Who's in the pipeline? In *Who will do science? Educating the next generation*, ed. W. Pearson Jr. and A. Fechter, pp. 1–21. Baltimore: Johns Hopkins University Press.

Walsh, F. 1998. Beliefs, spirituality, and transcendence: Keys to family resilience. In M. McGoldrick, ed., *Re-visioning family therapy: Race, culture and gender in clinical practice*, pp. 62–77. New York: Guilford Press.

Ward, J. V. 1996. Raising resisters: The role of truth telling in the psychological development of African American girls. In B.J. Leadbeater and N. Way, eds., *Urban girls: Resisting stereotypes, creating identities*, pp. 85–98.

Waters, M. C. 1996. The intersection of gender, race, and ethnicity in identity development of Caribbean American teens. In B.J. Leadbeater and N. Way, eds., *Urban girls: Resisting stereotypes, creating identities*, pp. 65–81.

Way, N. 1998. *Everyday courage: The lives and stories of urban teenagers*. New York: New York University Press.

Weiler, J. 1999. An overview of research on girls and violence. *Choices Briefs*, number 1. New York: Institute for Urban and Minority Education, Teachers College, Columbia University. Retrieved May 1, 2000, from http://iume.tc.columbia.edu/choices/ briefs/choices01.html.

Weinstein, R. 1998. Promoting positive expectancies in schooling. In N. Lambert and B. L. McCooms, eds., *Issues in school reform: A sampler of psychological perspectives on learner-centered schools* (pp. 81–111). Washington, D.C.: American Psychological Association.

Weinstein, R. S., C. R. Soule, F. Collins, J. Cone, M. Mehlhorn, and K. Simontachi. 1991. Expectations and high school change: Teacher-researcher collaboration to prevent school failure. *American Journal of Community Psychology* 19: 333–64.

Werner, E. E., and R. S. Smith. 1992. *Overcoming the odds: High risk children from birth to adulthood*. New York: Cornell University Press.

Williams, J. 1998. *Thurgood Marshall: American revolutionary*. New York: Times Books.

Willingham, W. W., C. Lewis, R. Morgan, and L. Ramist. 1990. *Predicting college grades: An analysis of institutional trends over two decades*. Princeton, N.J.: Educational Testing Service.

Wilson, K. R., and W. R. Allen. 1987. Explaining the educational attainment of young black adults: Critical family and extra-familial influences. *Journal of Negro Education* 56: 64–76.

Wilson, M. N., D. Y. Cook, and E. G. Arrington. 1997. African-American adolescents and academic achievement: Family and peer influences. In R. D. Taylor and M.C. Wang, eds., *Social and emotional adjustment and family relations in ethnic minority families*, pp. 145–55. Mahwah, N.J.: Lawrence Erlbaum Associates.

Wilson, M. N., ed. 1995. *African American family life: Its structural and ecological aspects*. No. 68 in the New Directions for Child Development Series. San Francisco: Jossey-Bass.

Wilson-Sadberry, K. R., L. F. Winfield, and D. A. Royster. 1991. Resilience and persistence of African-American males in postsecondary enrollment. *Education and Urban Society* 24: 87–102.

Wineke, W.R., and P. Certain. 1990. *The freshman year in science and engineering: Old problems, new perspectives for research universities.* University Park, Pa.: Alliance for Undergraduate Education.

Wyatt, E. 1999. Women gain the doctoral chase, *New York Times*, November 4, p. A17.

Yan, W. F. 1999. Successful African American students: The role of parental involvement. *Journal of Negro Education* 68: 5–22.

Yonezawa, S. S. 2000. Unpacking the black box of tracking decisions: Critical tales of families navigating the course placement process. In M. G. Sanders, et al., eds., *Schooling students placed at risk: Research, policy, and practice in the education of poor and minority adolescents,* pp. 109–37. Mahwah, N.J.: Lawrence Erlbaum Associates.

Yong, F. L. 1992. Mathematics and science attitudes of African-American middle grade students identified as gifted: Gender and grade differences. *Roeper Review* 14: 136–40.

Yoshikawa, H., and E. Seidman. 2000. Competence among urban adolescents in poverty: Multiple forms, contexts, and developmental processes. In R. Montemayor, G. R. Adams, and T. P. Guyllotta, eds., *Adolescent diversity in ethnic, economic, and cultural contexts,* Advances in Adolescent Development Book Series, vol. 10, pp. 9–42. Thousand Oaks, Calif.: Sage.

CPSIA information can be obtained at www.ICGtesting.com
Printed in the USA
LVOW13*1409261013

358738LV00004B/34/P